D1565530

THE TEACHING OF THE PARABLES

Peter Rhea Jones

BROADMAN PRESS
Nashville, Tennessee

To
my parents
Mildred Rhea Jones
Judge Robert David Jones
lifelong lay students of Scripture

© Copyright 1982 • Broadman Press
All rights reserved.
4213-71
ISBN: 0-8054-1371-5
Dewey Decimal Classification: 226.8
Subject heading: JESUS CHRIST—PARABLES//
JESUS CHRIST—TEACHINGS
Library of Congress Catalog Card Number:
78-054367
Printed in the United States of America
Unless otherwise indicated, Scripture passages
are the author's translation.

Contents

Preface

These studies of the parables are offered first of all as a textbook for college and seminary classes. Courses on the life of Christ or the teachings of Jesus as well as specialized classes on the parables or the kingdom of God could relate to this work. Students using the book are encouraged to read each parable in a translation and a Gospel parallel before reading the expositional studies. *The Cotton Patch Version of Luke and Acts* is especially recommended for its lively depictions of parables. Beginning students have been kept in mind when technical terms appear. Terms are not avoided but are quite often explained in passing or used with a synonym. Note also that the first chapter functions not only to tell the story of interpretation but also to introduce terms that are clarified even further in chapters 2 and 3. Some teachers may prefer to start with the second chapter as a first assignment rather than with the first because of the nature of the materials.

Preachers and professors will also find the book directed to them. Pastors will find fodder for both their teaching and preaching ministry. Each exposition concludes with hermeneutical exploration and homiletical beginnings. As a busy pastor, I know the press of preaching responsibilities and constantly search for helps that possess integrity. Congregations tend to respond to parables quite naturally. Pastoral experience has heightened my sense of the importance of outcome as well as careful analysis, though former students familiar with my teaching style would be shocked anyway if these expositions ended short of application. The style of these outcome sections is intentionally more colorful and popular.

Scholars and research students will find some different ideas and angles and many notes dialoguing with current opinion, graciously allowed by Broadman Press.

Disciplined study groups on college campuses or in local churches may also choose to engage in dialogue with the parables by means of this study, as well as that fascinating breed of lay theologians who are scattered about.

The primary concern in interpretation centers upon original meaning of each parable in the historical ministry of Jesus, yet with keen interest in the early church and the present church. Scholars perhaps will detect a greater than usual appreciation of Adolf Jülicher's study. This is because of his recognition of the importance of generalizing conclusions, the place of ethics in parable study, and his sensitive attention to literary forms and details. Also a suspicion of certain doctrinaire critical notions can be observed in relation to "critical orthodoxy," as never allegory, never an authentic interpretation or generalizing conclusion, never a scriptural basis (Old Testament) or citation. As is well known each of these absolutes has contradicting parallel among rabbinic parables. Could it be that Lutheran notions of law and grace, neoorthodox and history of religions interest in distinctiveness and uniqueness, and disdain for allegory because of certain rather puristic canons of literary criticism have caused some distortion requiring correction?

The mood herein is post-critical. As early as 1966, certain severe limitations of the historico-critical method began to be apparent. Though not then fashionable, I began with my dissertation on New Criticism to advocate a far more literary stress, which characterized my teaching career at The Southern Baptist Theological Seminary. Paradoxically, I remain intensely interested also in the quest for the historical Jesus and with Jeremias see the parables as firm foundation. Problems related to the recovery of original historical circumstance do not disappear into splendid certainty, of course, and it is unbecoming to dogmatize about stubborn perplexities. Nevertheless, careful speculation about the original setting is ventured.

The critical opinion that Mark stands as our earliest Gospel is accepted. It remains probable there were special saying sources (as Q), but they may have contained special Matthew (M) and Luke (L) material. Furthermore, the picture of the disciples functioning like rabbinic disciples is promising. Surely material such as the instructions to the disciples before the mission to Israel (Matt. 10) and the Sermon on the Plain (Luke 6) and certain parable speeches were committed to memory by the disciples.

The rabbinic sources used in documentation are thought of more as illustrative than probative. Primacy should still be given to material claiming to depict the pre-70 period, which names sages who lived then. The oldest works deserve highest claim (Mishnah, Tosefta, tannaitic midrashim) with the Talmuds taking a secondary place. Specialists must continue the presently vigorous reevaluation of rabbinic sources.

The distinctive angle in this book can be most clearly seen in the third chapter in its extended reflections on the literary aspect of the parables and in efforts to apply these insights through ensuing chapters. There is also a conscious effort to include some pastoral and some prophetic parables. Jesus, with his impressive combination of sugar and steel, created some parables like beatitudes and others like woes. Some of his parables dealt sensitively with anxiety while others slashed fiercely in search of sensitivity among the stubbornly resistant. Attention is also called along the way to certain parables that function as theodicies.

A concerted effort has been exerted to produce a readable style. Much of the critical detail and dialogue with scholars goes on in the notes rather than the text. Careful readers are, therefore, encouraged to read the notes appropriate to each chapter. Journals, a major resource, are generally documented with full title for the benefit of beginning students in order to present a less foreboding apparatus; but familiar resources frequently cited are abbreviated for convenience, such as the *Theological Dictionary of the New Testament (TDNT)* and the *Interpreters' Dictionary of the Bible (IDB)*. Standard tools and reference works are utilized and often assumed, such as Danby's edition of the Mishnah, Vermes' edition of the Scrolls, Hatch and Redpath's concordance of the LXX, lexicons by Bauer, Arndt, and Gingrich and by Liddell and Scott, grammars by Robertson and by Moulton and by Blass, DeBrunner, and Funk.

I have sought to be sensitive about exclusivistic language but not to be extreme in choosing alternatives. The problem cannot be resolved readily in any event. The words *woman, human,* and *person* contain the syllables *man* and *son,* for example. Frequently in the text *he* and *she* are mentioned simultaneously and occasionally the order is reversed. The term *man* is used generically but sparingly, but more often words like *humanity* appear in an effort to be inclusive.

I cheerfully acknowledge many to whom there exists real indebtedness, not least of which are fellow students of the parables. Former students in a decade of classes at The Southern Baptist Theological Seminary provided a graciously responsive, yet definitely stimulating, context for an annual series of lectures on parables. An invitation to write an introduction to current study of parables from the *Southwestern Journal of Theology* moved things along, as well as the opportunity to publish a study of the Compassionate Samaritan in *Perspectives in Religious Studies* and an exegesis of the seed parables in the *Review and Expositor*. Permission has been granted by the respective editors to a second use in a somewhat revised form. I am grateful to Southeastern Baptist Theological Seminary for the gracious invitation to present my views on the parables through the Spring Lectures of 1980. The fellowship with the faculty and president during those days was absolutely delightful. I am also indebted to Ronald Deering, head librarian of the Boyce library of The Southern Baptist Theological Seminary, and to Jane Lawson, previously periodicals librarian at Pitts library of Emory University and presently head librarian at Georgetown College, for their help and the use of extensive resources in their care.

Major aid came also from the typing pool at The Southern Baptist Theological Seminary. Much of the manuscript was written in Louisville and typed in rough and second draft by seminary secretaries. Charlotte Sprawls at First Baptist, Decatur, has carried the project through to completion with competence. Tom and Louise Davis and Howard and Ruth Connell thoughtfully provided Lake Burton hideaways for writing during a couple of vacation weeks that allowed the by-then extensive project to be completed. Dr. Judith King voluntarily produced an invaluable bibliography which, along with Kissinger's book, provided the primary guide to journal resources.

Ellen, my wife, has provided strategic encouragement at various stages. Our three children, Peter Rhea, Heather, and Ramsey, have evinced a genuine interest in how the book was going.

The dedication to my parents is inevitable. They taught by example their love for the Bible. Both took responsibility for a Sunday School class across many years and gave their best. They studied the lesson sometimes all week long and discussed it intelligently at the dinner table and collected a good theological library for a lay couple. They are so deserving of this modest dedication.

I record my affection for former teaching colleagues in Louisville who have shown interest along the way and my appreciation to my congregation in Decatur who have listened to sermons from parables.

My confidence in the parables as word of God from the Word of God has been enhanced by serious study. Our clumsy fingers lose many dear things in life. The parables and their meaning for our lives should not be among them. If I stir readers here and there to allow the parables to help them get in touch with their sort of existence and with the Teller I will be pleased.

PETER RHEA JONES

Decatur, 1981.

1 Report from the Trenches: Recent Study of Parables

Biblical criticism can seem so ineffectual in result and so impractical in value for the church, yet when the story of the interpretation of the parables of Jesus is followed, the result is impressive. The record is one of creative and constructive outcomes in the main. There is a marked sense of advance and progress in understanding.

For nineteen centuries interpreters, with a few impressive exceptions, treated the parables as simple allegories, and their interpretations now appear farfetched. These allegorical interpreters used the parables more as an arsenal of proof texts for current church doctrine than as a source for new insight. The next chapter recognizes that some parables contain a subordinated allegorical dimension, but the positive contribution of recent study has very definitely been to take with utter seriousness the original meaning of the parables in the historical context of the ministry of Jesus rather than to indulge in "allegory run riot." Indeed, the parables in their original import are better understood today, thanks in no small measure to Joachim Jeremias, than they have been known for many centuries—possibly since the first. Implicit in not a little of the critical analysis of the parables is a mildly disguised reverence for the authority of the Lord's words.

An academic anecdote tells of Adolf Schlatter, a famous conservative scholar, taking a new teaching post. One elated person was pleased at his appointment and exclaimed, "I understand that you take your stand on the Word of God."

The professor retorted, "I take my stand under the Word of God." He wisely saw that to take seriously the authority of the Scriptures the student must allow the original meaning to have authority in a constant criticism of personal opinion. He refused to stand above the Bible. The scholars who have led the way and forged ahead in parable research have refused to accept traditional opinion and ecclesiastical dogma as a substitute for inquiry. They have chosen to stand under the Word.

This report from the trenches of research, to orient and provide background for personal study, begins by selecting two influential scholars who have dominated the century and then goes on to feature quite recent trends.

The Big Two

The beginning of the modern study of parables should be reckoned from the epoch-making two volumes of Adolf Jülicher.[1] Interesting now is the fact that Professor Jülicher possessed a developed appreciation of the literary character of the parables. From his influence derive some of the modern terms used in parable analysis, such as the picture part and the object part, the *tertium comparationis* (the point of comparison), the similitude (a typical event in real life told in present tense), and the *exemplum* (not a comparison but an example to imitate). He insisted that parables were comparisons, not allegories, and that they contained only one point.[2] He did recognize that the evangelists and their sources as well conveyed a Hellenistic notion of parable as enigma, which allowed for allegory.[3] However, he demolished the allegorical approach and established the opinion that the parable has one basic meaning. As Norman Perrin put it, "One finds oneself thinking in terms of cobwebs being swept away."[4] Layers and layers of nonsense were removed when Jülicher returned to the autonomy of the text. His breakthrough was not accomplished without some distortion however.

Jülicher's error, from a literary perspective, grew out of his exaggerated separation of simile and metaphor. He took the position that a metaphor is nonliteral speech and the simile is literal speech, that a metaphor is a word that must be replaced by another while there is no need for a process of translation from the simile to its interpretation. It is a short step to the definition of an allegory as a string of metaphors. His hidden agenda apparently was to drive away all allegorical demons by literary definitions. He opposed treatment of the parables as allegories or metaphors. He did succeed in underlining the nature of parable as simile, but his definitions of parable and metaphor and simile are too indebted to Aristotle and insufficiently influenced by the parables of the Old Testament and the rabbis.

From a theological perspective, Jülicher's error (easier seen in the convenient light of hindsight!) lies in his simple mixing of the teaching of Jesus and the liberal theology of the late nineteenth century in which he lived. Jülicher imagined Jesus as forever uttering timeless truths and "scattering clever aphorisms about."[5] These timeless truths were "remarkably" like the theology of his own liberal German Protestantism. So Jesus appeared "an apostle of progress," a purveyor of general religious truths. These universal truths, abstracted by Jülicher, reflect too much his personal attitudes and situation, what has been called a "bourgeois attitude to life in a German university town at the end of the nineteenth century."[6] These general truths are sometimes theologically anemic. His actual interpretations are sometimes disappointing, often slack epigrams lacking eschatological glory. The great put-down came from a fellow student of parables: "No one would crucify a teacher who told pleasant stories to enforce prudential morality."[7] Any interpretation of Jesus must explain why the people killed him! Jülicher did succeed in turning a corner in our understanding of the parables. He effectively countered the excesses of allegorization. He recognized the ethical character of parables, a perspective presently in eclipse. Professor Jülicher is one of the two most significant scholars on the parables.

Joachim Jeremias, greedy for learning, has pursued his study of the parables over a lifetime with a relentless perseverance.[8] He lived in Palestine as a boy. Standing on the shoulders of the great C. H. Dodd, Jeremias has placed the parables clearly in the context of the historical ministry of Jesus. He wants to know what the parable meant the first time it was spoken. He has seen rightly the crisis nature of many parables, the implicit call to decision, and the critical importance of the Teller as well as the tale. The hearer or reader encounters Jesus as well as his story. Jeremias has a passion to return to the "very words of Jesus" (ipsissima verba) or at least to the "very voice of Jesus" (ipsissima vox). He is splendidly equipped both as a constructive form critic and as a master of Aramaic, probably the language of Jesus. Critically speaking, Jeremias has greatly strengthened the probability that nearly every parable goes back to Jesus—a critical conclusion that has enormous significance for the quest after the historical Jesus. One of Jeremias's former students went so far as to brand Jeremias's study "the greatest single contribution to modern knowledge of the historical Jesus."[9] His book *The Parables of Jesus* is exceptional.

Respect must not deteriorate into reverence however. Jeremias is a child of his time. For example, the neoorthodox theology has influenced his exegesis perceptibly. Time may show that he was unduly influenced by Dodd and that both collapsed the category of crisis parable too much to fit the coming catastrophe for Israel. Jeremias is quite right that the entire proclamation of Jesus is predicated upon conscious eschatological convictions and that the parables are never apart from eschatology. However, he has more than made his point and has said precious little about ethical content. If Jülicher centered on ethics at the expense of eschatology, Jeremias has focused on eschatology at the expense of ethics. In private conversation, he indicated that an ethical aspect is sometimes present in a parable but is relatively unimportant or secondary.

Jeremias, as historian, has downplayed the literary character of the parables as well because of his desire to reject any academic notion of these stories as literary productions when they should be conceived as spontaneous products in conflict circumstances. This has resulted in a "severely historical" approach. His insistence upon parables as interpretations of the Galilean ministry on the one hand (as the Sower) while rejecting allegorical interpretation out of hand on the other is a considerable inconsistency. Also, his form critical program while conservative may still prove to be somewhat severe in the light of further literary and midrashic studies.

Nevertheless no serious student of parables ignores the monumental work of Jeremias, and no serious student is free of influence from Jülicher. These two are the major figures of the century in parable research, though there were other distinguished pacesetters like Dodd, Cadoux, Fiebig, and Manson.

Recent Trends

Parable research and discussion have been especially lively in the past two decades and rather bold and experimental. Most study has been literary analysis in one way or another. It has not been dull. Much of it has taken place in university settings, and a conscious effort has been made to make contact with subjects other than religion and to communicate with modern people. Two patterns appear regularly. One is the tacit assumption of Jeremias as foundation, and the other is existential categories as framework. Furthermore, feminine interpreters have come into their own as have Americans. Study groups are in vogue.

New Hermeneutic. Out of the Bultmannian school has come an understanding of parables as "language events." Ernst Fuchs has broken new ground by putting the questions of a modern philosopher (Heidegger) to the parables.[10] He relates the parables to the language of the family where one speaks because one is understood and where time announcements are made.[11] Words claim their potential to create "a happening." The philosophical jargon in Fuchs' writing style has put off many sophisticated readers. To read Ernst Fuchs is to experience the stimulus of a mental hike.

Eta Linnemann, one of his students, has produced a constructive application.[12] She believes that the interpreter must use critical methods to get behind the Gospels and into position to hear the parables as the original hearers heard them.[13] She makes the interesting point that the original hearers were not Christians and that the parables are especially valuable for communication to a secular world.[14] The parables are language events through which Jesus audaciously announced the time of the kingdom of God, forcing the hearers to a decision about the Proclaimer of the message. The parables involved the unheard-of claim to speak for God and opened up a new possibility that did not exist before. Developing her idea of "interlocking," Linnemann portrays parable as a medium that interlocks the speaker and hearer because the speaker is willing to concede something to the hearers. The opposed judgments of speaker and hearer do not remain separate in the parable, but both leave their deposit upon the parable.[15] She recognized more than her predecessors the role of the hearer in the parable situation.

There is scarcely a dull page in Linnemann's book. It is now clear, however, that the New Hermeneutic, supported by her and her teacher, is more of a stimulus than a lasting program. This emphasis has been a reminder that the parables strike the watertable of our common existence and toll our being from beyond. There have been a few magical moments in many lives when the integrity of a speaker's personality and the truthfulness of his or her utterances were so cohesive and authentic that truth itself happened. Is not biblical preaching letting the Word happen again? The parables of Jesus were, indeed, language events because they created possibilities that did not exist before and that decisively altered the situation.

New Criticism. Dan Via produced a bell-ringing study in 1967, since translated into other languages.[16] He brought together the New Criticism[17] and the New Hermeneutic in a highly independent fashion and opened a new chapter in parable research. He reacted vehemently to parable work of recent vintage that concerned itself with the parable as history and a medium for theology at the expense of the literary nature of parable. He took on the giants and while he slew no Goliaths, he succeeded in changing the subject!

The exciting connection Via forged was between existence and drama. He saw the parable as dramatizing the ontological possibility of *the gain or loss of existence.* He further labeled certain parables as comic and others as tragic. The ontological possibility of losing existence is then aesthetically the tragic movement, while the possibility of gaining existence is aesthetically the comic movement. By tragic Via simply means a downward movement toward catastrophe and the isolation of the person from society; by comic he means an upward movement toward well-being and inclusion in a new or renewed society. An example of a tragic parable is the story of the Wicked Tenants (Mark 12:1-9), and the Unjust Steward (Luke 16:1-9) is a sample of comic form. This combination represents a positively brilliant bringing together of the existential, literary, critical, and eschatological. Via's engaging exegesis has real value since it makes contact with the secular world. The parables may be communicated in a fresh fashion when seen as comic and tragic, and a modern point of contact can be established, especially in college settings.

There are limitations. The interpretations are decidedly centered on the human side, too removed from the historical Jesus, too generalized and secular. After all, some of the original parables were openly religious in nature.

Parable as Metaphor. Amos Wilder, influenced by Fuchs and an influence upon younger scholars, prefers to speak of the parable as metaphor.[18] And metaphor is by no means an ornament in the speech of an eloquent speaker. True metaphor is more than a sign. The parables as metaphors impart to their hearers something of Jesus' vision of the power of God at work. While a simile clarifies, a metaphor reveals, providing a certain shock to the imagination. Wilder's recent book *Theopoetic* actually calls for a renewal of the religious imagination.[19] The brother of the playwright Thornton Wilder, he has sensitized a generation to the power of language and metaphor. When Amos Wilder speaks, scholars listen.

Robert Funk produced a potboiler of a book in 1966 entitled *Language, Hermeneutic and Word of God.*[20] Written at a time of exciting international hermeneutical conferences, the book dialogued with several philosophical issues but maintained a primary interest in the parable. Through metaphor a parable tells who one is, Funk held. He rightly objected to the reduction of a parable to an idea or a mere interpretation. He followed Dodd's definition of parable, especially the notion that the application of a parable was left imprecise by Jesus in order to tease the hearer into making his own application. After all, in metaphor the point must be discovered because metaphor is by its nature open-ended. Funk is uncomfortable with the model of a single historical meaning for each parable and calls in question the untouchable teaching of Jülicher that each parable conveys a single idea.

Funk, a kind of American Käsemann, has been highly provocative and catalytic. His thinking and studying about parables continue to develop, as when for a time he taught Kafka's parables at Vanderbilt, but it will be immensely unfortunate if he never publishes a major study concentrated on the parables.

Meanwhile Sallie McFague has recommended doing theology with the parables of Jesus as models for theological reflection.[21] This she sees as appropriate because of the metaphoric character of our Christian confession. Her program, like Funk's, is to isolate and understand the metaphors and not reduce to single assertions. "A metaphor is a word used in an unfamiliar context to give us a new insight," she writes. "A good metaphor moves us to see our ordinary world in an extraordinary way."[22] For example, she envisions the parable of the Prodigal Son as a metaphor of God's love. This famous parable is a nonreducible entity to be savored whole.

McFague points out that metaphor is the only legitimate way of speaking of the divine, that the kingdom of God is never defined but spoken of in metaphorical language, and that Jesus himself is a parable of God![23] As a theologian, she objects to traditional theologizing because it is so abstract and conceptual. She advocates a parabolic theology. She wants theologians who will express themselves with pictures and metaphors when speaking of the infinite with finite language. At least she would like to call forth and bless a group of intermediary theologians better able to distinguish between words that are dead and those that are alive, a concern incidentally that might free preaching from lifeless assertions about God. Images and metaphors communicate.

These efforts by Wilder, Funk, McFague, and others to understand parables as root metaphors have salutary effects, not least in consciousness raising. The temptation to substitute a paraphrase of a parable for the parable itself may be spurned. The parable as a whole will be left intact. The parables cease to be artifacts of history but function as appeals to the imagination.

Structuralism. Students of literary analysis, not content with a focus upon language and gaining momentum in university departments of religion, have moved on to study structure. Structuralism itself, spoken best with a French and Swiss accent, has gained ground in Europe as a philosophical alternative to Sartrian existentialism. Among other things certain analytical procedures suitable for literary analysis have emerged, and certain parable students have begun a fascinating experimentation of their own.[24] One French scholar, J. Delormé, announced gleefully and forcefully to a group of parable students, "The Germans examine problems. We study the text!" A new journal has arisen, called *Semeia*, dedicated to experimental biblical criticism. *Semeia* has devoted several issues to the application of structuralism to parables. The technical jargon of this new discipline has put off many scholars and is understood only by the initiated. "Entrance requirements" are high.

One of the leading exponents is John Crossan, an enormously literate scholar whose work, like that of Funk and Via, is still in progress. Avoiding many of the structuralist terms, Crossan nevertheless introduces the reader to a rarefied world in his primary book *In Parables*.[25] His book tickles the reader's cerebrum. There are many good insights like the fact that allegory is not a bad word to be used pejoratively, that parables are metaphoric expressions of Jesus' own experience of God, and that his parables are compositions of an oral poet. In a creative fashion, Crossan seeks to organize the parables under three rubrics: advent, reversal, and action. The first two are particularly telling. Advent becomes a fresh way of thinking about the kingdom's coming in the Sower and the Mustard Seed. Reversal parables imply how the coming of the kingdom unravels human security as in the Rich Man and Lazarus and the Pharisee and the Publican. Things are not as they seem. Indeed, in the light of the kingdom, matters may be reversed. Crossan is especially impressive commenting thus on the Good Samaritan:

> . . . the story challenges the hearer to put together two impossible and contradictory words for the same person: "Samaritan" (10:33) and "neighbor" (10:36). The whole thrust of the story demands that one says what cannot be said, what is a contradiction in terms: Good + Samaritan. On the lips of the historical Jesus the story demands that the hearer respond by saying the contradictory, the impossible, the unspeakable.[26]

So he heightens sensitivity to the proportions of reversal.

However, Crossan's most creative contribution to parable study may not lie in his application of structuralism, but rather in his attention to clusters of parables gathered around common metaphors. For instance, he singles out seed parables and servant parables. He grouped no less than nine servant parables and observed that "all concern a master-servant relationship *and* a time or moment of critical reckoning therein."[27] He is at his best analyzing the parable of the Unmerciful Servant (Matt. 18:23-34) as "a small masterpiece of dramatic choreography in three tightly integrated scenes."[28] Because there are so many servant parables, Crossan can speculate meaningfully about Jesus' creativity as a kind of restless probing of structure, repetitive variations on a theme. Crossan has moved on in recent publications toward studies more classically structuralist, observing universal patterns of fabulation and plot options.[29] But his most valuable breakthroughs have been in the detection and investigation of seed and servant parables. These and other clusterings mark a definite advance and may be of more lasting value. Perhaps Crossan will one day favor us with a book studying the parables according to the chief metaphoric systems. Meanwhile further fresh insights will emanate from structuralists in the next several years.

Sociology. In addition to the primary interest in literary analysis at the present time, there is a flowering of interest in the application of sociology to New Testament study generally and parables in particular. This challenging development is most promising and is another example of enrichment by interdisciplinary dialogue.[30] Previous scholars, such as Dalman, Jeremias, and Oesterley, have brought sociological matters to bear on parables already; but now we can expect a concerted effort that will enjoy substantial impact as it probes social dynamic.

One impressive practitioner, Kenneth Bailey, is chairperson of the Biblical Department at the Near Eastern School of Theology in Beirut. Not satisfied with standard scholarly tools alone, he insists that the parables be understood in their original cultural framework. He is also interested in the literary structure as put in a cultural context. Obviously sociology is exceptionally important for parables since they are not abstract theologies but slices of real life. As Bailey puts it, "The culture of the synoptic parables is that of first-century Palestine."[31]

Bailey advocates "Oriental exegesis," by which he refers to the present culture of conservative peasants, to Oriental versions of the Bible, and to ancient literature. He is at home with Arabic translations of the Bible and early Arabic interpreters. He adds illuminating background detail. Concerning the parable of the Lost Coin (Luke 15:8-10), he reminds us that a village was largely self-sufficient, making its own cloth and growing its own foods, so cash was a rare commodity. Furthermore, the lost coin probably came from a necklace so the loss of one coin spoiled the beauty of the whole necklace. Also the woman knew that the missing coin was somewhere in the house because her movement as a woman was severely limited. She had not been away.[32] He never tires of confusing the reader with facts! Bailey does make arguments from silence that are less than convincing and in his enthusiasm runs the risk of allowing his reconstructed background to take precedence over the text. He is comfortable with Duncan Derrett for some details and with T. W. Manson for some directions.

Richard Rohrbaugh, writing from the pastorate, singles out the hermeneutical problems caused by an agrarian Bible in an industrial age. As a preacher, he stresses the sociological conditioning of both biblical writer and contemporary preacher. The expository preacher must make some transpositions because the Bible arose in a preindustrial age and the American minister functions in an industrial era. Reflecting on the parable of the Rich Man and Lazarus (Luke

16:19-31), Rohrbaugh plays up the extreme social disparity. Desperate Lazarus belongs neither to the class of the urban poor nor to the rural poor of peasants but to "the relatively small group of outcasts that inhabited the gutters of every ancient city. Beggars, cripples, prostitutes, and lepers made up this group."[33] Rohrbaugh argues interestingly that the modern application must avoid individualized moralizing and must rather think of justice and address poverty issues by challenging the system.

Bailey and Rohrbaugh heighten the consciousness of the sociological factor, both historically and hermeneutically considered. More can be expected from this quarter. Just think about the various social positions and situations present in parables. There are kings, servants, householders, merchants, women, fishers, shepherds.

Comparative Midrash. Furthermore, attention must be called to the growing tendency to think of a parable as a midrash and to compare these expositions to rabbinic styles of scriptural interpretation. Several scholars are sensing how much in fact the parables are rooted in the Old Testament and Jewish exegesis. They are thinking of parables as developments of particular Old Testament texts. For example, the parable of the Compassionate Samaritan (Luke 10:25-37) has been seen as a sophisticated midrash on Hosea 6,[34] and behind the parable of the Ten Maidens (Matt. 25:1-13) may stand Song of Songs 5:1-5;[35] perhaps the parable of the Great Banquet (Luke 14:15-24) is a midrash on Deuteronomy 20.[36] A quiet revolution is brewing.

The scholars applying comparative midrash to parable study receive "bad press" or gross neglect, partly because of their own excesses and partly because they threaten presently established opinion, especially as relates to certain applications of form criticism and views of Jeremias regarding influence of the rabbis and the Old Testament. However, natural connections to earlier scholars such as Fiebig, the scholar who placed the parables in a rabbinic context, will likely be forged. The persons leading this effort include Earle Ellis, Birger Gerhardsson, C. H. Cave, J. Duncan Derrett, and James Sanders. Jeffrey Sharp, now a missionary and professor in Hong Kong, has written the first extensive analysis of this method, calling attention to various and separated individuals applying comparative midrash to parable understanding.[37]

The actual word *midrash* is not readily defined.[38] Generally it has to do with inquiry into Torah (as Ezra 7:10), expounding of a scriptural text. There is haggadic midrash (religious devotion and duty) and halachic midrash (regulation of conduct through law). Especially among the rabbis, midrash is a technical term used to describe scriptural interpretation. The form the midrash might take could be as varied as verse by verse exegesis, sermons, and even narrative, including parables.[39]

This model for understanding the parables has a future and has influenced this study toward a more persistent pursuit of Old Testament linkages. The fact that several parables are placed in explicitly exegetical contexts (Luke 7:36-50; 10:25-37; 18:18-30; Matt. 21:33-44) must be taken quite seriously and may be a clue to the original setting for some other parables.

Redactional Analysis. One other modern method, very important for understanding some of the newer studies, is the application of redaction analysis to parable study. Redaction analysis is a current procedure developed to discern the theology and intention of the final editor or evangelist. This method seeks to discover the way a particular Gospel or section in a Gospel was put together by the evangelist. It investigates the author's messages and purposes.[40] Biblical theology has been enriched generally as new theologians, so to speak, have come into their own. Luke, Matthew, and Mark have theological contributions to make.

This interest to find the message of the evangelist has been applied creatively to the parables, especially by Jack Kingsbury.[41] Centering on Matthew 13, he points out that all the parables in that extended chapter are kingdom-of-heaven in orientation, a central theological concept for the entire Gospel. The function of the chapter in the ground plan of the entire Gospel is to signal the "great turning point." Jesus came to the Jews but his mission was rebuffed, so he began to address them in the enigmatic form of parables. Jesus then turned to his disciples as the true people of God. The chapter can be divided into two main sections: verses 1-35 function as apology (parables to the Jewish crowds) and verses 36-52 function as instruction or paraenesis (parables to the disciples in private). This turning point had great relevance for Matthew's church because his congregation had carried on a mission to the Jews and had experienced failure. Thus the Lord addressed himself to the situation of the church.

Kingsbury went a further step and drew conclusions regarding Matthew's influence upon the seven parables in chapter thirteen. These parables possess characteristics strikingly similar to the rabbinic traditions. Also the kingdom-of-heaven focus falls upon the present reality. Stereotyped phraseology characteristic of the evangelist elsewhere in the Gospel is detected, and Kingsbury calls attention to the occurrence of direct speech as a typically Matthaean touch.[42]

Another redactional study of substance, carried out by Charles Carlston, concentrates upon the sixteen Markan passages that may be classified as parabolic.[43] Warning against the tendency toward an exclusive emphasis on the message of Jesus to the neglect of the contributions of the evangelists, he considers these authors as having equally serious theological purposes as Paul.[44] With particular care to detail, Carlston studies each Markan parable in its setting in Matthew and then in Luke to assess the accent of each evangelist before proceeding to Mark. The result critically is often to assign relatively little to Jesus and rather much to the evangelists. Though he calls attention to the temptation so to concentrate on the message of Jesus as to find an authentic kernel to every parable as Jeremias, he does not recognize the temptation to claim too much both for each evangelist and for a new method. Carlston has produced a complete study of all the Markan parables and has challenged students to think carefully about the critically conservative conclusions of Jeremias. His book also illustrates the risk of excessive applications of redactional analysis.

Some interest in the theology of the evangelist is pursued in this study, but this concern is secondary due to limitations of scope and purpose.

Conclusion

This brief presentation of the story of interpretation is intended to acquaint the student with the influences and backgrounds playing on study and to equip him or her to understand the issues independently. Many of these methods are applied throughout this study. Furthermore, some impression can be gained about the many angles of vision that may be applied to the understanding of parables, and a growing horizon can be one personal gain. Applications of many of these methods are made in following chapters and will be better understood in the light of this story of interpretation. Readers just may also become more thoughtful about even further breakthroughs and fresh approaches.

NOTES

1. Adolf Jülicher, *Die Gleichnisreden Jesu.* (Darmstadt: Wissenschaftliche Buchgesellschaft, 1963 [reprint of 1910 edition]).
2. Ibid., 1:44,49.
3. Ibid., 1:42.
4. Norman Perrin, "The Modern Interpretation of the Parables of Jesus and the Problem of Hermeneutics," *Interpretation*, 25:132 (1971).
5. Harald Riesenfeld, *The Gospel Tradition*, trans. E. M. Rowley and R. A. Kraft (Philadelphia: Fortress Press, 1970), p. 141. For histories of interpretation see especially Warren S. Kissinger, *The Parables of Jesus* (London: The Scarecrow Press, 1979). For brief treatment see the perceptive remarks of Jack Kingsbury, *The Parables of Jesus in Matthew 13* (Richmond: John Knox Press, 1969), pp. 1-11; and Perrin, pp. 131-148.
6. Ibid. It must be remembered in fairness, however, that Jülicher's universal truths, like Via's existential truths, represented an effort at hermeneutical and not merely historical exegesis.
7. C. W. F. Smith, *The Jesus of the Parables* (Philadelphia: Westminster Press, 1948), p. 17.
8. Joachim Jeremias, *The Parables of Jesus*, trans. S. H. Hooke, Revised Edition; (New York: Charles Scribner's Sons, 1963).
9. Perrin, p. 133. On the quest see J. M. Robinson, *A New Quest for the Historical Jesus*, No. 25 of *Studies in Biblical Theology* (London: SCM Press, 1959).
10. Ernst Fuchs, *Hermeneutik*, Third Edition (Stuttgart: R. Mülharschon Verlag, 1963), pp. 219-30 on parable. For an introduction to Fuchs see P. R. Jones, "A Critique of Patternism as a Hermeneutical Method" (Unpublished Ph.D. dissertation, The Southern Baptist Theological Seminary, 1968), pp. 63-83. For a careful treatment of the thought of the later Heidegger, see Vincent Vycinas, *Earth and Gods* (The Hague: Martinus Nÿhoff, 1961). See also J. D. Kingsbury, "Ernst Fuchs' Interpretation of the Parables," *Lutheran Quarterly*, 22: 380-95 (1970).
11. Fuchs, "The New Testament and the Hermeneutical Problem," *The New Hermeneutic*, Vol. 2 of "New Frontiers in Theology," ed. J. Cobb and J. Robinson (New York: Harper & Row, 1964), pp. 124-5.
12. Eta Linnemann, *Jesus of the Parables*, trans. John Sturdy (New York: Harper & Row, 1966). It was originally published in 1961.
13. Ibid., p. 46.
14. Ibid., p. 47.
15. Ibid., p. 27.
16. Dan Via, *The Parables* (Philadelphia: Fortress Press, 1967). Geraint V. Jones was a kind of precursor in terms of existential and literary sensitivities. See his *The Art and Truth of the Parables* (London: SPCK, 1964).

17. For introduction see Murray Krieger, *The New Apologists for Poetry* (Minneapolis: University of Minnesota Press, 1956); also C. E. Pulos, *The New Critics and the Language of Poetry* (Lincoln, Nebraska: University of Nebraska Press, 1958); and R. J. Foster, *The New Romantics: A Reappraisal of the New Criticism* (Bloomington, Indiana: University of Indiana Press, 1962). With new critics, Dan Via affirms the autonomy of an aesthetic object, subordinates the historical background, sounds the note for organicism, and allows for polyvalence.

18. Amos Wilder, *The Language of the Gospel: Early Christian Rhetoric* (New York: Harper & Row, 1964), esp. pp. 79-96.

19. Wilder, *Theopoetic: Theology and the Religious Imagination* (Philadelphia: Fortress Press, 1976).

20. Robert Funk, *Language, Hermeneutic and Word of God* (New York: Harper & Row, 1966).

21. Sallie McFague, *Speaking in Parables: A Study in Metaphor and Theology* (Philadelphia: Fortress Press, 1975).

22. Ibid., p. 4.

23. Ibid., pp. 76-86. In a review, I criticized her for using the literary genre *allegory* as a whipping boy, but in correspondence she indicated that she had modified her position.

24. On structuralism see the excellent application by Jean Calloud, *Structural Analysis of Narrative*, trans. Daniel Patte (Philadelphia: Fortress Press, 1976); and the introduction by Bill Stancil, "Structuralism and New Testament Studies," *Southwestern Journal of Theology*, 22:41-59 (1980). For a negative assessment of the relevance of structuralism for parable study see Perrin, *Jesus and the Language of the Kingdom* (Philadelphia: Fortress Press, 1976), pp. 204-205.

25. John Crossan, *In Parables: The Challenge of the Historical Jesus* (New York: Harper & Row, 1973).

26. Ibid., p. 64

27. Ibid., p. 96.

28. Ibid., p. 106.

29. John Crossan, *Finding Is the First Act: Trove Folktales and Jesus' Treasure Parables* (Philadelphia: Fortress Press, 1979).

30. For an informative introduction see Robin Scroggs, "The Sociological Interpretation of the New Testament: The Present State of Research," *New Testament Studies*, 26:164-179 (1980).

31. Kenneth Bailey, *Poet and Peasant: A Literary Cultural Approach to the Parables in Luke* (Grand Rapids: Wm. B. Eerdmans, 1976), p. 27. See also his more recent volume, *Through Peasant Eyes* (Grand Rapids: Eerdmans, 1980).

32. Ibid., p. 157.

33. Richard Rohrbaugh, *The Biblical Interpreter* (Philadelphia: Fortress Press, 1978), p. 77.

34. So J. Duncan Derrett, *Law in the New Testament* (London: Darton, Longman and Todd, 1970), pp. 208-227. I have argued previously that the parable centers primarily in Leviticus 19:18 and chimes in with Hosea 6:6-8 in "The Love Command in Parable: Luke 10:25-37," *Perspectives in Religious Studies*, 6:224-242 (1979).

35. So J. Massingberd Ford, "The Parable of the Foolish Scholars," *Novum Testamentum*, 9:107-123 (1967).

36. So J. Sanders, "The Ethic of Election in Luke's Great Banquet Parable," *Essays in Old Testament Ethics*, ed. J. L. Crenshaw and J. T. Willis (New York: KTAV, 1974).

37. Jeffrey Sharp, "Comparative Midrash as a Technique for Parable Studies" (Unpublished Ph.D. dissertation, The Southern Baptist Theological Seminary, 1979).

38. See Epstein, "Midrash," *The Interpreter's Dictionary of the Bible* (hereafter referred to as *IDB*), K-Q: 376-377 (1962); M. P. Miller, "Midrash," *IDB*, S: 593-597 (1976). For an effort at a precise definition of midrash as a literary genre, see A. G. Wright, *The Literary Genre Midrash* (New York: Alba House, 1967); and for a more accepted view of midrash as covering a wide range, see Renée Bloch, "Midrash," *Dictionnaire de la Bible*, 5:1263-1281. See also Sharp, pp. 2-39; also Roger le Deaut's critique of Wright, "Apropos a Definition of Midrash," *Interpretation*, 25:259-282 (1971).

39. Wright, pp. 52-59.

40. See R. C. Briggs, *Interpreting the Gospels* (Nashville: Abingdon Press, 1969), pp. 85-107; also R. T. Fortna, "Redaction Criticism, NT," *IDB*, S: 733-35 (1976); also Simon Kistemaker, *The Gospels in Current Study* (Grand Rapids: Baker, 1972), pp. 50-60.

41. Jack Kingsbury, *The Parables of Jesus in Matthew 13* (Richmond: John Knox Press, 1969).

42. Ibid., pp. 135-137. Direct speech, while prominent in Matthew, is by no means merely typical of the evangelist as later chapters will document.

43. Charles Carlston, *The Parables of the Triple Tradition* (Philadelphia: Fortress Press, 1975). He demonstrates considerable independence by restraint in his use of the gospel of Thomas. His work is done with unusual care and offers enormous help for the research student. The parabolic passages in Mark are 2:15 *ff.*,18 *ff.*,21 *ff.*; 3:22-27; 4:1-20, 21,22,24 *f.*,30 *ff.*; 7:1-23,24-30; 9:50; 12:1-12; 13:28 *f.*,34-37; 4:26-29.

44. Ibid., xi.

2 The Nature of a Parable

The second step in preparation for parables requires an opening orientation that sets out characteristics and establishes what to expect. Actually, one finds out the nature of parable by extended engagement with particular texts, and, further, every parable is unique.[1] The student, indeed, begins with what he or she is presented originally—the text. The text is the thing.

This chapter shares the result of study of the parable texts and study of other scholarly analyses. The first step in the introduction involved acquainting the student with methods developed for encountering the text devised by influential scholars, particularly of recent and present vintage. Bible study is done by the individual but by the individual-in-community. Breakthroughs forged by others enlarge horizons and allow for advance.

One suggestive model for provoking thought about the nature of the parable is the triangle.[2] A triangle delivers from the tendency toward one factor analysis. Consider the parables as three-dimensional.

The parables reach the reader as distinctive literary form within a literary genre called gospel. The parables happened two thousand years ago in an actual ministry set in Palestine, and they must be evaluated as past events. The parables also are still read and studied because of the grand assumption that they remain hermeneutically invaluable as Word of God.

Each side of the triangle should be contemplated until consciousness raising occurs. The literary side provides a natural beginning, though it must focus first on oral art.

Parable as Literary Form

The parables were oral events (and "language events") delivered by a poetic Prophet.[3] They enjoyed the life of living speech. They were spoken Word. They addressed hearers in ongoing life rather than readers removed from the experience. Jesus recognized that the parables were hearing events that required personal response. Though the parables exist now as written, they must still be "heard." Amos Wilder invites the fresh sensibility of childhood. He recommends naive reading: "Let the word and the words have their own untrammeled course"; hear the parables naively and afresh.[4] Indeed, the interpreter needs to experience the parable, not merely reduce it to a propositional meaning nor merely accept a scholar's opinion.[5] To recognize the originally oral character of the parable event is to find a clue and attitude regarding response. It is imperative to develop the discipline of reading the parables themselves with intensity. Modern dramatic readings may facilitate a "hearing."

Definition of a Parable. Recognizing first the uniqueness of each parable, it is then permissible to offer generalizing definitions as starting points to be tested. Though the parable is a recognized literary form both in the Greek and Hebrew world, it is well to begin inductively. Some of Jesus' parables are extended similes because they are comparisons with the use of "like" (*homoia*) or "as" (*hōs*). They are often comparisons that illumine the great thesis, the kingdom of God (Mark 4:30), which is itself a symbol. Especially in Matthew the kingdom is explicitly likened to leaven (13:33), treasure lying buried in a field (13:44), a seine (13:47-50), laborers in the vineyard (20:1-16), and a marriage feast (22:1-14). Notice certain sayings (Matt. 10:16; 23:27).

Yet some of the parables are extended metaphors. Consider certain cryptic statements as well (Luke 6:38; 13:32; Matt. 23:24). Jesus' accusation, "You brood of vipers" (Matt. 12:34) is definitely metaphoric. Metaphor, "a transaction between contexts" (I. A. Richards), plays a creative role in language. By its etymology, metaphor implies motion (*phora*) and simultaneous change (*meta*). It is a kind of metamorphosis. Aristotle put it, "When the poet calls old age 'a withered stalk,' he conveys a new idea, a new fact, by means of a general notion" (*Rhetoric*, 3:10). A metaphor is "giving a thing a name that belongs to something else" (*Poetics*, 21). Aristotle, who took the perceptive use of metaphor as a token of genius, understood metaphoric thinking as finding the similarity in dissimilar things (*Poetics*, 22:16-17).

Most of the parabolic sayings and narrative parables are extensions of metaphors, but the simple parables are extensions of similes.[6] John Crossan has gone so far as to say suggestively that the parables are metaphoric expressions of Jesus' own experience of God.[7] The present tendency is to denigrate simile, as well as allegory, in favor of metaphor, to the point of overstatement.[8] It is misleading to drive a wedge between simile and metaphor as though they are completely different. The venerable Aristotle saw them closely related since they always involve two relations (*Rhetoric*, 3:2). In any event, an actual parable of Jesus is more than a mere extension. It is an independent literary type.

Some advance toward definition may be had by recognizing *internal* juxtaposition as typical of parable. The word *parable* derives from a preposition and a verb. The verb *ballō* means "to throw" and the preposition *para* means "alongside." So a parable is a throwing alongside. The noun *parabolē* means "setting beside" and the verb *paraballein* means "to set beside," "to compare."[9] Scholars have regularly spoken of a point of comparison (*tertium comparationis*), by which is meant the point at which the story (picture part) and the intended application (object) coincide. In fact, the very essence of Jesus' parables lies in the presence of *internal juxtaposition*. For example, in the parable of the Two Sons (Matt. 21:28-32) observe juxtaposition in the two responses (R1 and R2) to the father's request:

R1   Verbal Refusal and Actual Obedience (v. 29)
R2   Verbal Acceptance and Actual Disobedience (v. 30).

Another and familiar example turns on the responses (R1, R2, and R3) to the wounded man in the parable of the Good Samaritan (Luke 10:30-37).

R1   Priest passes by (v. 31)
R2   Levite passes by (v. 32)
R3   Samaritan stops (v. 33)

Again in Luke 15 observe the juxtaposition between ninety-nine sheep and one sheep (vv. 3-7) and ten coins and one coin (vv. 8-10). The point is made explicit in Luke 15 by verse 7 and verse 10 and in Luke 10 by verse 36. The discovery of such juxtaposition does not lead to a simple, abstracted proposition or interpretation. Indeed, the juxtaposition demands the retention of the parable, but it also provides the crucial restraint. It establishes parameters for meaning. The juxtaposition does leave "the mind in sufficient doubt about its precise application to tease it into active thought."[10] The point of a parable should be sought internally in a juxtaposition.

Parable and Allegory. The distinction between parable and allegory in Gospel study is emphatically not a matter of mere rhetorical precision. The possible implications are far-reaching. For example, are the interpreters from the evangelists all the way up to Jülicher and A. B. Bruce in the nineteenth century incorrect? Is allegorical interpretation of a parable defensible? Does one settle for finding the main point of a parable and treat the details of a parable like dead limbs on a tree?[11] These major considerations should sharpen the beginning student's awareness of what exactly is at stake, in what may appear otherwise a seemingly pedantic discussion. With these matters singled out from the beginning, a start can be made toward distinction.

Generally an allegory is a series of pictures symbolizing a series of truths in another sphere. The details of the story are meant to have independent significance. Each detail is a separate metaphor. William Hull portrays allegory as follows:

Story

Application[12]

Such a story is composed then of what might be called metaphorical cryptograms. Allegories appeal to the initiated, to those in the know, to insiders. They may involve some breakdown in realism.

There are distinguished allegories in the history of English literature, among them Spenser's *Faerie Queene*, Swift's *Gulliver's Travels* and *Tale of a Tub*, and Bunyan's *The Pilgrim's Progress*, which are familiar. The Old Testament set a biblical precedent for allegories. Ezekiel 17, crucial for the parable of the Mustard Seed, develops an impressive incident of nature concerning great eagles and vines (vv. 3-8). The prophet followed with a very allegorical application (vv. 9-18). Again, Ezekiel spun an allegory of the cauldron (24:3-5) and appended an allegorical meaning (esp. vv. 9-14). The Hebrew word *mashal*, which had a very broad semantic field, was used to designate such allegories in the Old Testament.[13] There are other allegories, and the parables are themselves rather allegorical (as 2 Sam. 14:6-11).

The word *allegory*, however, never appears in the Gospels, and the Gospel parables can in fact be distinguished, though some parables have been classified as pure allegories. The parable of the Wicked Tenants (Mark 12:1-12), the classic case in point, is admittedly allegorical, but even it is not a simple allegory but an allegorical parable.[14] Some have suspected the parables of the Sower, the Seine, and the Marriage Feast.[15]

The parable, as distinguished from the allegory, contains an internal juxtaposition rather than a series of relatively equal points. Ian T. Ramsey holds rightly that the purpose of a parable is to lead to a "disclosure point," while allegory correlates two areas of discourse.[16] The allegory is necessarily reducible. Paul Ricoeur writes:

The allegory can always be translated into the text but can be understood by itself; once this better text has been made out, the allegory falls away like a useless garment; what the allegory showed, while concealing it, can be said in a direct discourse that replaces the allegory.[17]

The parable is otherwise. The structure of connections is simply closer in a parable. Even though the parables contain inescapable symbolic elements, these elements are made subordinate to the internal coherence of the parabolic story.[18] Furthermore, the parable drives toward participation rather than information. While allegory presumes participation, parable creates participation and as such is never expendable. The form of the parable is not a mere envelope but rather participates itself in a happening. "The hearer not only learns about the reality," says Wilder, "he participates in it. He is invaded by it."[19] Allegory and parable then are distinguishable, though not antithetical, and the parables of Jesus are not allegories.

The battle Jülicher fought has been won, and now scholars are more willing to admit that the line between allegory and parable can be too sharply drawn.[20] C. F. D. Moule actually calls in question the legacy from Jülicher that Jesus could not have used allegory and recommends the category "multiple parable" to cover those with a plurality of implications.[21] It is appropriate, indeed mandatory, to recognize the presence of subordinated allegorical dimensions. Many parables incorporate stock metaphors also that may be quite influential. The parables interpret the ministry of Jesus and responses to it. The parables assume the Old Testament. Excellent practical guidance comes from James Denney:

The golden rule is this: Don't try in the interests of an arbitrary theory to eliminate everything allegorical and so trim the texts into pure parables. On the other hand, don't allegorize to the point which mars the one lesson which every parable was meant to teach.[22]

Classification of Parables. The parables enjoy a certain range or variety in length, calling forth a traditional classification. C. L. Mitton, in a delightful fashion, portrayed Jesus' capability to turn people's ears into eyes, "Sometimes it is a still picture, like a single cartoon; at other times it is a series of moving pictures like a short story presented on a film."[23] Some ordering of subcategories can accelerate analysis.

1. Parabolic sayings (*Bildwörter*). These simple metaphors elaborate a picture, a brief utterance stating a fact of common human experience to be applied by the listener in context. For example, "You are the salt of the earth" (Matt. 5:13); "You cannot serve two masters" (Matt. 6:24); do not "throw pearls before swine" (Matt. 7:6). They are picturesque appeals to the imagination that nevertheless carry the famous authority of Jesus (Matt. 7:29). They remind somewhat of wisdom; and in the Apocrypha there are sayings in Ecclesiasticus such as, "How can the clay pot associate with the iron kettle?" (13:3), and "The bee is small among flying creatures, but her product is the best of sweet things" (11:3). The parabolic sayings of Jesus predominate in Matthew and in the Sermon on the Mount but are present elsewhere

(Luke 4:23; Mark 2:17*a*; 2:21-22). They are not proper parables, though they may be thought of as incipient or as "parable germs" (A. B. Bruce). The sayings are not pursued further in this study.

2. Simple Parables. These basic parables depict a typical situation, appeal to common experience, and are normally introduced by formulas of comparison. Some students prefer to label them as similitudes, but they are helpfully conceived simply as general situation. C. H. Dodd has suggested the simple grammatical test that while a parabolic saying has no more than one verb, the simple parable has more than one verb, and it is usually in the present tense.[24] A simple parable is more than a picture; it is a picture elaborated into a story. Examples include the paired parables of the Lost Sheep and Lost Coin (Luke 15:3-10) and the Tower Builder and the Warring King (Luke 14:28-32) and the Treasure and the Pearl (Matt. 13:44-45).

3. The Narrative Parables. These are stories in the sense of progression as they depict an interesting specific case. Examples include the very familiar parables of the Rich Fool (Luke 12:16-21), the Unjust Steward (Luke 16:1-8), the Good Samaritan (Luke 10:30-37), and the Wicked Tenants (Mark 12:1-9) among others. As Matthew reports a preponderance of the parabolic sayings, Luke contains many narrative parables. Jülicher was inclined to use the term *fable* for these imaginary stories narrated in past time, but he declined to avoid confusion with animal stories.[25]

There were certain laws of popular narratives that applied in a general manner to the narrative parables. There was conciseness of story, for example, as only necessary persons appeared. There was the law of the single perspective from which the story flows. Rarely were characters portrayed by attribute or were emotions mentioned. Subsidiary characters were described minimally. Motivation was usually absent in the presentation. Economy in description was observed. There was rich use of direct speech. The law of repetition called for reiterations. The law of end stress invited the most important thing to be described last. There was often an antithesis of two types.[26]

These narrative laws, while not binding, are valuable clues. Attention should also be given to the separate scenes or episodes in narrative parables. They may be divided into scenes that heighten awareness of the parable as a drama, clarify progress, and underscore contrast. Via, Eichholz, and Crossan have brought out the dramatic development and character of parables.[27] Indeed, a narrative parable is a dramatic story composed of one or more scenes constructed intentionally for intended effect, taken from daily life yet centered in a decisive circumstance.

Parable as Historical Event

Though the literary side of the triangular model for parable should not be neglected, the historical side should not be forgotten. The this-generation dimension of the proclamation of Jesus holds our feet to history. Scholars like Dodd and Jeremias saw in a clear-eyed way that Jesus announced the coming of the kingdom to a very particular time. So students press behind the literary Gospels to the parables as historical happenings, and critical scholars are optimistic about success. Historical study naturally begins with background.

Background. Jesus did not invent parables; he merely perfected the art. There are interesting antecedents in the Old Testament, and Jesus' parables stand in the tradition of the prophetic parables. The most famous and most instructive antecedent comes from Nathan's parable to King David, itself an historical happening.

There were once two men in the same city, one rich and the other poor. The rich man had large flocks and herds, but the poor man had nothing of his own except one little ewe lamb. He reared it himself, and it grew up in his home with his own sons. It ate from his dish, drank from his cup and nestled in his arms; it was like a daughter to him. One day a traveller came to the rich man's house, and he, too mean to take something from his own flocks and herds to serve to his guest, took the poor man's lamb and served up that (2 Sam. 12:1-4, NEB).

Nathan seized the teachable moment in a breathless game which the prophet played with his king's soul and his own life at stake. The parable functioned as a tool to get inside David's guard, to strike an existing moral blindness from his eyes. It had an element of surprise. "It strikes his victim with added force just because, as he listens, he does not expect that it is meant for him."[28] The parable evoked an outraged moral verdict before it dawned "for whom the bell tolled." David blurted out his kingly judgment only to get his comeuppance when Nathan then applied his parable to David's affair with Bathsheba (2 Sam. 12:5-14). Observe with James Smart, "It is the use of a parable not so much as a method of teaching spiritual truths, but as a means in a definite situation of revealing a man to himself."[29] This antecedent reminds of the elder brother sequence in Luke 15:25-32. There are several other parables in the Old Testament, including the nature parables of the Plowman's Work (Isa. 28:23-29) and the very important Song of the Vineyard (Isa. 5:1-7), which Jesus sang in his own manner. Ecclesiastes 9:13-16 represents a narrative parable. Consider also Amos's vision of the plumb line (7:8-9) and Ezekiel's picture of the wild vine (15:1-8). Nevertheless, the Jesus kind of parable remains notably scarce in the Old Testament and has most affinities with the prophetic tradition as especially the case of his parable of the Barren Fig Tree (Luke 13:6-9).

Incidentally little exists in the literature between the testaments to label parable. The so-called "Book of the Parables" in 1 Enoch 37—71 is not especially relevant.[30] The word *parable* or *mashal* there really means oration or discourse, and these discourses read like apocalyptic visions. The author himself described his work as "the Second Vision of Enoch" (37:1). The fact that these celestial journeys are called *meshalim* merely attests to the elasticity of the term. Some of Jesus' parables did bring an apocalyptic perspective, however, such as the Rich Man and Lazarus (Luke 16:19-31) and the Sheep and the Goats (Matt. 25:31-46).

Nor is Qumran promising. The Dead Sea Scrolls contain no parables. *Mashal* is to be found nowhere, though the hymns (IQH) contain striking metaphors and similes.[31]

More promising is Greek culture. Homer used parables extensively to illustrate events. There are 189 pure parables in *The Iliad* and 39 in *The Odyssey*.[32] Plato's speech was rich in similitudes which were taken from typical actions or relations. Parables were used in Stoic-Cynic diatribes to clarify philosophical ideas and to answer objections. Also some illustrations of Socrates were parabolic.[33] Influence of any direct kind is quite debatable, though Hellenistic influence in Palestine in the Ten Towns and beyond was considerable.

Foreground. Were the parables of Jesus beautiful examples of an established rabbinic art or catalysts for a later rabbinic flowering? Certainty is not presently possible because some specialists in rabbinics see the necessity of an extensive critical evaluation before dating and authentic residue can be creditably established.[34] Professor Jeremias gave a delightful lecture at The Southern Baptist Theological Seminary in which he allowed only one parable of Hillel, a charming joke to his disciples upon taking leave, as a rabbinic antecedent.[35] It is certain at least that a rich supply of rabbinic parables exists in the foreground after the Jesus era and that striking correspondences can be drawn.

Similarities of convention include the use of common metaphors like king, servant, and vineyard and introductions that may take the form of a question or stated comparison, as "A parable. To what is the matter like?" Some rabbinic parables state the intended comparison in the last sentence and/or append an application. Some have two climaxes, and some end with a question for the audience.[36] Rarely were direct expositions of rabbinic parables offered.[37]

The discontinuities also exist, however, like the fact that eschatological parables are rare among the rabbis. A famous entreaty in *Midrash Canticles* suggests not only the rabbinic regard for parables but also names their intended purpose: "Let not the parable be lowly in thine eyes, for through a parable one can attain to an understanding of the words of the Torah" (1:1). The conscious purpose of the rabbinic parables was to expound the Torah or the Scriptures,[38] but the parables of Jesus expound the kingdom. The difference is one more of content than form. Christian interpreters are further convinced that Jesus was the master of the parable art and that his parables contain a creativity and lifelikeness quite beyond the rabbinic parallels. It is natural to presume, in the light of Old Testament antecedents and rabbinic parallels in the immediate foreground, that others during the time of Jesus told parables.

Setting (Sitz im Leben Jesu). The principle of finding the life setting further invites the student to reconstruct how parables were interwoven into the ministry and meaning of Jesus. It belongs to a healthy and necessary "back to Jesus" campaign to give first place to what these texts meant originally. Popular impressions of parables as merely moralistic stories containing precious little gospel are innocuous and are best corrected by historical reconstruction. The discipline of seeking life setting also retains the authority of Jesus.

The actual occasions for the parables, not always possible to recover, were several, not merely one. Many arose out of conflictual situations in which Jesus met a barrage of criticism for his life-style,

ministry, and preaching with his parabolic answers. Beyond the parables, there are two major sets of controversy stories (Mark 2:1 to 3:6;
11:27 to 12:44 and par.) in which Jesus met criticism, as well as controversy miracles, which have affinity with the parables for Pharisees
and sinners. These answering parables accomplished two marvelous
feats simultaneously. They *exposed* the self-righteousness of opponents and *extolled* the kingdom of God. They put the activity of Jesus
in a fresh light. A nice case in point is the parable of the Playing Children (Matt. 11:16-19; Luke 7:31-35). The Baptizer had been faulted as
sternly ascetic ("neither eating nor drinking"), yet Jesus caught it
broadside for being a religious man who was life of the party ("came
eating and drinking"). Both were scorned iconoclasts. The parable
exposes the inconsistency of the two criticisms and the underlying pre-
supposition and defends the joy of table fellowship with sinners,
which anticipates the joys of the age to come.[39] But notice that Jesus
did not propose merely to win a point but a person. According to Jan
Lambrecht, "He wants to convince his opponents, not crush them; he
wants to win them over, not merely put them down."[40]

Other occasions for the parables included scholarly debate (as
Luke 10:25-37) and teaching settings (Mark 4:1-2).

Another and vital setting factor concerns discerning the function
of the Teller of the tales. One cannot obtain the full historical meaning
of the parable apart from the Parabolist. The parables are not merely
clever stories. They are proclamations by the eschatological Bringer of
salvation to interpret what God was doing in a unique moment. They
are veiled self-testimony.

A striking instance of "Christological penetration" appears in the
parable of the Strong Man Bound (Mark 3:23-27) when the exorcism
of demons caused critics to link Jesus with evil (v. 22). The counter
claim is remarkable. There is "no gentle Jesus, meek and mild, with a
pale Protestant face," no peaceful pastoral in response, but admission
of a campaign to roll back the powers of evil and make way for the
kingdom. Jesus claimed that a stronger One had bound the strong one
in a great ministry of liberation (cf. Luke 11:20). The Parabolist depicts himself as Conqueror as he exposes the inconsistency of his
critics.[41]

The Teller often emerges as Prophet, vis-á-vis Israel (Luke
13:6-9), religious leadership (Mark 12:1-11), and the cult (Luke

10:25-37; 18:9-14). In a similar vein, he is Defender of the religious outcast, Awaker of faith and Proclaimer of the kingdom (Mark 4:1-34), and even Son (Mark 12:1-11) and coming Son of man (Matt. 25:31-46). Critical opinion varies as to precise picture, but a widespread concensus recognizes with Otto Kuss, "Who will understand Jesus must seek to understand his parables."[42] George Beasley-Murray put it down,

Our Lord's message of the Kingdom is controlled by His consciousness that He embodies its authority and employs its powers; that by His acts of mercy and judgment . . . He opens its gates for the sons of men.[43]

And on the very last page of his magisterial study, Jeremias concludes, "In attempting to recover the original significance of the parables, one thing above all becomes evident: it is that all the parables of Jesus compel his hearers to come to a decision about his person and mission."[44] There is no security or safety when engaging in close study of the Teller's tales for his veiled kingliness invites obedient faith. It can be asserted that something of the historical Jesus, the mind of Christ, can be gleaned from the parables.

One intriguing postscript. The Speaker of parables was also a Doer of parables. Consider his parabolic acts. He chose twelve (Mark 3:13-19), a symbolic gathering of Israel; he received outcasts (Luke 15:1; 19:1-10), a direct correspondence to the parable of the great supper (Luke 14:16-24); he entered Jerusalem at Passover astride an ass (Mark 11:1-11), a symbolic gesture defining his kingship; he cursed the fig tree (Mark 11:12-14), a symbol of divine judgment on Israel; he cleansed the Temple (Mark 11:15-19), a statement of God's sovereignty over the cult (v. 17); and he seized upon the last supper (Mark 14:22-26), the bread and wine becoming themselves miniparables.[45] These prophetic signs, while far more eschatological, belong to the tradition of parabolic acts done by the prophets, such as Isaiah's nakedness (20:2 ff), Jeremiah's breaking of the earthen flask (19), and his purchase of a field while Jerusalem was under seige (32:6-25).[46]

Method. Parables as historical happenings require historical methods of analysis, including attention to backgrounds and use of the historicocritical method and beyond. Source Criticism is one comparative tool for assessing sources such as Mk., Q (a sayings source seen in material common to Matt. and Luke), M (special Matthean material), and L (special Lukan material). Excellent introductions to the method abound,[47] and the student of parables should assume the habit of studying each parable in a Gospel parallel, in English translation, though preferably a Greek text (Huck or Aland).

Form Criticism, another method, recognizes a twofold setting, that of Jesus and that of the early church (*Sitz im Leben Kirche*). Early Christians applied the parables creatively and afresh to new situations they encountered. Form Criticism, which groups similar materials such as controversies, miracles, parables, seeks to show the stages of development prior to final form.[48] This method along with Source Criticism is best learned by doing exercises. It has been applied carefully and severely to parables.

The mysterious gospel of Thomas also can be applied comparatively since it contains eleven parables common to the Gospels. It is not a gospel in the sense of a narrative, but is a collection of 114 sayings attributed to Jesus. The available text is a fourth-century Coptic manuscript found at Nag Hammadi in Egypt.[49] Scholars, especially Jeremias, regularly include the parables of the gospel of Thomas in their reconstructions, though Gnostic intrusions into its text make this perilous.

Even more attention fastens upon the four "hitherto unknown" parables present. Could it be that the gospel of Thomas preserves some authentic sayings, not previously available? The fact that a great many parables belong to only one gospel throw open the possibility that a few might have been missed by all the canonical Gospels. After all, it was recognized that everything of Jesus could not be and was not included (as John 21:25; Mark 4:33).

These four parables are here presented because of their unfamiliarity to the general reader.

Logion 8 (parable of the large fish).
The man is like a wise fisherman who cast his net into the sea, he drew it up from the sea full of small fish; among them he found a large good fish, that wise fisherman, he threw all the small fish down into the sea, he chose the large fish without regret.

Logion 21a (parable of the little children)
Mary said to Jesus: Whom are thy disciples like? He said: They are like little children who have installed themselves in a field which is not theirs. When the owners of the field come, they will say: "Release to us

our field." They take off their clothes before them to release it to them and to give back their field to them.

Logion 97 (parable of the jar)
Jesus said: The Kingdom of the Father is like a woman who was carrying a jar full of meal. While she was walking on a distant road, the handle of the jar broke. The meal streamed out behind her on the road. She did not know it, she had noticed no accident. After she came into her house, she put the jar down, she found it empty.

Logion 98 (the parable of the assassin)
Jesus said: The Kingdom of the Father is like a man who wishes to kill a powerful man. He drew the sword in his house, he stuck it into the wall, in order to know whether his hand would carry through; then he slew the powerful man.[50]

Of the four the first two are so Gnostic as to weaken their claim, but the second two are looked on with more favor. Ray Summers objects to the parable of the assassin because of its use of a murder illustration.[51] The parable of the jar has the best claim and could refer to the imperceptible coming of the kingdom until it has suddenly been seen to have arrived (as Mark 4:26-29).

Parables as Hermeneutical

The final side of the triangular model for parable understanding places the focus on the hermeneutical.[52] The parables themselves are hermeneutical explorations of the kingdom of God. They interrogated the original audiences, and they illumine existence today. They also move through symbolic story toward understanding and have a rightful and highly influential place in the proclamation of Jesus. The teaching of Jesus and the parables in particular have a crucial place in New Testament theology.[53] Jesus was a poetic theologian, one for whom truth was parabolic. Christian theology itself would be more balanced, more ethical, more kingdom-oriented if the teaching of Jesus were more genuinely incorporated.

The Great Thesis. The core concept around which all the parables revolve is the kingdom of God (*basileia tou theou*).[54] The kingdom functions regally as the presiding metaphor, as each parable gathers it up into its own metaphoric system.[55] Jesus came proclaiming the great thesis of the coming kingdom as portrayed in the summary statement in Mark 1:15. The parables portray it best.

The kingdom of God belongs to Old Testament thought as well,

especially in the motif of the kingship of Yahweh. In his inaugurating
vision, Isaiah saw "the King, the Lord of hosts" (6:5). The call to worship of a psalmist captured God's sovereignty:

> Lift up your heads, O gates!
> and be lifted up, O ancient doors!
> that the King of glory may come in.
> Who is this King of glory?
> the Lord of hosts,
> he is the King of glory! (24:9-10)[56]

Furthermore, the demand of the Ten Commandments implied the
sovereignty of God as does the covenant: "you shall be my people,
and I shall be your God" (Jer. 31:33). Yahweh manifested himself
further as sovereign over Israel's own king, as King of kings and Lord
of lords (1 Chron. 28:5; 29:23). Daniel 4 asserts the sovereignty of
God over the earth's kingdoms. At a climactic moment, Nebuchad-
nezzar affirmed the eternality of God's kingdom: "His sovereignty is
never-ending/and his rule endures through all generations (v. 34,
NEB). The ensuing account of Belshazzar's feast demonstrates God's
sovereignty over sovereigns, and Daniel 7 looks beyond the world's
empires.

Kingdom of God as such was not prominent in the apocalyptic
literature nor dynamic in the rabbinic literature, but it was over-
whelmingly central for the Zealots.[57] For them the kingdom came by
human hustle, but Jesus in the parable of the Seed Growing on its
Own (Mark 4:26-29) insisted charmingly that the kingdom comes by
divine initiative.

Jesus spoke of the rule of God through the metaphors of king,
father, and householder. He defined the kingdom in the Lord's Prayer
with memorable parallelism:

> Your Kingdom come,
> Your will be done
> as in heaven also upon earth (Matt. 6:10).

He portrayed the seeking and receiving grace of the kingdom in the
parables of the Lost Sheep, the Lost Coin, and the Lost Boy (Luke 15).
He spoke of the promise of the kingdom in the parable of the Mustard
Seed (Mark 4:30-32). He asserted the priceless value of the kingdom in
the parables of the pearl and the treasure (Matt. 13:44-46). He insisted

upon the necessity of obedience to the kingdom by hearing (Mark
4:1-9; Luke 16:19-31). To hear the Word is to accept the sovereignty
of God. He depicted the will of God for the disciple as one of compassion (Luke 10:25-37; Matt. 25:31-46). He sought to awaken faith.

Jesus himself was rooted in the will of God. The decisions during
the temptations expressed a commitment to God's will (Matt.
4:4,6-7,10). In Gethsemane came ultimate testing and profound struggle, "My father, if it is possible, let this cup pass" but followed immediately by the great willingness, "Yet not as I will but as you" (Matt.
26:39). Jesus saw his life from the affirmation of baptism, through the
mighty acts of the Galilean campaign, the mission of his disciples, and
his march to Jerusalem as oriented to God's will.

The precise timing of the kingdom, whether realized or thoroughly future, cannot be debated in detail. That Jesus claimed the
kingdom as present is critically clear from the famous logion in Luke
11:20, "But if it is by the finger of God that I cast out demons, then the
kingdom of God has come upon you" (RSV). The parable of the
Strong Man confirms it. The kingdom is certainly future at the Last
Supper (Mark 14:25). Jesus inaugurated the kingdom, but the kingdom's consummation stands in the future. The seed parables in Mark
4 are decisive. The kingdom is "already" and "not yet." The seed is
sown, the harvest will follow.[58] "Because . . . therefore."

Clusters. The teaching about the kingdom by the parables can be
grouped rather naturally, though not stringently. One cluster gathers
parables centered on the *crisis* of the coming kingdom. Like a drum
roll from the bowels of the earth came the announcement of Jesus, "I
have come to set fire to the earth" (Luke 12:49, NEB). Jesus addressed
the frivolous irresponsibility of his generation with a fierce word of
God. He spoke parabolically of the myopia of a generation that did
not know what time it was (Luke 12:54-56; Matt. 16:2-3) and emphatically in prophetic critique through fourteen "this generation" sayings
sprinkled throughout the Gospels (Mark 8:11-13,38; 9:19; 13:30;
Matt. 11:16; 12:38-42,45; 23:36; and Luke 17:25). He spoke further of
the imminence of catastrophe, the failure of national leadership. The
"parables of the times" confronted a nation with a call for sweeping
repentance.

Jesus centered upon a mission to Israel rather than one directed
primarily to Gentiles (Matt. 15:24; 10:5).[59] Like a Jewish prophet, he

saw Israel headed for national disaster. He predicted the ruin of the Temple (Mark 13:1-2) and the destruction of Jerusalem. His was a missionary intention to bring Israel to its mission as "a light to the nations" (Isa. 49:6). Jesus rejected the worldly hopes of nationalism in favor of his vision of the kingdom of God. Jesus warned the nation in the parable of the Barren Fig Tree (Luke 13:6-9) and challenged the leadership (Matt. 15:14; Mark 12:1-12).

The crisis of the kingdom was personal, as well as national. The personal crisis was nothing less than the decision to reorient one's whole being. One must undergo a conversion, a *metanoia*. Response is not optional; rather, it means life. Stake everything on the kingdom. This crisis of destiny demands decision. Indecision must end. "Alas for the man," writes Mitton, "who refuses God's moment, as though he had a right to make God wait for his own convenience!"[60] The individual is addressed in the parables of the Rich Fool (Luke 12:13-21) and the Rich Man and Lazarus (Luke 16:19-31), called in this study the parable of the Six Brothers.

Since the kingdom is future as well as present, it is also possible that Jesus spoke of the crisis of the consummation. The harvest is anticipated in some parables but portrayed graphically in others. The need is to be prepared for the advent (Mark 13:28,34). Keep your lamps burning (Matt. 25:1-13). The great separation (Matt. 24:40-41) will depend upon whether actual obedience to the will of God has occurred (Matt. 25:31-46).

Another cluster, regarding sinners and Pharisees, centers on grace and repentance. Jesus rarely, if ever, spoke directly of grace but rather of the ethic of obedience and with uncomfortable frequency.[61] This fact has created a stern image for some. Despite absence of the word *grace*, the gracious conduct of Jesus in his intercourse with sinners and tax collectors spoke with words of another coin.[62] Further, the compassion of the Messiah can be seen in the setting of the Sermon on the Mount, which places the grace of compassionate healing before and after (Matt. 4:23-25; 8—9), thus being faithful to Jesus' stress on demand and grace.[63] And the grace of the Beatitudes (esp. Matt. 5:3) forms basis for the commands. Grace, in its concrete form, also associates naturally with the whole healing ministry. The sick often ask for mercy (Mark 8:22; 10:47; Matt. 9:27). And there is that haunting invitation, "Come to me, all the ones who are working hard and have a heavy load, and I will give you rest" (Matt. 11:28).[64]

This emerging portrait of grace absolutely comes to life in the parables that proclaim the wideness of God's mercy, that explain his acceptance of sinners. These parables vindicate and challenge to repentance. It seems that the kingdom is quite exclusive, "For Sinners Only." All this cluster of parables is addressed to opponents among others, to scribes and Pharisees (Luke 15:2; 18:9; Mark 2:16), to Simon the Pharisee explicitly (Luke 7:40), and to the Sanhedrin (Matt. 21:23).[65]

Yet another cluster centers in the *conditions* of the kingdom. Jesus not only proclaimed the kingdom and portrayed its character but also invited persons to enter (Matt. 5:20; 7:21; 18:3; 21:31; 23:13; Mark 9:47; 10:15,23-25).[66] Obedience to God's will is necessary. The kingdom makes a demand so it is very appropriate to count the cost first, as in the parables of the Tower Builder and the Warring King (Luke 14:28-32). Entrance requires boldness like that of the unjust steward (Luke 16:1-9). A kingdom person cares concretely as she or he accepts the authority of the love command for ordering life (Mark 12:28-31; Luke 10:25-37).

These clusters, including the nature of the kingdom, are pursued with several examples from each in later chapters. The next step is to develop several significant hermeneutical characteristics.

Characteristics. In memorable fashion, several aspects can be noted.

First, the parables are *eschatological*, as hearers were living in an exceptional situation.[67] God was bursting into history. There was urgency. Life and history have meaning and purpose. Even in parables that are seemingly unrelated to the kingdom, there is reversal, a revision of values because of an otherworldly perspective, as in the Rich Fool and the Six Brothers.

Second, the parables are *existential* because they illumine existence. Jesus is often portrayed elsewhere as able to read the inner person (as Mark 2:8), but such understanding of oneself can be found within the parables, a capital reason why they stimulate contemporary response. Jesus could both expose a pale or petrified existence and feel the human struggle. The parables themselves strike the water table of common existence like deep calling to deep. Jesus intended to engage existence initially as he characteristically began, "Who among you . . .?" He knew, and the parable allows one to know, how it is to stand outside like the elder brother (Luke 15:28) or to be lost and to come to oneself and overcome estrangement (Luke 15:17).[68] The parables are intensely personal when the question arises explicitly, "What shall I do?" The parables adroitly expose inauthentic existence centered in values that do not last (Luke 16:19-31) and extol authentic existence centered in the things that matter and the things that last—the kingdom. Along the way the penny drops. Earthly stories have heavenly meaning.

Third, the parables are *ethical.* Note the interest within numerous parables regarding the attitude toward one's fellows, as the attitude of the Pharisee toward the tax collector (Luke 18:9-14), the elder brother toward his younger brother (Luke 15:25-32), the unmerciful servant toward his fellow servant (Matt. 18:23-35). The imperative of being religious *through* relationships comes through. Furthermore, the hearer is often required to form a moral verdict on some situations, such as the Two Sons (Matt. 21:28-32) and the Talents (Luke 19:12-27).[69] Further, the rousing call to repentance implicit in numerous parables invited participation in the kingdom and a new set of values. One can adopt the values of the Teller and love the things he loved, oppose the things he opposed, and value the things that he valued, and incarnate forgiveness, compassion, and grace.[70]

Fourth, the parables are *evangelistic.* Jesus appealed for a consent, to awaken a slumbering crowd, to stimulate a decision to enter the kingdom. The crisis parables require a response to emergency, the grace parables invite repentance, the parables on the coming kingdom seek faith, and those on the conditions of the kingdom demand obedience. The parables warrant change from hearers, invite faith. The Father's door is always open. The elder brother is not merely exposed (Luke 15:25-32). He is invited to "come to the party," to complete the story by swallowing pride and by tapping his toes. Robert Frost captured the invitation to participate in his poem, "The Pasture":

> I'm going out to clean the pasture spring;
> I'll only stop to rake the leaves away
> (And wait to watch the water clear, I may)
> I shan't be gone long.—You come too.

I'm going out to fetch the little calf
That's standing by the mother. It's so young
It totters when she licks it with her tongue.
I shan't be gone long.—You come too.[71]

Postscript

The study of parables has been approached by means of a memorable model. The triangle reminds the student of the necessity of encompassing the literary sensitivities, the historical realities, and the hermeneutical explorations. Each side of the triangle jealously demands its due and makes more likely the probability of asking the right questions.

NOTES

1. The stress taken here is phenomenological as first priority. The character of A. T. Robertson's scholarship, influence of the New Criticism, and study with Paul Scherer influenced this stance.
2. Others have suggested the model, including Norman Perrin, "Historical Criticism, Literary Criticism, and Hermeneutics: The Interpretation of the Parables of Jesus and the Gospel of Mark Today," *Journal of Religion*, 52:61-375 (1972).
3. See the important and insufficiently influential study by C. F. Burney, *The Poetry of Our Lord* (Oxford: Clarendon Press, 1925).
4. Amos N. Wilder, "The Parable of the Sower: Naivete and Method in Interpretation," *Semeia*, 2:135 (1974).
5. Both the "severely historical approach" (Via) and the "paraphrastic heresy" (Cleanth Brooks) should be avoided. See P. R. Jones, "Biblical Hermeneutics," *Review and Expositor*, 72:144-146 (1975).
6. So L. Mowry, "Parable," *IDB*, K-Q: 650 (1962). This helpful generalization must be assessed in each instance.
7. As John Crossan, *In Parables*, p. 52. See previous discussion in the prior chapter, especially references to Funk and McFague. Crossan, "Parable and Example in the Teaching of Jesus," *Semeia*, 1:88 (1974), raises another interesting issue in his insistence that the parables be thought of as "metaphors of a poet" rather than "examples of a teacher." This distinction rightly demands recognition of the irreducibility of the parables.
8. Adolf Jülicher, *Die Gleichnisreden Jesu*, 1:52-58, had gone to the other extreme in identifying all parables as extended similes. For a superb summation of Jülicher's view, see Jack Kingsbury, *The Parables of Jesus in Matthew 13* (Richmond, Va.: John Knox, 1969), pp. 1-3. Madeleine Boucher, *The Mysterious Parable: A Literary Study*, No. 6 of "The Catholic Biblical Quarterly Monograph Series" (Washington: Catholic Biblical

Association, 1977), p. 21, labels some parables as formal similes. R. Funk, "Structure in the Narrative Parables of Jesus," *Semeia*, 2:75 (1974), moving in the opposite direction, goes so far as to conclude that "in the transmission of the tradition, the metaphorical horizon of the parables of Jesus was lost—of all parables." This is too convenient for polyvalence and represents "a severely literary approach." For a brilliant treatment of metaphor, see Philip Wheelwright, *Metaphor and Reality* (Bloomington: Indiana University, 1962). See also Owen Barfield, "Poetic Diction and Legal Fiction," in *The Importance of Language*, ed. Max Black (New Jersey: Prentice-Hall, 1962).

9. F. Hauck, "*parabolē*," *The Dictionary of the New Testament* (hereafter referred to as *TDNT*) 5:745 (1967). The noun *parabolē* is used in the Gospels 48x and in Hebrews 2x.

10. C. H. Dodd, *The Parables of the Kingdom*, Revised Edition (London: James Nisbet, 1961), p. 5.

11. See Raymond Brown, "Parable and Allegory Reconsidered," in *New Testament Essays* (Garden City, N. Y.: Image Books, 1968), pp. 321-326, who rebels against the "prejudice against allegory." Interestingly, he connects this same prejudice to the tendency in Johannine studies to suspect all *ego eimi* sayings.

12. William Hull, Classroom Lectures, The Southern Baptist Theological Seminary in Louisville, Kentucky, Fall, 1960.

13. For a good introduction see C. H. Peisker, "Parable, Allegory, Proverbs," *The New International Dictionary of New Testament Theology*, 5:743-749 (1976). *Mashal* covers such a wide range, including riddle (Ps. 49:4), proverb (2 Kings 4:23), oracle (Num. 23:7), instruction (Prov. 10:1), poem (Num. 21:27), and taunt (Ps. 44:14) as well as allegory and parable.

14. Many scholars since Jülicher have considered the story clearly allegorical and therefore not from Jesus. Rudolf Bultmann, *History of the Synoptic Tradition*, trans. J. Marsh (Oxford: University Press, 1963), pp. 177, 205, dismissed the parable as a community product. Joachim Jeremias, *The Parables of Jesus*, p. 70, accepts a reconstructed form shorn of all allegorical additions. In particular, he rejects the overt allusion to Isaiah 5 because it was omitted by Luke and the gospel of Thomas. This parable is more overtly allegorical, but it belonged apparently after the entry and cleansing when the secret was no more. Matthew and Luke do have the son killed outside the vineyard, thus suiting more allegorically later events. However, the critical question whether there was originally a specific allusion to Isaiah 5 is in one sense unimportant because in any event it is too obvious to deny that the parable itself has the Song of the Vineyard in mind. Jeremias's impressive effort to demonstrate the uniqueness of the parables of Jesus has kept him from accepting the midrashic possibility. Further, the implicit *Heilsgeschichte* within the parable does not comport with Bultmann's *Heilsgeschehen*. Dodd, pp. 96-98, established the verisimilitude of the story in relation to absentee lords common in Palestinian experience.

15. See the discussion of Eta Linnemann, *Jesus of the Parables*, pp. 5-8. She does not consider the Wicked Tenants an allegory.

16. Ian T. Ramsey, *Christian Discourse* (London: Oxford University Press, 1965), pp. 6-13.

17. Paul Ricoeur, *The Symbolism of Evil*, trans. E. Buchanan (Boston: Beacon Press, 1967), pp. 163-164.

18. Of course, it is Via, *The Parables*, who has scored the organic point. William Doty,

"An Interpretation: Parable of the Weeds and Wheat," *Interpretation*, 25:192 (1971), makes the further point that the way God reigns, which has its analogues in terribly ordinary human events, must remain in parabolic form because it never yields a simple equation.

19. Wilder, *The Language of the Gospel*, p. 92. Wilder in context was referring to metaphor or symbol explicitly, but his intention is not misdirected.

20. As for example reflected in Crossan, *In Parables*, p. 9, who pointed out that many came to feel that allegory and parable were but ends of a sliding scale. He registers his own misgivings.

21. C. F. D. Moule, "Mark 4:1-20 Yet Once More," in *Neotestamentica et Semitica*, ed. E. Earle Ellis and Max Wilcox (Edinburgh: T. & T. Clark, 1969), pp. 95-113.

22. Summarized by A. M. Hunter, *Interpreting the Parables*, p. 95. James Denney's article was published in *The Expositor* for 1911.

23. C. L. Mitton, *The Good News*, No. 13 of "Bible Guides" (Nashville: Abingdon Press, 1961), p. 80.

24. Dodd, p. 7.

25. Jülicher, pp. 92-111. Cited by Kingsbury, p. 3.

26. Taken from Bultmann, pp. 188-192.

27. Via; Crossan; and Eichholz, *Einführung in die Gleichnisse* (Neukirchen-Vluyn: Neukirchener Verlag, 1963).

28. James Smart, "A Redefinition of Jesus' Use of the Parable," *Expository Times*, 47:553 (1935-36).

29. Ibid., p. 552.

30. See Matthew Black, "The 'Parables' of Enoch (1 En. 37-71) and the 'Son of Man,' " *Expository Times*, 78:5-8. He cites J. T. Milik, who registers severe questions about a pre-Christian date because the fragments of 1 Enoch from cave 4 cover every chapter except the parables.

31. So Peisker, p. 746. A cursory reading of the Hymn Scroll turned up numerous nautical similes referring to roaring seas and winds. Hymn E has quite an extended simile of the woman about to bring forth (vv. 7-12). The translation used is Vermes. The fact that the teacher of righteousness apparently did not speak in parables is a considerable stumbling block to those who would rush to a simplistic identification or influence theory.

32. Ibid., p. 744.

33. So Hauck, p. 746.

34. Samuel Sandmel, "Parallelomania," *Journal of Biblical Literature*, 81:1-13 (1962), has rightly warned against the careless use of Strack-Billerbeck; and Jewish scholars generally have objected to Christian apologetic use of rabbinic parables to favor Christian literature at the rabbis' expense. See Jacob Neusner, *Early Rabbinic Judaism* (Leiden: Brill, 1975); *The Rabbinic Traditions about the Pharisees before 70* (Leiden: Brill, 1971), who is very skeptical of reaching Pharisaic tradition prior to Jamnia and the Jewish War (66-73). In his popular book *From Politics to Piety* (Englewood Cliffs, N.J.: Prentice-Hall, 1973), p. 43, he raises major questions about the reliability of the Hillel traditions. Good but older sources are less skeptical, such as A. Feldman, *The Parables and Similes of the Rabbis* (Cambridge: University Press, 1927), p. 19. George Buchanan, "The Use of Rabbinic Literature for New Testament Research," *Biblical*

Theology Bulletin, 7:110-122 (1977), though very sympathetic to the problem of anachronism, does not believe a genuine impasse has been reached. He also reports that a Japanese student has collected more than three hundred rabbinic parables of great interest (p. 114).

35. Jeremias, Lecture at The Southern Baptist Theological Seminary in Louisville, Kentucky, Spring, 1969. In an earlier era, Fiebig found many. See his seminal work, *Die Gleichnisreden Jesu im Lichte der rabbinischen Gleichnisse des neutestamentlichen Zeitalters* (Tübingen: Mohr, 1912), pp. 7-82, 94-103.

36. Hauck, pp. 750-754. These correspondences are far too significant for there to be no connection. It may be there was simply a common source.

37. Roy Stewart, "The Parable Form in the Old Testament and the Rabbinic Literature," *The Evangelical Quarterly,* 36:146 (1964). He furnishes isolated examples (*Exod. Rab.* 2:2 and 30:24) and terms them curious divergences.

38. Ibid., p. 142; Feldman, pp. 2, 14-15; and Oesterley, *The Gospel Parables in the Light of their Jewish Background* (New York: Macmillan, 1936), p. 9. Jesus did expound the coming kingdom often with Old Testament texts so the contrast offered (Torah/Kingdom) is not absolute (Matt. 13:52). Indeed, kingdom is in the Old Testament. See Gunter Klein, "The Biblical Understanding of 'The Kingdom of God,' " *Interpretation,* 26:394 ff. (1972).

39. So Perrin, *Rediscovering the Teaching of Jesus* (New York: Harper, 1967), p. 121.

40. Lambrecht, "The Message of the Good Samaritan," *Louvain Studies,* 5:129 (1974).

41. A kind of *Christus Victor.* See Ragnar Leivestad, *Christ the Conqueror* (London: SPCK, 1954), p. 254, who relates the response to apocalyptic expectations of the destruction of Beliar.

42. Otto Kuss, "Zum Sinngehalt des Doppelgleichnisses vom Senfkorn und Sauerteig," *Biblica,* 40:641 (1959). Also E. Trocme, *Jesus as Seen by his Contemporaries,* trans. R. A. Wilson (Philadelphia: Westminster Press, 1973), p. 96.

43. George Beasley-Murray, *Preaching the Gospel from the Gospels* (London: Epworth, 1956), p. 107.

44. Jeremias, p. 230.

45. For even more possibilities, see C. Brown, "Parable," *DNTT,* 2:754 (1976).

46. Other enacted parables include Ezekiel 3:24-26; 4:1-12,24; 5:1-4; Zechariah 11; 1 Kings 11:30-32; and Jeremiah 25:15-33.

47. For example, T. W. Manson, *The Teaching of Jesus,* Second edition (Cambridge: University Press, 1935), pp. 22-44. The best application to the entire synoptic tradition is Major, Manson, and Wright, *The Mission and Message of Jesus* (New York: E. P. Dutton, 1938).

48. On form criticism see R. P. Martin, *New Testament Foundations* (Grand Rapids: Eerdmans, 1975), 1:132-136; R. C. Briggs, *Interpreting the Gospels* (Nashville: Abingdon, 1969), pp. 69-84; and Edgar McKnight, *What Is Form Criticism?* (Philadelphia: Fortress, 1969).

49. The Coptic manuscript is a translation of a second century Greek manuscript. For the interesting story of discovery and general orientation, see Ray Summers, *The Secret Sayings of the Living Jesus* (Waco, Texas: Word, 1968); Bertil Gärtner, *The Theology of the Gospel According to Thomas* (New York: Harper, 1961); and R. M. Wilson, *Studies in the Gospel of Thomas* (London: A. R. Mowbray, 1960). It is significant that the

parables are addressed to disciples and interesting that there are no allegorical explanations and no reference to Mark 4:10-12.

50. These translations are drawn from A. Guillamont and others (ed.), *The Gospel According to Thomas* (New York: Harper, 1959).

51. Summers, p. 71.

52. *Hermeneutics* is a comprehensive term for the interrelated acts of exegesis, interpretation, and exposition. Hermeneutics usually refers to the theory of interpretation. For a good traditional statement, see James Smart, *The Interpretation of Scripture* (Philadelphia: Westminster, 1961); also James Robinson, "Hermeneutic since Barth," *The New Hermeneutic*, ed. Robinson and Cobb (New York: Harper, 1964), pp. 1-7.

53. I am in severe disagreement with the cursory treatment of Bultmann, *Theology of the New Testament*, trans. K. Grobel (London: SCM, 1952), 1:3-32.

54. So Dodd, pp. 21-59; Jeremias, and many others. Peisker, p. 748, takes the view that there are two groups of themes, kingdom and repentance. The resulting stress on repentance is tempting, but if repentance is indeed reorientation of life around the kingdom, then it can be subsumed without strain.

55. On presiding metaphor, see Robert Heilman, *Magic in the Web* (Lexington: University of Kentucky, 1956); for a New Testament application see P. R. Jones, "A Structural Analysis of 1 John," *Review and Expositor*, 67:433-444 (1970).

56. The translation comes from Klein, p. 395. He stresses the enthronement psalms and other later sources. See also John Bright, *The Kingdom of God* (New York: Abingdon Press, 1963).

57. For this generalization, see Klein, pp. 397-399. See O. E. Evans, "Kingdom of God," *IDB*, K-Q: 19 (1962), who reckons with the fact that the apocalypses were centered on the final consummation of the kingdom.

58. The realized position, later modified, is represented by Dodd, p. 31; the thoroughgoing futuristic position occupied by A. Schweitzer and J. Weiss is recently defended by Richard Hiers, *The Historical Jesus and the Kingdom of God* (Gainesville, Fla.: University of Florida Press, 1973). For a critical analysis of leading options, see Perrin, *The Kingdom of God in the Teaching of Jesus* (Philadelphia: Westminster, 1963). He considered that the kingdom as present and future has been firmly established (p. 185). See George Ladd, *A Theology of the New Testament* (Grand Rapids: Eerdmans, 1974), pp. 57-134, for a valuable conservative statement.

59. See Jeremias, *Jesus' Promise to the Nations*, trans. S. H. Hooke, No. 24 of "Studies in Biblical Theology" (London: SCM, 1958), pp. 25-39.

60. Mitton, p. 85.

61. See James Moffatt, *Grace in the New Testament* (London: Hodder & Stoughton, 1931); also Bultmann, *Jesus and the Word*, trans. L. Smith and E. Lantero (New York: Scribners, 1958; German in 1934), pp. 57-132.

62. See Ernst Fuchs, *Studies of the Historical Jesus*, trans. A. Scobie, No. 42 of "Studies in Biblical Theology" (Naperville, Ill.: Alec Allenson, 1964), pp. 20-22.

63. See W. D. Davies, *The Setting of the Sermon on the Mount* (Cambridge: University Press, 1964), pp. 433-434.

64. On this synoptic thunderbolt from the Johannine sky, see A. M. Hunter, "Crux

Criticorum—Matthew 11:25-30—A Re-appraisal," *New Testament Studies*, 8:241-248.
65. So Jeremias, *The Parables of Jesus*, p. 124.
66. See Todd Wilson, "Conditions for Entering the Kingdom According to Matthew," *Perspectives in Religious Studies*, 5:42-53 (1978).
67. Not all scholars consider every parable eschatological. Exceptions include Hauch, Manson, Lohmeyer. Certainly not all parables are explicitly eschatological or eschatological in the universal sense, for some are personally eschatological. Others are eschatological because of context.
68. See the haunting treatment by Geraint Jones, *The Art and Truth of the Parables* (London: S. P. C. K., 1964), pp. 167-205.
69. So Bultmann, *History of the Synoptic Tradition*, p. 192.
70. There are modern ethical problems at the level of story, like assumption of the institution of indenture (Luke 17:7) and imprisonment for debts (Matt. 18:23). Current literature, especially Jeremias, is least satisfactory at the point of interest in ethics, but see Crossan, p. 80; Manson, *Teachings*, pp. 70-72; G. Aulén, *Jesus in Contemporary Historical Research*, trans. I. Hjelin (Philadelphia: Fortress, 1976), pp. 41, 135-141.
71. E. C. Lathem (ed.), *The Poetry of Robert Frost* (New York: Holt, Rinehart, and Winston, 1969), p. 1. Called to my attention by M. L. Soards.

3 Special Literary Considerations

There has been a new awakening to the literary dimensions of the Bible in recent years, and the awakening has led to creative new ideas and fresh insights. Clearly the parables are art forms from an oral poet, and we have received them in literary form on the pages of the Gospels. They deserve to be treated from the literary side by their very nature, and a greater awareness of what is going on in the parable can be one definite outcome.

The literary side has been introduced already, first of all in the chapter on the story of interpretation where several new movements and methods were described. In the last chapter, the literary aspect of parable was portrayed in balance with the historical and theological considerations. Both backgrounds and teaching are quite important in this study and function as constitutive factors in understanding, but the literary side cries out for far more concentrated attention, and this chapter ventures some fresh suggestions about certain literary characteristics. It will be seen that these literary points illuminate the historical and theological interests.

Master Metaphors

When parables are grouped for analysis rather than studied one at a time, patterns emerge that provide broader direction. Common metaphors appear in a number of parables scattered through the Gospels. For instance, there are seed parables, such as the parables of the Sower, the Seed Growing of Itself, and the Mustard Seed. Quite appropriately this group of parables linked by a common seed metaphor focuses on the nature and coming of the kingdom of God.[1] Each parable taps the metaphor distinctively. Also John Crossan has singled out the numerous master/servant parables and a time of critical reckoning present in each.[2] As the student begins to group the parables in this new way, fresh insight can come. It is a helpful discipline to learn and apply.

Particular attention should be accorded what might be called the householder parables, for example. The master of the house *(oikodespotē)* features in several parables and functions decisively. The title can simply mean house steward but came to be used of a person of considerable authority. For example, in the parable of the Tares (Matt. 13:36-43), a master or landowner remained in charge despite the enemy's sabotaging activity. He refused to panic and instead asserted that ultimately he would in fact separate the wheat from the tares. In the parable of the Laborers in the Vineyard (Matt. 20:1-16), the landowner acted aggressively to gather workers throughout the day. When he paid all alike, his authority and fair play were challenged (v. 12). He responded to the grumbling sovereignly and interpretively! He justified his fairness and insisted upon his right as householder to full right of disposal. His expression of his sovereignty is classic, "Am I not allowed to do what I choose?" (v. 15, RSV).

Again, in the parable of the Wicked Tenants (Mark 12:1-12 and par.), the owner sent representatives during harvest time who were badly treated. Undeterred, his intentions unwavering, he dispatched his son. The wicked tenants imagined that they could murder the heir and be sovereign themselves, but the lord of the vineyard came and gave the vineyard to others (v. 9). The concerted effort to foil the owner of the vineyard failed.

So far examples have been drawn from Matthew (M) and Mark (Mk.). The remaining householder parable stands only in Luke (L).[3] In the parable of the Great Banquet (Luke 14:16-24), invited guests made excuses and absented themselves. None of them came, but the resourceful master ordered servants to bring others from the streets to the banquet. He intended a banquet. The guest list changed, but a banquet there was!

Once the householder group of parables, unified by a *master* metaphor, appears, several patterns can be seen. One important detail in each case is that the master is also called "lord" *(kurios)*. In secular usage, *kurios* is "the one who has the power to control and give the word."[4] Thus does the householder act, though with flexibility. In each parable, the master's will is challenged and seems on the brink of being thwarted. In each case, the challenge is met, whether from resistance, criticism, opposition, or rejection. The response is even, firm, never impetuous. The householder is never at a loss for words. After each setback, sovereignty or authority is reasserted in a fresh and convincing manner. The master's will will be, but significantly freedom remains. Some refuse to accept the master's will for themselves.

The master should not be simply equated with God, but certainly this figure is intended to point to the sovereignty of God active in the ministry of Jesus. Both Epictetus and Philo apply the term to God, and it is used of Christ (Matt. 10:25).[5] Surely these householder parables concern the will of God and represent answers (theodicies) to genuine questions and hostile criticisms, such as the apparent powerlessness or weakness of God or his seeming injustice. These issues arose from the teaching and action of Jesus, and the householder parables are sensitive responses. They all posit freedom and sovereignty. They indicate that some can resist God's will but that God's will reasserts itself in fresh and final ways.[6] The parables insist on the freedom of grace, God's right to do as he pleases. There is an awesome note regarding the ultimate authority of judgment held by and exercised by the master. These householder parables are overtly kingdom-of-God oriented.

Another famous and associated figure in several parables is the *king*, natural for kingdom parables. Regal stories appear especially in Matthew, and royal parables were often fashioned by Jewish rabbis.[7] One text in Matthew describes God as the great King (5:35). God is often King in biblical literature. Isaiah called Yahweh King (6:5), as did Micah and Jeremiah. The most numerous and important references are found in the Psalms, especially the coronation chapters (47; 93; 96; 97; 99).[8]

One parable dominated by a king is the Unmerciful Servant (Matt. 18:23-35). The king acted with both the strength of mercy and the strength of judgment. In both instances, he is in sovereign control. In the parable of the Sheep and the Goats (Matt. 25:31-46), the king as eschatological judge separates in sovereign fashion. This royal figure is actually the messianic Judge at the end time, but he speaks for God (v. 34).[9] In the parable of the Marriage Feast (Matt. 22:1-10), the king does not rest until the marriage feast is finally crowded with guests. The feast refers to the great messianic banquet and the indiscriminate inclusion of sinners and the self-exclusion of others.[10]

The kingly parables refer indirectly to God and portray the sovereignty of his grace and judgment. Once again the will of God is at stake, and people imagine erroneously that it can be ignored. The unmerciful servant assumes he can get by with cruelty (Matt. 18:28-30), the unrighteous at the last judgment challenge the fairness and accuracy of the royal verdict (25:44), and invited guests presume that a spurned wedding invitation is inconsequential (22:5). One should not dally with a kingly God. His sovereignty may be challenged subtly, but it will prevail. His will is forgiveness among persons, compassion to the needy, and response to the call. You cannot enter the kingdom without obedience.

Yet another small set of parables features a *father* figure. It is well known that Jesus expressed his own sense of sonship and the nature of God by "my Father" and *abba* (Mark 14:36; Gal. 4:6).[11] The naming of father in a patriarchal society calls up association with authority and lordship, though the father in Jesus' parables reaches quite beyond. In the parable of the Two Sons (Matt. 21:28-31), the issue is obeying the father's will (v. 31). One refused initially, insisting upon his own will instead, but later repented and obeyed (v. 29). The other son glibly agreed to the father's will but failed to do it. In the parable, the possibility for apparent and real refusal exists and the corrective that seeming and doing may be quite reversed in reality. The parable exposes religious hypocrisy. It assumes the duty of filial obedience to the Heavenly Father. Interestingly, in Matthew's Gospel the will of God is consistently linked to the title *Father* (6:10; 7:21; 12:50).[12]

In the parable of the Compassionate Father and the Angry Brother (Luke 15:11-32), the father figure fairly dominates both segments. Here Jesus' picture of God as Father comes to powerful expression. This father speaks with great authority a definitive word to each son (vv. 22-24,31-32), yet his sovereignty allows for freedom and personifies grace. His compassion clangs with the elder brother's anger. Also in the parabolic saying about good gifts (Matt. 7:9-11; Luke 11:9-13), there is assurance that what is given in answer to prayer by the Heavenly Father will really be good.[13] His very nature is gracious Giver.

Each of these metaphoric systems (householder, king, father) points the understanding of God's nature espoused by Jesus. The several parables in each system tap the common metaphor distinctively. They also give content to definitions of the kingdom as "the reign of God." They underscore the familiar assertion that the parables' core concept is the kingdom. Furthermore, the kingdom has to do with God's will, and God's will does not require a rigid evacuating of human freedom but neither is his will vanquished. The God suggested is sovereign. Jesus' personal activities function within that will, act out and define that will. These parables explain the ministry of Jesus and the God and kingdom to which he pointed through metaphoric systems.[14]

Parable Form

A Rhetorical Question. Another informing return from literary analysis derives from attention to actual form of parables, not content with abstract definitions of what they are supposed to be. For example, notice how rhetorical questions characterize parables. The less known parable of the Servant and his Wages in Luke 17:7-10 moves entirely by means of two rhetorical questions. Although unusual, this parable points beyond itself to the nature and function of many parables. Both the parable of the Lost Coin (Luke 15:8-9) and the Lost Sheep (Luke 15:4-6) take the form of engaging questions from common experience answered by a second half. The twin parables of the Tower Builder (Luke 14:28-30) and the Warring King (Luke 14:31-32) begin as lengthy questions, giving the entire parable a rhetorical cast.

Consider how the parable of the Unjust Steward (Luke 16:1-8) depends for its structure upon four questions:

1) What is this that I hear about you? (v. 2*b*)
   (A fundamental question that creates the crisis)
2) What will I do? (v. 3*b*)
   (A key existential question with a clear resolution in v. 4*a*)
3) How much do you owe my master? (v. 5*b*)
   (This enlivens the dialogue of transaction)
4) How much do you owe? (v. 7*b*)
   (This completes the double dialogue section)

These questions make the parable what it is. They engaged the original hearers.

Final rhetorical questions at the climax of parables imply the very nature and purpose of parables. The parable of the Rich Fool ends with the absorbing question, "Then whose will these prepared things be?" (Luke 12:20). The question is so devastating an answer is unnecessary, yet an answer involuntarily arises in the hearer! At the end of the parable of the Wicked Tenants (Mark 12:9), the Teller asks, "What will the lord of the vineyard do?" The parable of the Good Samaritan involves the hearer explicitly, requiring audience participation, "Which of the three do you believe was neighbor?" (Luke 10:36).

Rhetorical questions then should be taken into consideration when thinking of the nature of a parable. They appear as introductions, climaxes, and vehicles for defining a dilemma. These questions engaged the hearers personally—expecting an agreeing nod in one area of life that carries over into another.

General Situations. These questions invariably point to common experience. This leads on to further insight. A great many parables are introduced by the the words "Who among you . . .?" *(tis ex humōn).* This direct appeal to the immediate hearers expected an affirmative response. It invited listening. This direct address "seeks to force the hearer to take up a definite standpoint."[15] This question is never used in Mark but is prominent in parables peculiar to Luke (11:5; 14:28; 15:4; 17:7). Three parables common to Luke and Matthew (Q) contain the expression (Matt. 6:27 and Luke 12:25; Matt. 7:9 and Luke 11:11; and Matt. 12:11 and Luke 14:5). These parables make free use of future tenses and the subjunctive mode. They appeal to conventional wisdom and not to atypicality or "cracks in reality."

Observation of the frequent interrogative format unearths a larger grouping of parables that helpfully may be classified as general situation.[16] These parables have the strength of concurring with common sense and general experience. They are reminiscent of the wisdom sayings in that respect. They established a point of contact and inspired confidence that the speaker knew what he was talking about. They derived from sympathetic observation of life, or as the academic phrase has it, "concessions to common experience." Additional examples include parables of Wineskins (Mark 2:22) and the Patch (Mark 2:21), the Mustard Seed (Mark 4:30-32), and Weather Signs (Luke 12:54-56).

In the typical occurrences, through which Jesus communicated so naturally, there was no theological idea inherently present. It was his interpretation and application that were startlingly creative and gave point to an ordinary, recurrent event. It is clarifying to determine this classification early in the process of personal study.

Specific Situations. The other primary type of parable then is specific situation. Not a few of those parables distinctive to Luke belong to this category and characteristically refer to a certain *(tis)* person, as a certain Samaritan (Luke 10:30), a certain man had two sons (Luke 15:11), a certain rich man (Luke 12:16; 16:1,19).[17] This expression signals the reader immediately that a specific situation parable may be expected, an extended narrative utilizing past tense. The experiences narrated may be exceptional and surprising.[18] Some parables, like the Rich Man and Lazarus and the Pharisee and the Publican, smash stereotypical religious ideas. These stories seem constructed "to invade one's hearing in direct contradiction to the deep structure of one's *expectation.*"[19]

Within the specific situation grouping, there is a triad that might be called the compassion contrast parables. These three are the Compassionate Father and the Angry Brother (L), the Unmerciful Servant (M), and the Compassionate Samaritan (L). These are the only ones where compassion figures, and in all three instances the contrasting structure is the key to their interpretation. Each adds to the portrait of compassion, and in each there is a foil or contrast.

Another fascinating subcategory is the "refusal parable." Careful reading and comparing discovers the frequent appearance of "I do not will" *(ou thelō)* as a critical indication of intent. It is emphatic in the Two Sons where it expresses self-will in opposition to the father's will (Matt. 21:29). It is telling in the Compassionate Father and the Angry Brother to describe the refusal of the elder son to enter the festivities (Luke 15:23). It is revealing as a summary of the refusals to the wedding (Matt. 22:3) in the parable of the Marriage Feast and of the refusal to be merciful in response to a prostrate plea (Matt. 18:30).

The form of the refusal parable is surely authentic because it is present in three M parables and three L parables. In two instances the refusal is temporary and in both of these inappropriate (Two Sons, Unjust Judge). In two instances, there is a refusal to enter a feast and each concerns Pharisees (Prodigal Son, Marriage Feast). In one way or another, refusal to do the will of God is involved in all but one instance.[20] These are negative examples of wrong responses. They are intentional, responsible refusals. The refusal parables recognize the wrongness and reality of human pride, hypocrisy, cruelty, and rejection of the divine offer. Clearly these too are kingdom parables, testifying to the cruciality of human obedience to the will of God and response to the invitation of Jesus. In turn, they anticipate the great unwillingness of Jerusalem (Luke 13:34) and stand in stark contrast to the great willingness of Gethsemane (Mark 14:36). These parables speak not only of the sovereignty and grace of God but also of human responsibility.

Direct Discourse

One other literary characteristic, surprisingly neglected but immensely important, is the striking prominence and strategic function of direct discourse in the parables.[21] It is an eye-opening experience to color in red all the direct speech and to count the relative number of words in a particular parable given over to it. For example, in the Rich Fool (Luke 12:16-20), sixty-two words (original Greek) are direct discourse, twelve words more introduce speeches, and only six words are simple narrative, and they set up the situation. In the parable of the Barren Fig Tree, ten words introduce direct discourse, fifty words constitute direct speech, and seventeen words establish the narrative situation. Actually one cannot speak of the nature of the parables generally without including human conversation in the understanding.

A proof text for the importance of direct discourse is surely the explicit invitation to pay attention to what the judge says (Luke 18:6). Must not Jesus, as narrator, have delivered the direct discourse portions of his stories in an animated and communicative fashion and interpreted his own parables by his tone of voice? At any event, it would be a crime to deliver the Unjust Steward in a monotone.

The speeches often function in lieu of elaborate narrative descriptions and move things along, economize on words, avoid belabored details, and enhance appeal. They add specificity, color, vividness, and lifelikeness. They contribute the liveliness of overheard conversation and the privilege of tuning in on someone talking to himself about vital matters. Most importantly the speeches, as narrative devices, make transparent the motive of principal characters. This greatly aids interpretation and is a piece with Jesus' ethic of the inner intent (Matt. 5:28).

The *interior soliloquy* or internal monologue appears in numerous parables at critical junctures.[22] A primary character may simply talk to himself on a matter of enormous personal concern. The unclean spirit in the parable of the Evil Spirit says to himself, "I will return to my house from which I came" (Matt. 12:44, RSV; Luke 11:24, RSV). The dishonest steward spoke with himself swiftly (Luke 16:3), debating inwardly how he would deal with his destiny. The prodigal son had quite a reckoning with himself (Luke 15:17-19). There are actually two revealing internal monologues in the parable of the Wicked Tenants (Mark 12:6,7). The unjust judge revealed in soliloquy that his motive for granting the widow's request had nothing to do with his sense of justice (Luke 18:4-5). These soliloquys are crucial exegetically because they clarify situations as seen by the speaker and lead toward resolution of some kind. The poignant existential dimension is apparent.

Final speeches, in accordance with the law of end stress, are often determinative. Two parables, for example, contain two climactic speeches that establish the outlook of the entire story and express its purpose. The father addresses the prodigal indirectly (Luke 15:22-24) and the elder son directly vv. 31-32). The king addresses the righteous (Matt. 25:40) and the unrighteous (v. 45) with a key revelation. Other parables conclude with classic final speeches, such as Laborers in the Vineyard (Matt. 20:13b-15), the Great Banquet (Luke 14:23b-24), The Compassionate Samaritan (Luke 10:35), and the Tares (Matt. 13:29-30). These last words settle the outcome and are internally interpretive.

Dialogues also feature frequently and function to center the focus and offer crucial explanations. Several parables are dominated by dialogue, and some contain two separate exchanges. There is quite a lot of variety. One pattern is "question and answer." In the parable of the Good Seed (Matt. 13:24-30), there are two questions and two answers. In an apparent state of confusion and near panic, servants request an explanation (v. 27). A direct answer follows crisply explaining cause of the weeds and leading abruptly to a second question regarding the next course of action. The two part answer requires one approach for the time being and quite another at harvest (vv. 29-30). Another question and answer exchange appears in workers in the vineyard (Matt. 20:6-7) rounded out by a directive.

Another pattern might be named conveniently "protest and

explanation." The elder brother protests his father's extravagance toward his younger brother with an angry indictment, which is lengthy enough incidentally to expose his real feelings and the basis for them. The father responds with a kindly but critical explanation. Most of the parable of the Sheep and the Goats (Matt. 25:34-45) is comprised of two dialogues.

I. Address to the Genuinely Righteous (vv. 34-39)
   A. Blessing (vv. 34-36)
   B. Protest (vv. 37-40)
   C. Explanation (v. 40)
II. Address to the Unrighteous (vv. 40-45)
   A. Woe (vv. 41-43)
   B. Protest (v. 44)
   C. Explanation (v. 45)

The explanation each time acts as the key revelation that expounds the principle of judgment. The extensive dual discussion of the principle of judgment provides quite an opportunity to develop a perspective. Powerful internal juxtaposition in the two addresses, especially between beatitude and woe, demonstrates that this famous account is, indeed, a parable. Likewise, in the second dialogue found in the Workers in the Vineyard, there is complaint (Matt. 20:12) and elaborate defense (vv. 13-15).

The protest and explanation pattern gave occasion for Jesus to name certain hostile attitudes he encountered. By expressing them himself in parable, he put them out front in an honest fashion so they could be faced, aired, and evaluated. The answer could also be heard by the critics in a less intimidating and more objective setting of story. The critical hearer may realize that the Teller understands how persons of another persuasion like themselves may feel and think. They may also see the Teller's actions in a corrected light.

"Requests" or petitions appear, as in the parable of the Rich Man and Lazarus (Luke 16:19-31). After the narrative establishes the reversal situation, the dialogue dominates the parable. The elaborate dialogue between the rich man and Abraham constitutes the heart of the story. A noticeable pattern of petition to "father Abraham" appears with a resisting response and explanation. There are three petitions with corresponding denials, or more accurately two with the second debated twice. In the parable of the Ten Virgins (Matt. 25:1-13), two requests are made and denied (vv. 8,9; 11,12). In both of these parables, the denial is resounding and startling. A different twist appears in the Friend at Midnight (Luke 11:5-8) where a remonstrance follows a request.

A somewhat different dialogue is that of "report and response." In the parable of the Pounds (Luke 19:11-27), the narrative discourse sets the stage and direct discourse enlivens it. Three servants report, and thrice the master responds. He blesses and rewards in the first two instances and condemns the third. Significantly, the dialogue with the third is very lengthy and the clue to intended emphasis. Certainly the Teller expects the hearer (reader) to contrast the two kinds of report/response. The parable of the Talents (Matt. 25:14-30) follows the same structure.

Other types of dialogue appear, like the basic "negotiating dialogue" in the Unjust Steward (Luke 16:1-8), where the pattern question, answer, directive appears twice (vv. 5-7). It enhances the impression of decisiveness in a business crisis. In the Barren Fig Tree (Luke 13:6-9), there is the unexpected interchange in which the master gives a directive and a responsible and respectful voice asks for delay in its application. Directives, incidentally, are very common throughout the parables. A directive/response pattern appears in the parable of the Two Sons (Matt. 21:28-32).

Conclusion

Recognize then that conscious attention to the literary character of parables greatly enhances awareness of what is going on and can equip the individual student to do his or her own quite competent analysis. Be sensitive to master metaphors as you read the entire parabolic corpus. Develop the habit of deciding immediately whether a parable is a specific or general situation. Always mark any direct discourse early in study and watch how the dynamic interchanges then highlighted enliven the parable and touch the dramatic imagination.

NOTES

1. See J. D. Crossan, "The Seed Parables of Jesus, "*Journal of Biblical Literature,* 92:244-66 (1973); and P. R. Jones, "The Seed Parables in Mark," *Review and Expositor,* 75:519-538 (1978).

2. Crossan, *In Parables,* pp. 96-120. Amos Wilder, "The Parable of the Sower," *Semeia,* 2:140 (1974), suggests that the master-servant relation evokes the archetype of authority.

3. The fact that this metaphor appears in M, L, and Mk. should caution the scholar in regard to radical redactional theories. Other spanning patterns are mentioned in notes throughout this book.

4. W. Foerster, "*kurios,*" *TDNT,* 3:1086 (1965). This is certainly the case with the lord of the house in the parable of the Unjust Steward (Luke 16:2,8).

5. Noted by Moulton and Milligan, *The Vocabulary of the Greek New Testament,* p. 441. The word *oikodespotē* is used in an everyday sense in Matthew 24:43, Luke 12:39, and Mark 14:14. It is used eschatologically of God or Christ in Luke 13:25.

6. The perspective has affinity with those familiar categories of God's circumstantial will and his ultimate will popularized by Leslie Weatherhead, *The Will of God* (New York: Abingdon Press, 1944).

7. Adolf Schlatter, *Das Evangelium des Matthaus,* Second Edition (Stuttgart: Calwer Verlag, 1960), p. 559, pointed out that the Jewish kingly parables begin with the formula *basilei sarki kai haimati.* For an early study see Ignaz Ziegler, *Königsgleichnisse der Midrasch* (Breslau, 1903).

8. G. Von Rad, "*Basileus,*" *TDNT,* 1:567-71 (1963).

9. Ibid. The messianic King and God as King come together nicely in Chronicles. The Davidic King rules in the kingdom of God (1 Chron. 17:14; 28:5; 29:23). J. A. T. Robinson, *Twelve New Testament Studies,* No. 34 of "Studies in Biblical Theology" (London: SCM, 1962), pp. 82-83, strongly suspects that the evangelist has inserted the figure of a king into all the parables concerning a king. Assuredly Matthew was attracted to parables relating to a king. However, Luke contains one king parable (14:31); and this picture of God is common biblical metaphor and to be expected of one who spoke so often of the kingdom of God. Robinson correctly sees the parable as a combination of parabolic, apocalyptic, and ethical teaching. Robinson could be correct about the evangelist inserting the royal image, but it is more normal for a king to speak to people than a shepherd to converse with sheep! David Hill, *The Gospel of Matthew* (Greenwood, S. C.; Attic Press, 1972), p. 330, goes so far as to say that the only parabolic features are the shepherd, the sheep, and the goats. This remark represents a failure to appreciate the place of direct discourse in parables.

10. Matthew 22:1-10 may be a parallel to Luke 14:16-24, or they may be originally discrete. One can argue that Matthew's propensity for kingly figures led him to tell the same story of a king. On the other hand, one can also argue that "a certain man" is Lukan. It does seem likely that Matthew 22:7 is a clue to the date of the Gospel and that 22:11-14 should be separated.

11. See Joachim Jeremias, *The Central Message of the New Testament* (New York: Charles Scribners Sons, 1965), pp. 9-30. He points out that *abba* was far too familiar and irreverent to the Jewish mind as a word for God. This is a uniqueness of Jesus'

concept of God, and it belongs especially to prayer. It is informative to note that the concentrations of God as Father are in the Fourth Gospel, 1 and 2 John, Paul, and Matthew, especially Sermon on the Mount.

12. G. Schrenk, "Thelēma," TDNT, 3:56 (1965), points this out as a distinctive. He sees the usage influenced by synagogue forms and the new estimation of the name of the Father very much in the heart of the evangelist.

13. Bread and fish were the ordinary fare of simple folk living around the lake (Mark 6:38). The parable of the Wicked Tenants as well, already mentioned, does imply father in the sending of a son (Mark 12:6).

14. It is also illuminating to observe the several primary worlds from which the parables take their life. Surprisingly, fishing, carpentry, and the cult are not frequent settings. Rather the worlds of family, commerce, and farming (including viticulture and shepherding) reappear most often. The parables provide tremendous sociological data for understanding Galilee. The family and commerce settings have decided communicative potential for urban society.

15. Jeremias, Parables, p. 103. There are apparently no contemporary parallels, but the idiom occurs in the prophets (Isa. 42:23; 50:10; Hag. 2:3), though not as an introduction to a parable.

16. I owe the term to a passing reference by H. K. McArthur, "The Parable of the Mustard Seed," Catholic Biblical Quarterly, 33:198-210 (1971). In correspondence with Sam Williams dated March 31,1979, McArthur equated his term "general situation" to Jülicher's similitude. He defined it as a recurrent event in nature or human relations, a way of saying "This is the way things happen." He observed that many rabbinic parables began, "In the custom of the world. . . ," and went on to compare or contrast the behavior of God.

17. See Jeremias, "Tradition und Redaktion in Lukas 15," Zeitschrift für die neutestamentliche Wissenschaft, 62:174 (1971), who argues 1) that "a certain man" is a Semitism, and 2) that Luke sometimes prefers aner in a passage with parallel in Mark (Luke 8:27; 4:33; 6:6; 9:25, 20:9). The critical problem is complicated so far as parables are concerned. The "certain person" parables stand in L. The natural test is Luke 14:15-24 and Matthew 22:1-10.

18. See R. W. Funk, "Structure in the Narrative Parables of Jesus," Semeia, 2:51-73 (1974), who shows a common pattern of Determiner and Respondent 1 and 2. Some have an additional respondent (r). See also Norman Huffman, "Atypical Features in the Parables of Jesus," Journal of Biblical Literature, 97:207-220 (1978). I think that the best case for atypicality can be made for some of the specific situation parables.

19. So J. D. Crossan, "The Good Samaritan: Towards a Generic Definition of Parable," Semeia, 2:94 (1974).

20. The exception is the parable of the Pharisee and the Tax Collector. The publican refuses to lift his eyes to heaven (Luke 18:13). The parable of the Pounds includes a parenthetical aside in which a delegation expresses unwillingness to accept their would-be king (Luke 19:14).

21. Some, including Jülicher, have sensed something of the intrinsic importance of direct discourse in the parables. Mary Ann Tolbert, Perspectives on the Parables: An Approach to Multiple Interpretations (Philadelphia: Fortress Press, 1978), reflects this sensitivity. It is the particular emphasis of this study but much remains to be done. It is

very remarkable that so much specific dialogue has been retained by the tradition. One might have expected more abbreviation and summation of speeches as Matthew 18:13. The fact that speeches are prominent in all strands suggests that they were characteristic of the original parables. A few parables by their nature, such as the seed parables, do not require direct discourse.

22. I have opted for such terms as *interior soliloquy* or *internal monologue* because these speeches are private thoughts and less formal than a dramatic soliloquy or dramatic monologue. The Rich Fool approaches a dramatic monologue. The category *soliloquy* is technically preferable.

Part I

The Sure Coming of the Kingdom

4 The Parable of the Sower and the Soils

Jesus offered a gift to disciples and preachers and a challenge to hearers with his well-known agricultural account of a sower's experience and soils' response. The reader or hearer quickly imagines a lone sower on a hillside and envisions the fourfold field on which he stood. The story leaves a lasting impression, both regarding farming and faith. The interpreters of this very familiar picture should neither lose sight of the obvious nor disdain discovery of more insight because they are not playing in a theological sandbox but are instead engaged by a striking Word of God. The parable becomes an impetus to hearing and hoping for those with ears to hear.

The Markan record of the parable stands very close to that of Matthew, a sign of faithfulness and the early importance of the text.[1] Mark's parable does speak of the seed in the singular, while Matthew has the plural. The report of the yield comes in ascending order in Mark (4:8c) and in descending sequence in Matthew (13:8b). Luke's form of the parable, more lean and spare, differs more extensively in detail but contains the same rudiments.[2] Support for the basic parable comes from a triple tradition.

Understanding of the outdoors incident can begin by initial attention to the life situation.

The Life Situation

Two major impressions are created by the evangelist Mark regarding public response to Jesus up to the parable speech. One is that of resistance to his teaching authority by the Pharisees. In open conflicts, Jesus was accused of blasphemy, table fellowship with sinners, failure to fast, and breaking the sabbath (2:1 to 3:6). He became unacceptable in the synagogues. Such concerted opposition occasioned the first strategic withdrawal from the towns and synagogues (3:7). As with other prophets, Jesus met skepticism, misunderstanding, indifference, disbelief, and open hostility. Ironically he was also driven from the towns because of his enormous popularity. This point, extraordinarily important for the setting of the parable, is accented emphatically by Mark. There was a popular acclaim of almost hysterical proportions in response to his healing ministry (1:45; 2:2,13,15; 3:7-8). His family came for him (3:31-35). Of necessity, he taught in the country by the lake in a boat. Thus, two natural forces compelled Jesus into the open-air stage of the Galilean ministry. The Pharisees assigned the worst motives to his actions and plotted against him (3:6). The crowds hounded him relentlessly.

Interpreters must pay more attention to the literary context indicating a large crowd in all three Gospels:

Mark 4:1	a very large crowd	(ochlos pleistos)
Matthew 13:2	great crowds	(ochloi polloi)
Luke 8:4	a great crowd	(ochlou pollou)

Both Mark and Matthew reported that it was necessary for Jesus to enter the boat. This situation may very well explain his choice of parable, and this setting should caution students from turning the story entirely into a teaching for disciples.

The Agricultural Picture

A sower with cheerful abandon hand cast the seed over several kinds of soil with various results. Evidently the seeds were dropped on unplowed ground, sowing preceding plowing, and then later were plowed in. This point has been controverted especially by K. D. White, who regarded such an agricultural procedure "a wasteful and slovenly proceeding."[3] He attacked Jeremias and Dalman, claiming that their reconstruction is palpably absurd. He brought forward texts indicating the more normal sequence of plowing and then sowing (Jer. 4:3; Isa. 28:24, Hos. 10:11 f.). Jeremias responded in a very spirited fashion, especially defending his beloved former teacher Dalman,[4] and seems to have the best of it.

Possibly an actual sower on an adjacent hillside sowed a field, and Jesus spontaneously pointed to his activity as a clue to the kingdom. Such a sower would scatter seeds from a sowing cloth hung about him or would gather high his outer garment to make a seed pouch. The hard ground upon which some seed fell was probably the public path beaten down by pedestrians. The rocky ground reflected the peculiarity of the Palestinian hill country and the region of Capernaum in Galilee. Commonly underlying limestone reached almost to the surface of fields in some places. This thin crust of earth meant too little top soil. The first morning's sun would scorch a plant breaking though the soil too quickly because of shallow depth. The thorny ground assumes presence of thorns that sprang up during the summer. The good ground received the seed, and the plant grew according to schedule and produced an astounding crop.

Incidentally, there is a charming old Arabic story that when Allah was creating the world he entrusted all the stones to two angels, each with one full bag. As they flew over Palestine one of the bags broke and spilled half the stones intended for the whole world.[5]

The yield at the climax of the parable is exceptional. The ascending order in Mark, at the climax of the parable, is highly dramatic as hearer or reader is swept along.[6] The harvest ran as high as a hundredfold.[7] Jeremias reported that a ten-times harvest was counted a good harvest and a yield of seven-and-a-half average.[8] The hundred-times harvest was most exceptional but apparently not unheard of.[9]

Meaning and Implication for the Audience

The parable as presented in Mark is as the first delivered to a pressing crowd, one that had forced Jesus to a floating pulpit. For such an eager crowd, Jesus chose or created spontaneously the parable of the Sower. In the light of the life situation as reported by Mark, this should not be lightly disregarded. Could it be that Jesus fashioned the parable in a kind of count-the-cost tone? At any event, Mark especially stressed the hearing response both at the outset with the call, "Hear" (akouete, 4:3a) and at the end, "Who has ears to hear let that one hear" (hos echei ōta akouein akouetō, 4:9b).[10] It would appear that Jesus addressed the crowd with a kind of reality therapy. Not everyone flocking to his standard would stay. This corresponds nicely to the picture of the eager crowd, pressing Jesus to an aquatic podium. A positive note of hope for the would-be committed disciple comes as well with the potential success of good soil (4:8). [Is the point rather like that of the last parable in Matthew's Sermon on the Mount

(7:24-27)?] It may well be for the crowd a challenge to right hearing, the importance of attentive hearing.[11] Jesus was not taken in by their display of fawning followship. Though the Galilean enthusiasm was at its height, Jesus wished "to throw hearers back on themselves in self-examination."[12] Jesus presented a searching challenge to expose the depth and character of the crowd's initial flurry. The interpretation provided at least a paradigm for responsible hearing: the good soil (1) hears the Word and (2) receives it and (3) bears fruit (Mark 4:20). Significantly, all three Gospel accounts of the parable record the invitation for those with ears to hear.

For the disciples, who may have been discouraged by the vicissitudes of the Galilean campaign, the parable must have come as great encouragement. The parable included the stern reality of failure rather than an ignoring of it but pointed triumphantly to the astonishing harvest. Jesus wanted his disciples to be convinced of the power of preaching the kingdom, as well as the realism of unreceptive responses. Consider what terrific value this parable had "formationally" upon the missioners Jesus sent later to Israel. In the Markan framework, Jesus had already chosen the twelve for the purpose of sending them out to preach (3:14). The parable is encouragement to sowers because sowers sow with a yield in mind. Some seed will fall on good soil. This application to the disciples is nearer the popular view of Jeremias.[13] So the disciple is steeled by the reality of rejection as something already experienced and as something to expect if one risks sowing the Word. William Neil put it, "The farmer does not lose heart although he knows that much of his work will come to nothing."[14] The disciple need not be thrown by predictable failure and hostility. The proclaiming disciple is also buoyed by the realistic expectation of a colossal harvest.

However, the internal juxtaposition within the parable is surely that of the three unproductive soils and the fourth by way of contrast. There is glaring contrast between no harvest whatsoever in three instances and a stupendous harvest in the other instance. It is emphatically not four equally important soils, for three stand over against the fourth. Hence the parable is allegorical but not an allegory. Given the juxtaposition of two kinds of soil, it is imperative to retain the force and value of both in interpretation. It is not only valid but essential to insist upon the warning of the one and the hope of the other. The parable is not only a rugged recognition of failure and opposition but also a call to faith because of what God will do with the good soil. Indeed, the parable itself is a proclamation of the kingdom. It was an invitation to faith to respond to the proclamation. It seeks to awaken faith. It points to the harvest of the seed. The parable expressed not only the faith of Jesus but also his observations of what was already going on. Jesus was a realist, but his view of reality included God. The peddlers of despair turned out to be wrong. Jesus saw a harvest. The hearer had to trust that he was right.

The imagery of sowing itself is noteworthy. In the Old Testament, sowing sometimes has a metaphorical use in the sense of sowing righteousness or evil. Significantly, God himself sows in several prophetic passages (Hos. 2:23; Jer. 31:27; Ezek. 36:9; Zech. 10:9). In these striking texts God addresses Israel in a kind of renewal of the covenant. There is promise of an increase of human and animal life and a strengthening of Israel. These passages are promises of the New Age. Sowing is "a recognized metaphor for God's action in bringing about the New Age."[15] Could it be that the parable had in mind divine action in the New Age inaugurated by Jesus acting for God?[16] If so it would strengthen the traditional title, "Parable of the Sower."

A second intriguing question comes to mind. Is the parable in some sense a kind of model or archetype of election? That is, God moves toward all persons. He sows with cheerful abandon. Seed falls on different soils. Some choose to reject. Some seed meets with response. To those who decide to respond and to persevere belongs the lavish future. Emil Brunner, in his observations on the parable, took the position, "Reception does not depend upon God, neither on the sower nor on the seed; it depends upon man's decision."[17]

The Parable Interpretation (Mark 4:13-20 and par.)

The interpretation of the parable in the Gospels, especially Luke, reflects the struggles of the early church with the demonic and desertions.[18] It is a moving sermon to the church to stand fast. Three basic *causes of desertion* emerge from the several Gospels. First is the failure to understand (Matt. 13:19). They have heard the word (Mark 4:15; Matt. 13:19; Luke 8:12); it has been sown in their heart, but Satan has come along and snatched away the word. Luke made it explicit that this group had not yet believed and been saved (8:12). The seed that fell on the path met with no response. The supposition for Matthew is that understanding must precede conversion (13:19a). One suspects that his church saw the need to instruct catechumens until the peril of misunderstanding was past. Mark stressed more the role of Satan, with the Roman Empire in the background.

Second, persecution and tribulation are causes of desertion. This is explicitly persecution because of the word (Mark 4:14; Matt. 13:21c) related to the picture of the rocky ground. This group heard the word and responded, but the plants had no real root. In time of stress, they "fall away" (Mark 4:17; Matt. 13:21; Luke 8:13). They were scandalized and deserted. Luke reported that they believed for a little while and then quit in time of temptation (8:13). Luke reflected a strong conviction about the necessity of perseverance.

Third is worldliness. Mark classically named three diversions that choked the word: the cares of the world, delight in riches, and desire for other things (4:19). Mark knew that one "must realize not merely that he does not draw his life from this present world but also that if, in self-concern, he cares for the things of this world, he will fall victim to the world."[19] Each Gospel recorded the need to bear fruit. Luke called for perseverance (8:15). Mark identified the good soil meaningfully as those who hear the word, accept it, and bear fruit.

So Mark and the others rightly related the parable to the experience of the church and could do so because of the coping power of the Word of God in new situations.

All three interpretations were freshly applied in a pastorally sensitive fashion, but it may very well be that behind all three lies a dominical explanation as well.[20] Many scholars assign the interpretations strictly to later church exposition. Reasoning generally includes the fact that the application is so allegorical, the fact that some later church concerns are addressed, the fact that words are present common to the epistles but absent in the Gospels.[21] These considerations are significant, but strong arguments favor the interpretation. Jesus was putting the false starts and ignition failures of his Galilean ministry into perspective. He observed a shallow eagerness on the part of some and eventual desertion from others, as well as the hard resistance his ministry met. He saw his ministry in cosmic conflict with the demonic from his temptations through the exorcisms. The three interpretations speak of the evil one.[22] The emphasis on hearing is present

prominently in Mark's parable, but significantly all three versions of
the parable conclude with the challenge to those who would hear
(Matt. 13:9; Mark 4:9; Luke 8:8). There were other private disclosures
to disciples (Mark 4:34; 7:17-23; 9:28 *ff.*; 8:1; 9:31; 10:32-34; 13:3 *ff.*).

The Purpose of Parables

It is now possible to tie some loose ends together by pointing out
the unity and interrelationships of Mark 4:1-20 and par. and by making a stab at Mark 4:10-12 and par. Certainly as it stands not only is
Mark 4:1-34 an extended parable speech but also 4:1-20 is a closely
knit unit. However, the influential analysis of Jeremias has had the
result of dividing this score of verses into three separate parts. A
major catalyst for division has been the enormously troublesome
statement on the purpose of parables. The three sections are as follows:

> Section One: The Parable (vv. 1-9)
> Section Two: The Purpose of Parables (vv. 10-12)
> Section Three: The Interpretation of the Parable (vv. 13-20)

Of these three sections, Jeremias assigns the parable to Jesus and the
interpretation to the later church and considers 4:10-12 as coming
from Jesus but misplaced by the evangelist into this parable chapter.[23]

The bothersome statement on the purpose of parables, that will
not go away, is as follows:

And whenever he was alone, the ones with him along with the twelve began
asking him about the parable. And he was saying to them, "To you has been
given the mystery of the kingdom, but to those outside everything comes in
parables, that 'While seeing they may see and not perceive, and while hearing
they may hear and not understand, lest they turn and be forgiven' " (Mark
4:10-12).

Both the other evangelists also reported this most difficult text that
seems to suggest that the purpose of parables is obfuscation, intentionally misleading people in order to keep them from being redeemed!

Matthew retained more of the word order of Isaiah (LXX) and
included a long additional verse from Isaiah, which explained that the
people were developing hardness of heart by human choice (Matt.
13:15). This extra verse alleviates the problem of apparent meaning
considerably. Surely the "hard ground" of the parable correlates

nicely to "hardening of heart." The people of Israel rejected God's Word, as in earlier eras.

The next breakthrough is to connect the interpretation of the parable with the purpose statement. Observe how all three accounts interpret each receiving of seed as involving hearing the word explicitly.[24] This application relates not merely to the parable but directly to the stress on hearing in the purpose statement. Another notable connection between the interpretation and the purpose statement is the reference to people's hearts (Matt. 13:19; Luke 8:12,15).

An hypothesis is in order. Could it be that Jesus had Isaiah 6 in mind as he developed his parable about the sower? It may well be that the parable is a kind of kingdom comment or midrash. If this is true, it helps to tie the three sections together. The parable, the purpose statement, and the interpretation all focus on reception. The parable, based on the coming kingdom, goes beyond Isaiah and projects a great hope, as well as a great rejection.

Many stubborn problems remain. Much ink has been spilled regarding the word *(hina)* that introduces the Markan citation of Isaiah, but it could be simply a device to introduce an Old Testament quotation and to imply fulfillment.[25] Certainly the parable itself is "a vigorous way of stating the inevitable," as C. F. D. Moule has put it.[26] The parable does go beyond rejection to anticipate acceptance and great result.

The fundamental issue of the intended use of the parable must still be faced. Is the kingdom a mystery intentionally hidden from outsiders to obstruct understanding and salvation?[27] Are parables excluding agents? The parallel parables from the rabbis certainly performed an educative function rather than any effort to confuse and to exclude.[28] The parables of Jesus themselves surely stimulated illumination and invited decision and response. On the other hand, based on Old Testament varieties of *meshalim*, a parable can include enigmatic sayings, puzzles, and riddles.[29] And admittedly most of the parables are not blatant nor is the meaning completely obvious in each instance nor is the relevance of the parable to the moment in history and to the Teller completely apparent. The parable teases the mind and imagination toward recognition. Just as it took faith to overcome the messianic secret (the true identity of Jesus), so faith is required to hear a parable aright. The use of the word *mystery* may have referred not so much to intellectual incomprehension but to an obtuseness arising from a hardness of heart.[30] That is, some "resist understanding because they are determined to do nothing that will alter or change their ways."[31] The Pauline usage had to do with temporary hardening of Israel (Rom. 11:25). Surely both the kingdom and the parables were a mystery perceived only by a faith to see in tiny beginnings and in a veiled Messiah, God's presence.

This reading avoids a rigid determinism and leaves open the possibility for anyone to be good soil. As Brunner helpfully put it, "You are not the rocky ground, the thorny field or the trodden path; you become the one or the other, depending on your reaction to God's Word."[32] T. W. Manson had it right early on when he concluded:

> It is the man himself who places himself in one category or another, and that simply by the response which he makes to the parables. Those in whom religious insight and faith are awakened by the hearing of parables press into the inner circle for more.[33]

So the parable, purpose statement, and interpretation reflect on the mystery of rejection actually experienced within the ministry of Jesus in Galilee. Jesus drew a parallel in Isaiah's prophetic ministry and spoke with impressive realism and powerful expectation. Many in Israel chose to reject, and Jesus defended and explained his ministry and its reception with the authority of the Scriptures.

It remains to discover the coping power of the parable for contemporary life. It is as relevant as a key fitting into a lock.

Model for Managing Despair

A glass of water introduced a striking television advertisement for the Peace Corps. The issue presented to the viewer—how shall you describe the glass? Shall you say half empty? Then the Peace Corps would not want you. Or would you call it half full? Then you are a promising candidate. Actually the glass stood half empty as well as half full, and it is imperative to recognize both.

Ernest Campbell has observed that seventy-five years ago Christian congregations could be characterized by a general sense of guilt. About a decade ago, some of those same congregations could be characterized by a general sense of doubt. Campbell reads the typical contemporary congregation as beset with a general sense of discouragement.[34] The half-empty feeling pervades many Christian lives, but the parable of the Sower is "the parable to end despair."[35] How? It provides a model for managing despair. It accounts for the empty half and interprets the full half.

For one thing, the parable *faces failure*. The glass stands half empty. It is not healthy or helpful to be rosy and positive about negative facts by sheer denial. The Galilean campaign itself met stubborn resistance and stinging rejection. Jesus admitted the reverses and setbacks openly and identified with the disciples' despair. Contemporary Christians too have known disillusionment in advocating the Christian faith and in personal failures. Discouragement descends when one first finds out that some people demonstrate absolutely no openness but rather stiff, impenetrable resistance. There exists no chance in some instances, as in the case of the seed thrown on hard ground immediately gulped down by hungry birds. Some refuse out of hand because they are morally insensitive persons for whom callousness has become a way of life. Their hearts seem as hard as anthracite. Some appear past feeling, their anxiety anesthetized.[36] They constantly place the Bible at the bottom of their reading list.

Resistance arises not just from the secular life into which Christian truth can find no entry. There are also hardened saints, those who only come to the sanctuary for one more coat of varnish, who consistently oppose any fresh invasion of spiritual truth. Such resistance of hardened sinners and hardened saints surprises and discourages disciples. With penetrating perception Buttrick faces facts:

There are people at Niagara Falls who hurried from that marvelous torrent to a cheap and crowded carnival: they did not understand that thunder-majesty! There are people to whom the Fifth Symphony is only a farrago of sounds: they do not understand Beethoven's spirit-rapture.[37]

Jesus recognized the reality of shut minds. And he bids his disciples face failure and name resistance and not ignore it, as though it never happened. Face failure, however, *do not accept all of the blame.*

Sometimes expectations are raised sky-high by a sudden sign of personal interest and are then dashed by disengagement. An intense interest in Christian faith may be expressed. One may be encouraged initially by the possibility of a promotion, by a romantic overture, or by an offer of friendship that fails to materialize. We know people who are like converts on the first ballot, persons profuse with praise and extravagant in enthusiasm, but who do not last. Such personal encounters and experiences are deflating.

Some are eager to get on board the Christian faith but have failed to count the cost. They fail to stick it out to the finish. Alexander Findlay has put it bluntly, "Indeed, it is not easy to be a Christian; but it is *easy to start*."[38] One church announced its intention to present new members on a particular Sunday. One man telephoned the church office to say he was sorry he could not be present on that day. Later on in the same week he called back again cheerfully. "I made a mistake," he explained, "the Rams are playing out of town Sunday. I can be there after all."[39] Sometimes promising specimens are strangled by competing interests and cluttered lives. David Redding, recognizing the practical way Christians break the King of kings down to a buck private, says, "Christianity is fighting a losing battle in so many of our lives, not because we are bad, but because we are too busy with our briefcase of second rate stuff."[40]

Jesus ministered to the despair of his disciples. He understood how his first twelve felt, and he faced the failure with them. He not only encourages Christians to deal with disillusionment but also to understand its causes. He both registered the rejections and explained the anatomy of rejection. From the standpoint of sowers, Jesus invited honesty in naming the half emptiness, to face the failures, but not to accept all the blame.

Taking responsibility for your own life comprises the parable's second message for managing despair. Jesus refused to incur liability for decisions belonging to others. Rather he spoke to the crowds on the beach eyeball-to-eyeball. The listener of the parable then and now is under the awful obligation, not to compliment or criticize, but to decide. "The Word of God," declared Thielicke, "is not a feast for the ears but a hammer."[41] From the side of the soils, the parable offers further direction for managing despair.

Increasingly, modern psychologists encourage people to take charge of their lives rather than give in to the feeling that they are helpless victims or leaves blown in the fall wind. Rollo May, who sees modern persons' most pervasive tendency as thinking of themselves as passive, points with alarm to the undermining of will and the undercutting of individual responsibility. He writes forcefully, "Indeed, the central core of modern man's 'neurosis,' it may be fairly said, is the undermining of his experience of himself as responsible, the sapping of his will and ability to make decisions."[42] He recognizes this modern malady that deprives persons of personhood and calls for a recovery of will. "It is in intentionality and will that the human being experiences his identity," he believes.[43] This corrective toward responsibility from a leading psychologist encourages a perennial conviction of Christian faith. Some forms of "neurotic religion" also increase dependency and even invite individuals to remain infantile.

My former professor, Donald Macleod, makes a crucial distinction between listening and hearing that speaks both to the parables and to responsibility. Sensing the urgency of Jeremiah, "O earth, earth, earth, hear the word of the Lord" (22:29), Macleod distinguishes listening as a passive role while genuine hearing involves personal confrontation and stirrings of conscience. In prophetic fashion in his sermon "Don't Just Listen: HEAR!" he makes his point:

We are a generation of listeners who have almost lost the sensitivity and competence to hear. Listening is like watching the scenery from the window of a fast moving train; hearing is getting off at the station and becoming involved in the human struggle.[44]

Jesus expects followers to get off at the station, to do something about their problems besides drowning in despair.

The other clue from Jesus' model for managing despair comes with the colossal harvest beyond human expectation. The disciples were mesmerized by the failures. We often dwell on the half-empty glass, but the same vessel contains much water. Jesus pointed to a fantastic outcome in that part of the story that predicts, that includes his faith hunch, his breakthrough beyond the malaise. *Count on God* when wrestling with despair.

Failures exist in life and constantly seek to call trumps. They can be persuasive and well-nigh overwhelming, but faith steps in with resources. Faith points forward to exciting, hopeful results. The parable invites preachers and witnesses to continue sharing despite setbacks because good ground there is. The glass is not empty. The parable also encourages hearers, as it suggests invitingly what God can do. Persons haunted by brooding despair can look beyond their own private resources to God.

A minister emigrated from England to America in the seventeenth century. Friends forecast a bright future for this scholar, but he died within a year of landing on our shore. He left a personal library of two hundred books and seven hundred pounds of English money to a new college. The school today maintains a thousand professors and a student body of ten thousand. At the time of death, John Harvard's effort and promise seemed completely frustrated, but God had not finished.[45]

Face failures realistically but do not accept all the blame. Decide to take charge of your life rather than flounder. Do not give up. Count on the God who specializes in harvests.

NOTES

1. So Lohmeyer, *Das Evangelium des Markus*, Twelfth Edition (Göttingen: Vandenhoeck & Ruprecht, 1953), p. 83.

2. The primary differences include the introduction, the addition "it was trampled on" (8:5c), the terse lack of moisture explanation (8:6b), and the omission of the three yields. Luke was especially interested in the second and fourth part, both in the parable and the interpretation.

3. K. D. White, "The Parable of the Sower," *Journal of Theological Studies*, 15:305 (1964).

4. Joachim Jeremias, "Palästinakundliches zum Gleichnis vom Sämann (Mc. IV:3-8 par.), "*New Testament Studies*, 13:48-53 (1966/67). Jeremias credits Gustav Dalman as being the first who made the parable understandable. To counter White, he corresponded with the Director of the Theodor-Schneller-Schule in Amman for corroboration! He depends a great deal on *Shab* 7.2 and b. *Shab* 73b, but points out that the warning in Jeremiah 4:3 shows that it was a practice in Old Testament times. W. G. Essame, "Sowing and Plowing," *Expository Times* 72:54 (1960/61), confirms sowing preceding plowing by appeal to Jub. 11:11, an especially valuable parallel. P. B. Payne, "The Order of Sowing and Plowing in the Parable of the Sower," *New Testament Studies*, 25:123-129 (1979), in a well-documented article pictures an autumn sowing of wheat. Payne produces good evidence both for plowing before and after and considers the parable "sufficiently generalized to apply to almost any sowing in Palestine" (pp. 128-129). Birger Gerhardsson, "The Parable of the Sower and its Interpretation," *New Testament Studies*, 14:187 (1968), argues that it would be uncommon for a Palestinian field to have all these different kinds of soil. Rather the parable is a forced agricultural illustration.

5. Reported by Charles C. McDonald, "The Relevance of the Parable of the Sower," *Bible Today*, 26:1825 (1966).

6. The parables are markedly different in the description of the harvest. Matthew 13:8 presents a descending order. Luke 8:8 reports only the hundred-times result. Presumably the ascending order captures the original wonder. It is no small fact that both Matthew (13:23) and Mark (4:20) repeat the size of the harvest, thus accentuating its prominence there also. Some who favor the authenticity of the interpretation also play down the size of the harvest. This seems quite unnecessary.

7. Bruce Metzger, *A Textual Commentary on the Greek New Testament* (New York: United Bible Societies, 1971), p. 83, speculates that behind the Greek *hen* probably lies the Aramaic sign of multiplication and so could be translated "times."

8. Jeremias, *The Parables of Jesus*, p. 150n.

9. White, p. 302, cited Varro, *De Re Rustica*, 1, 44, 2, which reports returns of a hundred grains in the foothills of Gilead, near Gadara. See also Genesis 26:12. Some scholars think the harvest is not so exceptional and that the thirty, sixty, hundred result refers to the number of grains on a single ear.

10. The invitation to hear is often the sign of a mashal (Prov. 5:1; 12:17; Ecclesiasticus 3:1; 16:22).

11. So Vincent Taylor, *The Gospel According to St. Mark* (London: Macmillan, 1959), p. 251.

12. A. B. Bruce, *The Parabolic Teaching of Christ* (London: Hodder & Stoughton, 1893), p. 18.

13. Jeremias, *The Parables*, p. 151. The parable is not so much a contrast of seedtime and harvest. This parable is not that near the Mustard Seed and the Seed Growing on Its Own. It seems more a contrast in growth outcomes. Jeremias's view of encouragement was preceded by Justin, *Dial.*, 125, who applied the parable to the Christian preacher who should not become faint-hearted.

14. William Neil, "Expounding the Parables: The Sower (Mark 4:3-8)," *Expository Times*, 77:76 (1965).

15. K. Grayston, "The Sower," *Expository Times*, 55:139 (1943-1944).

16. This would constitute an eschatological assertion by Jesus. The implication of a divine sowing would bespeak the New Age. There is then a realized dimension, but it is more an inaugurated eschatology. The harvest is still future. Of course, this is contrary to C. H. Dodd, *Parables of the Kingdom*, pp. 135-137.

17. Emil Brunner, *Sowing and Reaping*, trans. T. Wieser (Richmond: John Knox, 1964; German edition, 1946), p. 14.

18. Luke brazenly utilized terms of systematic theology (*believe* and *be saved, fall away, hold it fast*), revealing beautifully the church of his time reflecting on the parable and applying it. W. C. Robinson also points this out in his article "On Preaching the Word of God (Luke 8:4-21)," in *Studies in Luke-Acts*, ed. L. E. Keck and J. L. Martyn (Nashville: Abingdon Press, 1966), pp. 131-138. He identifies Luke 8:4-21 as a discussion not so much on parables as on the Word of God. Noting the "Christianization" observed above, he sees Luke presenting a parable about Christian preaching. He singles out the addition in 8:12 as the most striking, and rightly recognizes Luke's concern about people rejecting Christian preaching.

19. R. Bultmann, "*merimnaō*," *TDNT*, 4:591 (1967). He concluded, "For his life is in fact controlled by that for which, about which, after which, before which and concerning which he cares." B. E. Thiering, " 'Breaking of Bread' and 'Harvest' in

Mark's Gospel," *Novum Testamentum,* 12:1-12 (1970), takes Mark 4:14-20 as an anticipation of the history of the reception given to the gospel in different parts of the world. Not short of inventiveness, he speculates that the rocky ground points to Peter-like behavior and to Rome scorched by Nero. The good soil refers to countries north of the Mediterranean. These references are the mysteries of 4:11!

20. The interpretation is customarily rejected, as Dodd, *The Parables of the Kingdom,* p. 145. More recently, however, two students have reopened the question. B. Gerhardsson, pp. 165-193, argues that Jesus told the parable with the interpretation in mind and in fact patterned on the Shema. That is, the failures were due to the refusal to hear with the whole heart, whole soul, and whole might. D. Wenham, "The Interpretation of the Parable of the Sower," *New Testament Studies,* 20:299-319 (1974), brilliantly attempts a critical reconstruction.

21. For example, Eduard Schweizer, *The Good News According to Mark,* trans. Donald H. Madvig (Richmond: John Knox, 1970), p. 96, summarizes the arguments against the interpretation. He sees it as deterministic as it stands because the nature of the soil cannot be changed. He does see value, nevertheless, in the interpretation because the situation of the early church is more like ours today. For a different view dealing with a problem in Mark's Greek, see P. B. Payne, "The Seeming Inconsistency of the Interpretation of the Parable of the Sower," *New Testament Studies,* 26:564-568 (1980). For a balanced statement of arguments against authenticity and counter considerations, see C. E. B. Cranfield, *The Gospel According to St. Mark* (Cambridge: University Press, 1959), pp. 158-161.

22. Recall also the parable of the Strong Man (Mark 3:27; Luke 11:21 *f.*). Each Gospel uses a different designation *(ho poneros,* Matt. 13:19; *ho satanas,* Mark 4:15; and *ho diabolos,* Luke 8:12), but significantly all include reference.

23. Jeremias, *The Parables of Jesus,* rejects the interpretation on linguistic grounds (pp. 77-79), accepts the parable especially because of its Palestinian character (pp. 149-150), and considers the purpose statement as a misplaced logion (pp. 13-18).

24. For example, note Matthew 13:19,20,22,23; Mark 4:15,16,18,20; and Luke 8:12,13,14,15.

25. As I. H. Marshall, *Commentary on Luke* (Grand Rapids: Wm. B. Eerdmans, 1978), p. 323. *Hina* is usually purposive, can be imperative or consecutive (so that . . .) or causal or relative.

26. C. F. D. Moule, "Mark 4:1-20 Yet Once More," in *Neotestamentica et Semitica: Studies in Honour of Matthew Black,* ed. E. Earle Ellis and Max Wilcox (Edinburgh: T. & T. Clark, 1969), p. 100.

27. The term "outsiders" *(tois exō)* surely reflected early church usage and referred to those outside the Christian community, yet the basic distinction of those entering the kingdom and those outside is quite appropriate to Jesus. Interestingly, only Paul and Mark use the technical construction *tois exō.* See 1 Corinthians 15:12-13, 1 Thessalonians 4:12, and Colossians 4:5 where the expression refers to those outside the church. Mark uses *exō* in several passages, the most interesting of which is 3:31-32—wherein an "outsider" is one who does not do the will of God. Among the rabbis outsiders were those who did not accept the *halakah* of the scribes *(Meg.* 4:8; *Sanh.* 10:1). In Josephus, the reference is to foreigners *(Ant.* 15, 314). In the LXX note 2 Maccabees 1:16-17.

28. So Moule, p. 97. Also John Bowker, "Mystery and Parable: Mark IV. 1-20," *Journal of Theological Studies*, 25:301 (1974).
29. So J. Drury, "The Sower, the Vineyard, and the Place of Allegory in the Interpretation of Mark's Parables," *Journal of Theological Studies*, 24:367-368 (1973). Drury is far more telling in his critique of Jeremias than he is in supporting his own position.
30. As Madeleine Boucher, *The Mysterious Parable: A Literary Study*, No. 6 of "The Catholic Biblical Quarterly Monograph Series" (Washington: Catholic Biblical Association, 1977), p. 84. Bowker, p. 307, identifies *mustērion* to that which constitutes or identifies Israel in its special relation to God.
31. Bowker, p. 315. Bowker has succeeded in typing together Mark 4:1-20 in a quite convincing fashion. See also Cranfield, "St. Mark 4:1-34," *Scottish Journal of Theology*, 4:398-414 (1951) and 4:49-66 (1952). I am personally indebted to Cranfield for calling my attention to Moule's article, and interestingly to Moule as well because he called my attention to Cranfield's article. Neither made mention of his own!
32. Brunner.
33. T. W. Manson, *The Teaching of Jesus*, Second Edition, (Cambridge: University Press, 1955), p. 76. For his celebrated thesis concerning Mark 4:10-12 that Jesus quoted from the Targum on Isaiah and that Mark misunderstood the Aramaic due to the ambiguity of the particle, see pp. 77-79. For further orientation to this thorny problem, see G. V. Jones, *The Art and Truth of the Parables* (London: SPCK, 1964), pp. 225-230.
34. Ernest Campbell, *Locked in a Room with Open Doors* (Waco: Word, 1974), p. 55.
35. William Barclay, *The Gospel of Mark*, "The Daily Study Bible," Second Edition (Philadelphia: Westminster, 1956), p. 94.
36. See Wayne Oates, *Anxiety in Christian Experience* (Philadelphia: Westminster, 1955), pp. 100-108.
37. George Buttrick, *The Parables of Jesus* (Grand Rapids: Baker, 1973, reprinted from 1928 edition), p. 45.
38. Alexander Findlay, *Jesus and His Parables* (London: Epworth, 1950), p. 75.
39. G. Kennedy, *The Parables* (New York: Harper, 1960), p. 175.
40. David Redding, *The Parables He Told* (New York: Harper, 1962), p. 92.
41. Helmut Thielicke, *The Waiting Father*, trans. J. Doberstein (New York: Harper, 1959), p. 56.
42. Rollo May, *Love and Will* (New York: Dell, 1969), p. 182.
43. Ibid., p. 241.
44. Donald Macleod, "Don't Just Listen: HEAR!" *The Princeton Seminary Bulletin*, 3:57 (n.s., 1980).
45. Cited by Barclay, *And Jesus Said* (Philadelphia: Westminster, 1970), pp. 23-24.

Mark 4:30-32;
Matthew 13:31-32;
Luke 13:18-19

5 The Parable of the Mustard Seed

This vignette likening the kingdom to mustard seed has enjoyed a noticeable popularity and familiarity. Christians have drawn considerable inspiration from this durable word of God. Like the other seed parables, it has "the smell of the country about it" and is associated with the open-air phase of Jesus' ministry around the lake.[1] The mustard seed parable belongs to what has been called the triple tradition because Matthew and Luke include it, as well as Mark. Indeed, the gospel of Thomas contains its own account as well.

Critical Analysis

These four accounts of the parable tell a roughly similar development of a mustard seed into an astonishing plant, but the differences are noticeable. For example, on a relatively minor point, Matthew says that the seed was sown in a "field," Mark on the "earth," Luke in a "garden," and Thomas on "tilled ground."[2] Generally speaking Mark and Luke stand apart from one another, and Matthew is a kind of middle term. In general, it does not appear that either Mark or Luke is dependent on any other Gospel.[3] Matthew appears to have combined the traditions of Mark and Luke. Apparently then Luke reflects Q, though perhaps abridged; Mark reports the Roman tradition; and Matthew combines Mk. and Q.

The source-critical opinion that two independent reports underlie the three Gospels has led naturally to champions for each. C. H. Dodd opted for the Lukan form (Q) as original, as have a surprisingly large number of others.[4] While some would be suspicious of Dodd's reasons for jettisoning the Markan form, H. K. McArthur, in a thorough study, feels that Dodd has reconstructed a Q form of the parable that reaches back to the forties. McArthur's confidence in Q and his preference for the past tense settled the matter for him.[5] Others choose Mark because his picture more realistically reflected conditions[6] or because his record explained why a mustard seed was selected.[7]

The decisive point to note, both form-critically and exegetically, is that Luke and Matthew portray the parable in the past tense. The Lukan story is a running *narrative* of three stages after sowing, each introduced by *and (kai)*. It contains no comment or interpretation, as it were, but economically records growth, becoming a tree, and the arrival of the birds of heaven.[8] Mark, on the other hand, is not a narrative but a general situation, a critical literary observation absolutely necessary for clarifying this problem and for solving it. Simply observe the subjunctives and the present tenses. Note that whereas a definite man sowed in Matthew (13:31c) and Luke (13:19b), there is no man or past orientation in Mark. Mark's general situation is far more likely for the time of Jesus, whereas the past tense narrative form reflects the perspective of the later church.[9] Furthermore, the Markan form contains internal contrast, as do many other parables, and it most faithfully reflects Palestinian conditions. The gospel of Thomas also supports it.[10]

Textual Commentary

The parable itself is introduced by a remarkable double question: "How shall we compare the kingdom of God, or in what parable will we put it?" A few similar rhetorical introductions to other parables are found in the Gospels[11] and among later rabbis,[12] but perhaps the most important Jewish precedent is Isaiah 40:18: "To whom then will you liken God, or what likeness compare with him?" (RSV) Both introductions are forms of Semitic poetry, posing the possibility of a likeness for God; but while Isaiah's rhetorical question expected a negative answer, Jesus supplied a parable.[13] Also observe the style conveyed by the deliberative subjunctive and the plural "we" which would have involved the hearers. "The inclusion of the hearers is especially evident."[14] This double question leading into the parable provides quite a glimpse into the nature and function of parables. A parable here is a comparison with the use of "as" (*hos* in 4:31a). It is the use of pictorial language to communicate about ultimate reality.

In Mark 4:31-32, the kingdom is compared to a tiny mustard seed that grows into a great bush. The seed is precisely the black mustard

(*Sinapis nigra*), grown in fields both for the grains supplying a sharp tang and for the leaves which were cooked like greens.[15] The *Mishnah* contains sayings about the smallness of the mustard seed as does one other saying of Jesus (Mark 11:23 and par.)[16] While the mustard seed may not be absolutely the smallest seed, it is so tiny it requires 725-760 to weigh a gram (28 grams = an ounce).[17] Jesus was speaking proverbially. Even today, mustard grows to a height of two-and-a-half to three meters (eight to ten ft.) around the Lake of Gennesaret.[18]

The parable observed that the tiny mustard seed becomes the greatest of the shrubs[19] and has such large branches that birds nest in its shade (4:32a).[20] Birds today seek out the shade of its big leaves and nibble on the mustard seeds.[21] It is possible that these are "Gentile birds," an allegorical allusion to the nations coming to join the Jews in the blessings of the end time.[22] The result clause in the last verse (v. 32d) is rather climactic, dramatizing the ample size and success of the mustard bush.[23] So the final trait of the parable confirms the indication of the introduction which announced instruction relative to the kingdom of God.[24]

Old Testament Promise

The concluding reference to the birds of heaven roosting in the branches and enjoying the shade calls to mind Old Testament pictures of tall trees providing shade and food. The classic texts are in Daniel 4, Ezekiel 17 and 31. The tall trees refer to kings and kingdoms and protection and are apt pictures of Pharaohs (Ezek. 31:6) and kings (Dan. 4) protecting their subjects. God's sovereignty plays in because he topples the trees so that the living may know that the Most High rules the kingdom of men and gives it to whom he will (Dan. 4:13-14). The mighty cedar of Lebanon is proud of its height, but foreigners will cut it down, and the sound of its fall will make the nations quake (Ezek. 31:1-16). The mighty cedar is an apt symbol.

These Old Testament passages, which contain verbal parallels with Mark 4:32d (Dan. 4:12,21; Ezek. 17:23; 31:6), belong to the general background of the parable.[25] However, the single text that definitely should be most closely associated is Ezekiel 17:22-24. All the other passages utilized the imagery and dealt with God's sovereignty but are focused negatively on human kingdoms experiencing God's wrath. The parable is not related to judgment but represents rather a very positive picture.[26]

Ezekiel 17:22-24 is preceded by riddles about great eagles planting cedars (vv. 1-6,7-10), followed by an application asserting the sovereignty of God (vv. 11-21): "You shall know that I, the Lord, have spoken" (17:21, RSV). Then, however, follows the promise of a very positive act of divine sovereignty. The Lord God will break a twig from a lofty cedar and *plant* it on the mountain height of Israel. It will become a noble cedar "and under it will dwell all kinds of beasts; in the shade of its branches birds of every sort will nest" (17:23, RSV).[27] Here is a great picture of a messianic kingdom, and the chapter ends on the divine resolution, "I will do it" (RSV).

Now Jesus was boldly declaring by his parable that what God had promised to do in Ezekiel 17 he was now doing in his ministry! The problem he faced stemmed from a hasty interpretation. The people expected a mighty cedar. Jesus spoke of a mustard seed.[28] Note, however, that even in Ezekiel the cedar begins as a "cutting" and is planted and will become a noble cedar (17:22-23). Even so, Jesus was taking a seed and planting just as Ezekiel promised. He selected the mustard seed primarily because of its proverbial smallness that results in the greatest of all shrubs.

Basic Interpretation

The parable assumes Ezekiel 17 and claims that in the ministry of Jesus at that very moment God is planting his messianic kingdom. Jesus sought to persuade his hearers concerning the decisive importance of that moment. The eschatological intervention of God has begun.[29] Certainly the kingdom Jesus presided over was the smallest kingdom in the Fertile Crescent! It was a burlesque of a kingdom. "Can something so contemptibly small be pregnant with the great purpose of God?" asked Hunter.[30] The disciples of the Baptizer admitted their doubt related to expectation (Luke 7:18-19). So Jesus imaginatively thought of the microscopic seed that could become a lofty bush. After all, one should not measure the importance of what is going on by its size. One certainly cannot limit future or intrinsic importance by present size.

Once again the exegetical clue lies with an internal contrast, and, if you please, the interpretation is virtually present within the parable. The meaning lies in the contrast between the smallest seed (*mikroteros*, v. 31c) and the greatest shrub (*meizōn*, v. 32b), with the realization that the latter grew from the former.[31] The emphasis is clearly not on stages of growth. Rather, the Parabolist wished to awaken faith in what could and would happen. Jesus believed and invited others to believe that God was beginning something new in Israel, that his sovereignty paradoxically was already being expressed in the planting of a mustard seed and the ultimate triumph of God would eventuate. This included the Gentiles. Jesus believed that "many will come from east and west and recline at table with Abraham and Isaac and Jacob in the kingdom of heaven" (Matt. 8:11). Jesus appealed to the imagination. Have you the imagination to find a kingdom in tiny beginnings and to project a gigantic outcome?

What the Kingdom Looks Like Today

In Vatican City, there remains an impressive fountain which symbolizes the size of the Roman Catholic Church. The various continents where there are many Catholics are indicated at the corners. A Protestant reaction to this statement in stone may well be critical. The fountain suggests an inappropriate spiritual power, a sense of empire parallel to the sense of secular empire, as in the courtyard of Buckingham Palace in London. The fountain conveys "triumphalism" rather than the church on mission.

Yet the Roman fountain does communicate how far flung is the Christian church. The church is international. It is interracial. Christians are many. The church is not merely regional or national. The dozen disciples have become an enormous assemblage. Many cultures and continents claim Christ. Advance through storm has actually taken place.

The fountain evokes ambivalent feelings and raises pointedly the question, What does the kingdom look like today? In the time of Jesus, the kingdom looked like a mustard seed. In the *eschaton* it will look like a bush. What about the present? Seed or bush or both?

Like a Mustard Seed. The actual career of Jesus resembled a mustard seed, did it not? His was a lowly stable birth. It seems that "The Almighty hid the Crown Jewel in a fork of hay."[32] Jesus came from a modest home and learned the carpenter's trade. He eventually became a rabbi without credentials and commanded a congregation without clout. He was a homeless teacher of religion. Messianic expectations certainly ran headlong in the opposite direction. George MacDonald in "The Holy Thing" captured the situation adeptly,

> They all were looking for a king
> To slay their foes and lift them high:
> Thou cam'st, a little baby thing
> That made a woman cry.

The "little baby thing" was as unremarkable as one mustard seed. It should also be recognized that Jesus' values remind of mustard. He was impressed by a cup of cold water. He was beside himself about a widow's gift of mites, and he memorialized her sacrifice. His values were startling. Now the career of Jesus, his crowd of disciples, and his values provide a primary clue for finding the kingdom today.

The kingdom is there when a Christian tutors a disadvantaged child, when a struggling Sunday School class comes into being, when a legislator presses for justice (the will of God), when the gospel is proclaimed in a little mission church. God is doing his thing. Sometimes, however, magnitude is substituted for faith and little efforts are passed by unheralded. A chairperson of a missionary meeting claimed that he founded a growing Christian group in India. He startled his listeners because he had never been out of England. He went on to support his claim impressively. When he was five he wanted to give his penny to the missionaries but was not willing to put his penny in the Sunday School box. The pastor happened to be a family friend and also friend to a missionary in India. To please the child the minister sold him a copy of the New Testament for his penny and instructed him how to mail a package to India. The boy wrote his name on the flyleaf and sent it. The missionary later gave it to a poor native who had trudged miles to procure a Bible.

Not another word was heard for twenty years. Then a missionary, visiting a remote village, found a delightful response to the words of the gospel. He started asking questions and found the people knew Christ and followed him. No preacher had ever been there. They produced the worn New Testament under the palm trees, a New Testament with a boy's name in it![33] Only a seed, a seemingly inconsequential act of a persistent youngster, but the outcome exceeded appearances.

The kingdom today is most often as small as a seed, and only faith notices. Never be daunted in starting something small. Never imagine that a venture's intrinsic spiritual value is measured by magnitude. A youth musical muses how

Just one man in a world full of sin
Is like one star in a sky full of stars.
But just one man can change his world
If he will try.

When Jesus left the carpenter's shop to follow his Father's summons, perhaps no one perceived what a history changing event was in the making.

The Roman fountain can misleadingly imply that the kingdom is easily recognized without faith because it is like a cedar of Lebanon or a full blown bush. The kingdom is very often today like the mustard seed, is it not? God is still making new beginnings. God is still planting seeds around the world. Respect the "infinitude of the little." Obsession with size is obscene.

Like a Bush for Birds. The Roman fountain stubbornly reminds, however, that a miracle in history transpired. How vast a tree from so small a seed. The modern disciple is allowed to see what the first twelve could not. Jesus was right. Then his band seemed trivial, dwarfed when contrasted with the Roman Empire. Now the Empire touted by Pilate and Herod is gone. The gospel went forward to penetrate the culture of Greece and to live on. The subsequent history of Christianity vindicates the truth of the mustard seed story. Elton Trueblood, calling the church the most powerful force for good in the world, points out, "It has, indeed, been a miracle of history more striking than any one miracle performed by Jesus in His earthly career."[34] The poor little fellowship Jesus started has become an earthshaking presence. Of course, the church must not be equated simplistically with the kingdom, which is where God's will is done.

The church does need to continue becoming the bush that provides shade for all people. The "Gentile birds" include all ethnic groups. Church growth is a natural and healthy expectation. Some are so devoted to the seed that they lack the imagination to celebrate the bush and the birds. Church growth is now on the agenda again and an entire movement in the USA has gathered momentum and some regard. It has come forward with principles and methods.[35] One of those moments in history has arrived when the Christian community needs to extend its ministry and reach "the unchurched American" and the unchurched world.

Church growth that matters must be authentic however. Church growth should not be measured principally or solely from a numerical basis. Real church growth is conceptual, incarnational, organizational, and numerical.[36] *Conceptual* growing dares to go beyond the spiritual *ABCs* as the writer of Hebrews insisted: "Let us go forward, then, to mature teaching and leave behind us the first lessons of the Christian message" (6:1, TEV). Horizons need to expand. Superficial understandings need to give way to depth. Lay theologians can come into being who read the Bible seriously, who also read Tournier and Trueblood and Barclay and Stagg and Moltmann and Moody. In-depth seminars for lay Christians can be initiated.

Church growth with integrity includes *organizational* advance. Paul expressed concern for organization in 1 Corinthians 12 and throughout Ephesians and the Pastoral Epistles. Such organizational growth includes efficiency and harmony but is potentially far more creative. The gifts of disciples need to come into play. Good casting is required. Gifts of helping, witnessing, loving, and ministering can be brought together sensitively with needs.

Church growth must be *incarnational* growth. A growing church, by definition, is one where Christians are growing in ministries. The very self-understanding of Jesus was expressed in the clarification that he came not to be served but to minister. A group that understands itself as his disciples must be like him in this vital clarification. The growing church must incarnate his love, incarnate his kindness, incarnate his concern for the poor and social justice. Church growth is not merely "nickels and noses" but healed hurts. Both the Great Commission and the love command carry the Lord's authority and touch the essence of the church's mission.

Church growth does legitimately include *numerical* growth, for the gracious inclusion of new people extends ministry. Concern for the spiritual well-being of other people and not just one's own is Christian. A congregation with an open-ended fellowship welcoming new people has the spirit of Christ. The explanation of the mission of Jesus involves inclusion of outsiders in the fellowship of faith (Luke 19:10). The Book of Acts records positively and enthusiastically numerical progress on strategic junctures (2:41; 4:32-34; 5:14-15; 6:7; 12:24; and 19:20). Acts does make it clear who grows the church numerically. "The Lord added to the church. . . ."

The bush for birds can be glimpsed in our world and can expand horizons. A community for every nation on earth is aborning for those with eyes to see.

NOTES

1. A. M. Hunter, *The Parables Then and Now* (Philadelphia: Westminster Press, 1971), p. 35.
2. H. K. McArthur, "The Parable of the Mustard Seed," *Catholic Biblical Quarterly*, 33:201 (1971), has shown that Q probably had "field" and that Luke accommodated to a Hellenistic audience. Jewish custom excluded mustard from gardens and confined it to the larger fields (see *M Kilaim* 3:2 and *T Kilaim* 2:8). This restriction was not characteristic of the Hellenistic world which regarded mustard as a garden plant. The reference of the gospel of Thomas to "tilled ground" apparently has Gnostic overtones.
3. For a very different view see David Wenham, "The Synoptic Problem Revisited: Some New Suggestions about the Composition of Mark," *The Tyndale Bulletin*, 23:31-35 (1972). His most telling argument is that Mark's use of Matthew would explain the awkwardness of the Markan style. Ernst Lohmeyer, *Das Evangelium Kritisch des Markus*, "Kritischexegetischer Kommentar über das Neue Testament" Eleventh Edition (Göttingen: Vandenhoeck & Ruprecht, 1951), p. 88, pointed out many infelicities earlier.
4. C. H. Dodd, *Parables*, pp. 152-154. He concluded, "The Kingdom of God is here: the birds are flocking to find shelter in the shade of the tree" (p. 154) and related the parable interestingly to the meals with sinners. Others include Jülicher, B. T. D. Smith, and C. W. F. Smith.
5. McArthur.
6. Norman Perrin, *Rediscovering the Teaching of Jesus* (New York: Harper, 1967), p. 157, pointed out that Matthew and Luke spoke too freely of a tree, and that Mark was correct that shade would have attracted the birds.
7. W. G. Kümmel, *Promise and Fulfilment*, trans. Dorothea M. Barton, No. 23 in "Studies in Biblical Theology," Third Edition (London: SCM Press, 1957), p. 130.
8. On the basis of the Lukan narrative the arrival of the birds of heaven is climactic, the end of an unswerving growth. Otto Kuss, "Zum Sinngehalt des Doppelgleichnisses vom Senfkorn und Sauertieg," *Biblica*, 40:645n (1959), recognized the arrival of the birds was an event (*Ereignis*). He rejected Mark's universal observation as reflecting his situation and favored Luke. This allows room for the development of the church in history. It also reopens Flew's question whether Jesus intended to gather a community. Issues like realized eschatology or a developing kingdom on earth and even early catholicism lurk in the background!
9. McArthur, p. 201, recognized himself that other general situation parables normally began with a question. Further descriptive work on the phenomenology of the parables is needed, especially on the general situation parables. Such work could establish patterns, parallels, and exegetical clues for understanding this particular type.
10. The identification of the mustard seed as the smallest seed, the omission of tree (*dendron*), and explicit reference to a large branch. I am indebted for my translation of

the gospel of Thomas to A. Guillaumont *et al.* (eds), *The Gospel According to Thomas* (New York: Harper, 1959).

11. As Matthew 11:16 introducing the parable of the children in the marketplace, the parallel (Luke 7:31) has two parts. More interesting because of reference to the kingdom is Luke 13:20, introducing the parable of the leaven. Other Old Testament parallels include Psalm 8:5 and 14:1.

12. See H. Songer, "A Study of the Background of the Concepts of Parable in the Synoptic Gospels" (Unpublished doctoral dissertation, The Southern Baptist Theological Seminary, 1962), pp. 166-170.

13. H. Bartsch, "Eine bisher übersehene Zitierung der LXX in Mark 4, 30," *Theologische Zeitschrift*, 15:126-128 (1959), made the provocative suggestion that Jesus' parable said that today it is possible to speak of the likeness of God, the very thing the prophet reckoned as impossible. One can gain not only the form parallel from Isaiah but also the purpose of the parable speech. He also argued for Mark 4:30-34 as a unit and 4:30 as a real parallel to 4:10-12 because the parable remains a veiled speech (*en homoiōmati*).

14. Blass, Debrunner, Funk, *A Greek Grammar of the New Testament*, p. 147 (280).

15. C. H. Hunzinger, *"sinapi,"* Theological Dictionary of the New Testament, 7:288 (1971).

16. *Nid.*, 5.2, makes the comparison "as little as a grain of mustard seed." Also *Nazir*, 1.5. Cited by Hunzinger, p. 288. The smallest known seeds (in the microspermous families), devoid of food reserves, are found in orchids, saprophytes, carnivorous plants and total parasites. Some seeds weigh as little as 0.001 milligrams or about 3.5 hundred-millionths of an ounce. See "Seed and Fruit," *Encyclopedia Britannica*, Vol. 16 of "Macropedia," Fifteenth Edition (Chicago: Benton, 1976), 482. Jesus spoke proverbially, not literally.

17. Ibid., p. 289.

18. Ibid., p. 288.

19. Of course, Matthew and Luke say tree, and the suggestion has been offered that the parable may have meant the mustard tree (*Salvadora Persica L*). Hunzinger, p. 289, puts this to rest by his observation that the mustard tree is not of outstanding size among trees. Furthermore, while the *sinapis nigra* is classified among the *lachana*, the mustard tree is not.

20. Wilhelm Michaelis, *"kataskenoo,"* TDNT 7:389 (1971), insists that temporary alighting is not meant but permanent nesting because of the Old Testament influencing passages and the saying of Jesus (Matt. 8:20; Luke 9:58). Robert Funk, "The Looking-Glass Tree Is for the Birds," *Interpretation*, 27:5 (1973), seems more accurate in his contention for summer roosting, seeking shade and seed. After all, the plant is a fast-growing annual (consequently mostly hollow) and would not provide spring nesting.

21. Hunzinger, p. 288n.

22. In extra-canonical literature *Eth. Enoch*, 90:30-42. Taylor, p. 270, considered it reasonable that Jesus thought of Gentile nations.

23. The clause is introduced significantly by *hōste* both in Mark and Matthew and should be translated "so that." Maximilian Zerwick, *Biblical Greek*, trans. Joseph Smith (Rome: n.p., 1963), p. 121, has helpfully pointed out that while *hōste* with the indicative means actual realization, *hōste* with the infinitive need not indicate the actual

event. This grammatical detail would also support the thesis of a positive general situation parable. Furthermore, *dunasthai* itself allows this rather than something already happened. Note the word order.

24 So J. Dupont, "Les paraboles du sénevé et du levain," *Nouvelle Revue Théologique*, 89:905 (1967).

25. IQH 8:4-9 and 6:14-17 echo the language. A. Dupont-Sommer, *The Essene Writings from Qumran*, trans. G. Vermes (Gloucester, Mass.: Peter Smith, 1973), p. 226n, speculated that the words "all the beasts of the thicket shall graze" was a prediction by the Teacher of Righteousness that his community will become an immense tree spreading over the whole earth.

26. Further research should be done in the area of comparative midrash applied to the parables generally and particularly to the parable of the mustard seed.

27. The reference to shade for the birds connects Mark and Ezekiel 17 even closer.

28. Funk, p. 7, in a stimulating fashion suggested that all cedars will be brought low, including Israel's proud hope, and the insignificant mustard plant will bear Israel's true destiny. The kingdom will not arrive as a mighty cedar but as a lowly garden herb. This selection of mustard seed by Jesus was asserted with comic relief. The implication is a call to an unpretentious venture of faith.

29. So Dupont, p. 910.

30. A. M. Hunter, *Interpreting the Parables* (London: SCM, 1960), p. 43.

31. The intentional contrast is highlighted by Matthew by means of *men* and then *de*. Strikingly in Mark *hotan* is used twice, having the effect stylistically of parallel moments: one moment of sowing states the smallness, and the other states the growing and resultant shade.

32. David Redding, *The Parables He Told*, p. 57.

33. Reported by Leslie Weatherhead, *In Quest of a Kingdom* (New York: Abingdon-Cokesbury, 1944), pp. 123-124.

34. Elton Trueblood, *Confronting Christ* (New York: Harper, 1960), p. 33.

35. The American leader is Donald A. McGavran. See his *Understanding Church Growth* (Grand Rapids: Wm. Eerdmans, 1970). For excellent background and orientation see Peter Wagner, "Recent Developments in Church Growth Understandings," *Review and Expositor*, 77:507-519 (1980). For a thorough and balanced assessment of the American church growth movement, see Larry L. McSwain, "A Critical Appraisal of the Church Growth Movement," *Review and Expositor*, 77:521-537 (1980).

36. So Orlando Costas, *The Church and Its Mission* (Wheaton: Tyndale House, 1974). See also his *The Integrity of Mission: The Inner Life and Outreach of the Church* (New York: Harper, 1979), where he discusses in-depth growth (pp. 47-53), in life-style growth (pp. 54-60) and numerical growth (pp. 38-47). He is not lukewarm about evangelism. He sees the need for a vibrant evangelistic atmosphere that is reflected in prayers, hymns, and sermons (p. 41). By conceptual growth he thinks of broadening understanding and becoming aware of the social conditioning of theology in its culture. Isn't it vitally important to recognize the church leadership now coming from South America? South American Christianity is making converts and growing. This is also the part of the world where liberation theology is so insistent.

6 The Parable of the Seed Growing on its Own

It is quite rare to stumble into a parable in the Gospel of Mark that is found only there. Mark is not exactly chock-full of parables to begin with, and the other two Synoptic Gospels report Mark's other parables, but for some fascinating reason this parable was not repeated by the other evangelists. Conjectures about its omission have ranged from the possibility that its meaning was just not clear enough to the theory that Matthew preferred to substitute the parable of the Tares.

Because the parable is less prominent and not really as familiar as some parables, it is especially interesting to study. The tantalizing possibility exists that if the meaning of the parable can be recovered, then a major breakthrough in finding Jesus' perspective on the kingdom of God is also possible.

A study of this exquisite simile should move through several stages of analysis toward an outcome. As a clarifying beginning for an understanding of this less familiar but important parable, it is more helpful than ordinary to set out how certain representative scholars have solved the mystery of its meaning. Exposure to the classic options can be consciousness raising and can nudge the student toward choosing and formulating a view of his or her own from the beginning. Read the parable several times before proceeding.

Classic Interpretations and Titles

Several patterns appear. For one thing, nearly all the leading interpretations recognize that the Greek word *automaté* (v. 28) is the key.[1] For another, most serious students observe that the parable contains a contrast.[2] Also most see the comparison as some form of encouragement. So even the variety in interpretation contains a surprising unity upon which to build. Representative interpretations are presented here under titles for the parable because naming a parable, after all, is tantamount to interpreting it.[3]

1. *The Allegory of the Sower-Reaper.* The traditional allegorical explanation identified the sower as Christ. The harvest symbolized the judgment; the sleeping and rising, Christ's death and resurrection. The admission of not knowing (v. 27) allowed for human free will.[4] R. C. Trench, who referred the sower primarily to Jesus, saw three stages of individual spiritual growth implied in the blade, the ear, and the full corn in the ear.[5]

Such allegorizing is excessive and obviously vulnerable when equating sleeping and rising (v. 27a) with the death and resurrection of Christ, "how he did not know" (v. 27) with allowance for free will, and the blade, ear, and full seed (v. 28) with stages of spiritual growth. The possible identification of the sower as Christ or the harvest as judgment cannot be flippantly dismissed. However, and in candor, it ought to be stated that other more cautious interpretations flirt with allegory too.

2. *The Parable of the Confident Sower.* This "optimistic" interpretation is associated with Karl Weiss, who has written extensively on the parable.[6] He delineated three truths: (a) Jesus established his kingdom on earth (v. 26); (b) he hoped confidently for success (v. 27); and (c) this hope moves certainly to completion (vv. 28-29).[7] Optimism becomes the ground thought of the parable. Weiss insisted that this portrait of the confident sower is superior to the common stress on passivity, which short-circuits the last component of the parable, because his approach takes and retains the unified wholeness of the parable.[8] Thus he opted for the optimism of Jesus and claimed that each part of the parable plays a constitutive role in his construction.

The emphasis upon optimism as such seems shallow, but Weiss' interpretation enjoys a certain unity. Something of the cheerful faith of Jesus is captured. His reinterpretation provoked real debate from his fellow Catholics.[9]

3. *The Parable of Gradual Growth.* Nineteenth-century scholars (such as J. Wellhausen and B. Weiss), influenced by liberal and evolutionary thought frames, attributed a development or process to Jesus' kingdom teaching. Paul Feine insisted that Jesus placed the immanental understanding alongside the apocalyptic. He posited an imman-

ental, slow, and secret developmental process inherent in the description of germination and growth (vv. 27-28). Secondly, he pointed out that the sower can do nothing other than trust the seed. He must wait.[10] So our parable functioned beautifully as a foil against excessive apocalyptic expectation, though Feine did wind up with a primary and secondary interpretation.

A. B. Bruce placed stress on "the blade, the ear, and the full corn" and proposed an interpretation of "progress according to natural law, and by stages which must be passed through in succession,"[11] though he individualized considerably. Adolf Jülicher, the nineteenth-century parable specialist, maintained consistently his one-point principle adroitly by setting down the meaning as *the certainty of the development of the kingdom*, though he found Mark's influence upon the last verse of the parable.[12]

The stress on gradual growth (which can be related to a postmillennial stance and even process theology) fails to emphasize the harvest and usually imports notions of ethical development not obvious from the parable's content. While the version of the interpretation bearing all the trappings of nineteenth-century agenda has been discredited, the idea of a gradual growth still claims proponents.

4. *The Parable of the Harvest.* Ironically both the well-known Albert Schweitzer with his thoroughly futuristic view and Dodd with his realized eschatology found the center of gravity in the harvest (v. 29). The Dodd scenario is particularly impressive, as he found God as the one doing the sowing, the stages of growth belonging to the Old Testament era, and harvesttime referring to the present crisis of the ministry of Jesus. The climax of a long process has arrived, "something has now happened which never happened before."[13] He pictured Jesus as standing in a ripe crop (Matt. 9:37-38; Luke 10:2). So Jesus fulfilled the expectations of the Baptizer. Thus Dodd was able to make much of the stages of growth as providential antecedents, as it were, to avoid a lapse of time before the second advent and to relate the harvest via the prophet Joel in an electrifying fashion to "the fullness of time."

Scholars, such as Vincent Taylor, have followed this line;[14] but one of the most interesting new writers, John Crossan, has a variation he dubbed "the parable of the Reaper." Following the gospel of Thomas and deleting verse 28, Crossan is persuaded that the emphasis is totally on the farmer. But note the surprising affinity to Dodd's interpretation which centers on the harvest. Both saw fulfillment then and there in the ministry of Jesus. For Crossan, the parable is a stirring call to action, a call to reap.[15] When most interpretations settle on the seed or the growth or the harvest, it is intriguing to see someone move from the side of the farmer to call for action when most interpreters stress the opposite, the patience and passivity of the farmer.

5. *The Parable of the Patient Farmer.* Bearing some similarity to the "confident sower," this view, in contradistinction to the preceding approach (4), relates the time of Jesus to seeding and waiting. This favored analysis not only centers upon the seed growing *automatē* but also upon the contrast between the passivity of the farmer and the activity of the seed. Jeremias, who classified the story as a contrast parable, reckoned that the seed grew unceasingly without the farmer taking anxious thought or active steps. The decisive beginning is made, and people shall wait patiently upon God (as Jas. 5:7).[16] Norman Perrin, a sometime student of Jeremias, placed this parable in his chapter "Jesus and the Future" and wrote of "the lesson of patient waiting, in sure confidence that what has been sown will be reaped, that what God has begun he will bring to a triumphant conclusion."[17]

The conviction that the kingdom comes without human care has been championed as the essence of the parable by various other scholars (Hauck, Calvin, Schleiermacher, Johannes Weiss, Schlatter, and Lohmeyer)[18] and may well be in the target area. Its focus on the believer waiting gains from the fact that the farmer as a character continues throughout the parable, but it makes too little of growth and harvest. One possible difficulty from one vantage is that the one who harvests and the one who sows and waits are the same. Indeed, it could be that antithetical aspects are present in the inactivity during the growth and the initiative at harvest.[19] N. A. Dahl, in fact, singled out the contrast between the farmer's passivity during the time of growth and his hurry to put in the sickle at the moment the grain is ripe.[20] This latter ingenious theory attempts to take seriously two centers of gravity in a holistic fashion and deserves further reflection, though it prefers a very subtle comparison over a very obvious one.[21]

These classic portraits of the parable provide options, stimulate the mind, and hint at the implications each contains. However, the interpreter must not merely select one he or she likes but must interact with the text itself.

Literary Analysis

This economically told parable is notable for the prominence of the subjunctive mood and the resulting hypothetical cast, though appealing to an ordinary and familiar situation. Indeed, Mark 4:26-29 is a general situation parable. The structure breaks naturally into three parts as follows:

1. Sowing (v. 26)
2. Growing (vv. 27-28)
3. Reaping (v. 29)

Through the three parts the one character, the sower, appears. It should then be noticed that he is busy in part one and three but by no means activating in part two. Indeed, the seed may very well sprout while he sleeps! He is planter and harvester but not grower. The parable establishes an internal comparison, a *tertium comparationis* within the parable.

Structural analysis then exposes the prominence of part two which comprises two verses,[22] apparently the parable's center of gravity.[23] These verses are telltale because they contain two comments within the story. The reader or hearer is told that the sower did not know how the seed grew (v. 27c) and that the earth bears fruit *automatē* (v. 28a), two interpretive asides.[24] These comments appear to be primary pointers to meaning. They, especially verse 28a, are a kind of explanatory break in the narrative, an important literary-critical point. Indeed, the thesis or revelation from nature may appear at verse 28a: the earth bears fruit "automatically."

Textual Commentary

Attention to detail can further the investigation, building upon the results of our literary analysis. From verse 26 ("thus is the kingdom of God, as . . .") it should be underscored just how particularly the parable is kingdom-oriented *(houtōs)*. The kingdom is not, however, like a person but rather like the entire parable as an extended simile. The subjunctive mood begins in verse 26 and continues.

In verse 27a, it is established that after sowing the man went on his usual course in a relaxed manner, without taking anxious thought. The critical point is how to render verse 27c *(hōs ouk oiden autos)*. Is it that he did not even know *when* the secret germination under the ground took place? He may have been sleeping. The growing had already begun, and he was unaware ("when he did not know").[25] Or is it rather that he did not know *how* the seed germinated and grew ("how, he does not know," NEB)?[26] The context favors the second possibility because of the beginning thought in the next verse.

The opening assertion of verse 28*a*, possibly the thesis of the parable, is intrinsically important, especially the meaning of *automatē*. It can be translated as "without visible cause" and imply "without human work."[27] It can be translated "of itself" (RSV, NEB) or "out of its own power."[28] It can be expressed as "without recognizable cause" and even "worked *by God*."[29] In Leviticus 25:5,11 (LXX), the word is used and does relate to plants and means "on its own" or "of itself." In 2 Kings 19:29 (4 Kings 19:29, LXX) a similar usage appears. In both of these cases, it is volunteer growth without fresh planting. Two other usages suggest indirectly an act of God (Josh. 6:5; Job 24:24), as does the only other New Testament usage (Acts 12:10). "Without human agency" will fit all of these Old Testament usages with the implication of divine agency added in the latter three. The same may be said for Mark 4:28. However, the parable is not overt reference to divine miracle.[30] "The Biblical authors do not feel a contrast: the processes of nature are due to the wonderful work of the creator."[31] To summarize, retaining the independence of the parable as agricultural story, *automatē* refers in the first instance to the soil and seed producing growth on their own without the further agency of the farmer.[32] Hebrew hearers associated nature's processes with God, and the fact that this statement ("the earth bears fruit on its own") is the key revelation in a parable about the kingdom of God makes it clear that its application leads to an affirmation of God's action. So "the seed should sprout and grow" (v. 27*b*) contrasts with "should sleep and rise night and day" (v. 27*a*), and "as he *himself* does not know"[33] and "the earth bears fruit on its own" are commentary on the contrast.[34]

The last verse completes the cycle of sowing and harvest: "But when the crop permits, immediately he puts in the sickle because the harvest has come." The introductory words "but when" (*hotan de*) complete a series.[35] *Hotan*, a temporal particle commonly referring to "a definite action in the future but concluded before the action of the main verb," mitigates against the simple equation of verse 29 to the present moment of the ministry of Jesus.[36] The postpositive *de* can be an adversative particle suggesting general contrast[37] or a continuative particle suggesting transition.[38] Both *hotan* and *de* signal a climax of growth. The sower enjoys the benefits of nature's grace and eagerly harvests its result. He immediately puts in the sickle. The language (v. 29*bc*) recalls Joel 3:13, a highly eschatological passage, but the words *must* first be allowed to carry the parable as parable to completion. The temptation to excessive allegorizing lurks here, and the difference frankly between the Joelic judgment note and the parable should moderate one's assessment.[39] Harvest is a natural metaphor for the end time, and it may well suggest this parabolically. But as in the parables of the Tares and Nets, it is more a latent eschatological completion with the center of gravity elsewhere, but quite necessary for the wholeness of the parable. I wonder if "immediately" *(euthus)*, a favorite Markan word, is the evangelist's emphasis promising there will be no delay once the kingdom harvest is ready.

Possible Setting *(Sitz)*

Mark 4:1-34 is almost certainly a composite, though the seed parables might have been uttered together by Jesus. The overall setting is teaching crowds from a boat on the seashore (4:1-2,35-36), but at times Jesus addressed only the disciples (4:10), and at other times it is ambiguous. Mark 4:26-29 could have arisen from a formal teaching setting early in the Galilean ministry in which Jesus took the initiative. He may have been explaining and expounding the kingdom to the crowd. Perhaps he was still establishing the burden of his proclamation, setting down the great thesis. So this may have been a parabolic communication about the kingdom to the eager crowd, a clamoring impatient group. There are indications that the disciples themselves could be caught up in feverish expectation of the kingdom (Luke 19:11; 24:11; Acts 1:16). There could have been self-appointed militants (Zealots) pressing for violence as the manner of bringing in God's rule.

Could there be an actual clue to the setting in the expression "how he himself did not know" *(hōs ouk oiden autos, v. 27c)?* The hearers could have been feeling or articulating their own uncertainties about the nature of the kingdom. They may have wondered how the kingdom came or entertained unwholesome opinions about bringing in the kingdom so the parable interlocked existentially with their misapprehensions or queries.

Basic Interpretation

In drawing the analysis together, one negative conclusion requires immediate attention. The parable is emphatically not an allegory in the usual sense, though subordinated allegorical dimensions are present. The sower may not be identified simply with Jesus because the farmer in the parable is sower, sleeper, and reaper. Nor does the farmer know what the Teller knows.

The literary analysis uncovered the middle section on "growing" (vv. 27-28) as the center of gravity and verse 27c ("how, he himself did not know") and verse 28a ("the earth bears fruit on its own") as key internal explanations. The textual commentary concluded that verse 27c be understood as he did not know how and *automatē* in verse 28a be translated as "on its own." The quest for a setting came up with the speculation that the issue to resolve through the parable was how the kingdom comes. On this foundation a basic interpretation may be ventured.

The kingdom comes by miracle, by a wonder deed of God. The seed germinates and grows *on its own*. The seed and soil conspire. The sower is planter and harvester but not grower. Even as he sleeps,[40] the seed and soil conspire, so he is dependent upon nature's grace. He neither causes the seed to grow nor understands how it develops. "The sower's sleeping and rising night and day are, so to speak, repeated acts of non-participation."[41] The seed's growth is independent from the sower. The development from seed to harvest is God's deed, God's wonder.[42] The kingdom on its own appears without human agency, a perspective not only delimiting the role of the sower but also affirming the capability of seed and soil.

The parable shows that the sower had no instrumentality in the crucial growing. The sower did not, cannot, need not cause the seed to grow. This negative angle of vision functions to highlight the royal independence of the soil. Existentially the role of the believer is seen as one of dependence or grace, of confidence in the outcome, certitude about the completion of the commenced process. There is the good news that humanity need not make the kingdom come. So the parable inveighs against "endeavors to force the coming of the kingdom or to build it—by a revolution like the Zealots, by exact calculations and preparation like the Apocalyptists, or by complete obedience to the law like the Pharisees."[43] Patience, however, is not as near target as confidence in God, patience possibly having become too strong a category because of the influence of James 5:7.[44] To focus primarily on the farmer, furthermore, is entirely too anthropocentric as the positive side of the interpretation shows.

The parable indicates that the seed does in fact grow and will reach completion, that the earth bears fruit of its own. This picture from nature can be appropriately called "the self-growing seed," but even better would be "the earth bearing fruit on its own." The parable affirms the power of God, the sure effecting of the kingdom by divine sovereignty. The kingdom is surely coming because God is actively engaged. The parable was and is *an invitation to faith*. Indeed, it seeks to awaken faith. It was not merely pastoral encouragement or didactic corrective. It was for Jesus an expression and advocacy of faith. He had eyes to see what God was doing through his ministry and its inevitable outcome. He believed that in his ministry the kingdom was dawning. He was sure that the kingdom had germinated, would grow, and would attain harvest. Faith then was to see the kingdom in the ministry of Jesus, to recognize God at work in a unique fashion. Faith was to share Jesus' faith that God was not only making a beginning but would just as surely complete it out of his sovereignty. This last thought is the purpose of the final verse.

The parable of the earth bearing fruit on its own contains a dramatic tension, an internal juxtaposition, then, between the sleeping farmer and the sprouting seed. The parable teaches that the kingdom has a power of its own, that it is God-given. No one need worry. It is a stiff rebuke to feverish trust in human hustle. The confidence of Jesus that he would impart to those with ears to hear is well expressed poetically by George Buttrick: "Let the seed be buried deep in the earth: it would germinate and find the sun."[45]

Message for Now

Implicit Warning. After wrestling with the meaning then in the historical ministry, it is imperative that meaningful study ask after message for now. The parable functions presently as an indirect ad-

monition about *getting in too big of a hurry.* The seed story rebukes a
feverish overactivity. Christians can panic at the sight of the unfin-
ished business of the church and try to do too much in too short a
period of time. A Christian ought to be a living audiovisual aid, but a
disciple can come to feel personally propelled like a 33 record set on 78
rpm or as a movie reel speeded up outrageously, as is sometimes done
for humorous effect.

Urban Americans often pace themselves in a constant rush. One
frequent visitor to America recorded his several impressions of the
priority of its citizens. On his first visit to the USA, he came to the
conclusion that the great desire of the Americans was for power. On
his second visit, he decided rather that the great appetite of Americans
was for money. Upon yet another journey's finish, he concluded that
the great commitment of Americans was to speed. The third impression stuck as a lasting opinion of one foreign traveler.[46] Fatigue,
suppressed anger, tension, and spiritual dissatisfaction can result from
being in too big of a hurry. After a year's study away, my greatest and
least wanted adjustment upon returning was to the taken-for-granted
American push.

Jesus, on the other hand, with his sensitivities and gifts, could
have ministered madly to suffering and sinning, in a nervous fashion.
Rather he made strategic spiritual retreats with a handful of disciples
whom he taught lasting realities worth sharing with still others. The
Man with a quiet center spoke with exceptional power because he had
first spoken with the Father. He could give the best hours of the day to
prayer because "he knows that while he rests in eternity it is not that
nothing is happening but that in doing this he is rather giving place to
God's Spirit, that then God is working and the seed is growing."[47] As
an act of faith, Jesus saw God working in his ministry and expected
the inevitably good results to follow. He knew that the sowing was
happening and an irresistible harvest would surely follow.

The parable speaks helpfully to those driven or pushed, to those
uncritically committed to being workaholics. Serious Christians and
ministers are often overwhelmed by how much needs to be done and
may suffer from an unconscious omnipotence complex. When faced
with a day or days with heavy demands, remember the Christian insight of Bovet who clearly believes that it is not how much you accom-
plish quantitatively in a day that counts but how much of what you

do is what God wants you to do.[48] That attitude also seems to lead toward meditation on what God is doing. The farmer actually was unconscious while the seed grew. Thank God we cannot, do not, and need not make the seed grow. "There are Christians," said the great preacher Frederick Robertson, "who are anxious for growth. They scratch and dig away at the root—Wait!"[49]

The parable also cautions about getting *too big for our britches.* We have at our disposal the technology to rape nature and to use up our resources greedily and too rapidly. Exhausting fossil fuels in a very few generations by a very few highly developed technological societies amounts to a lack of belief in the future. Astonishing technological capabilities sometimes serve to convince some people only of unlimited benevolent outcomes.[50]

Today there exists impressive technological agriculture with its mechanized farming and artificial fertilizers. The scientist can even make a synthetic seed. If analyzed, it contains all the properties of a natural seed. There is just a single difference—it will not grow.[51] Farmers are sowers and reapers; but despite indiscriminate claims, they are not growers. It is God who gives the growth. Emerson asked once, "What is a farm but a mute gospel?" Jesus spoke of a seed that grows mysteriously, miraculously, and irresistibly by God's grace.

Confidence in God. Surely the positive encouragement of the parable for today lies in the possibility of accepting Jesus' vision for one's own. This parable, which has the "tang of the human and the glow of the divine," depicts the kind of farmer who milks his cows and mends his fences and sleeps deeply. The seed grows of itself without the farmer turning a hand in the growth process. His part is planting and harvesting; the growing comes as gift. It is a parable of agricultural grace.

A distinguished American surgeon was questioned about what he relied on when he operated. He simply answered, "Medical grace." He meant the natural healing power residing in the human body which works by itself.[52] So it was with the seed in the parable, and so it is with our relationship to the kingdom.

As a pastor in rural communities, I knew many farmers who were not only deeply religious but who also possessed what might be called a "natural faith." They worked hard at planting and reaping, did the weeding and fertilizing, but years in the fields taught them that growing is nature's gift. It is no coincidence that many preachers in our day grew up living on "mute gospels"—farms. They know intimately nature's grace.

The parable kindles hope. George Buttrick said that it was "spoken in the mood of unshakable confidence—as though He held the future in the hollow of his hand."[53] The kingdom can be counted on. Trust in God.

> Have faith in God, he's on his throne;
> . . . .
> He cannot fail, he must prevail;
> Have faith in God, have faith in God.

This confidence in God's wonder deed should not be applied one-sidedly however. To take the accent of the parable as license for disengagement is highly inappropriate. A famous theologian once accused another famous theologian of "transcendental irresponsibility" because the latter's theology seemed to accent divine activity exclusively. One-sided emphasis upon divine sovereignty at the expense of human responsibility led one wag to write a parody of the well-known hymn "Rise Up, O Men of God" as follows:

> Sit down, O men of God
> His Kingdom He will bring,
> Whenever it may please His will,
> You cannot do a thing.

In the parable, the farmer did in fact play a crucial part in both sowing and reaping, cooperating with nature. We are fellow laborers with God. The image of a duet or a dance for our collaboration with God is creatively suggestive.[54]

Pastoral Applications. One of John Steinbeck's characters in *The Winter of Our Discontent* observes that his wife falls asleep gently—while he experiences more trouble—because she assumes a life after death and gives herself to sleep trustfully. The farmer in the parable could let himself go, let the seed do its thing, and he could sleep. The marvelous picture of the sleeping farmer and the sprouting seed is worth savoring!

Sometimes sleep eludes when worry and tension hover over bedtime. Psychologists are prone to ask what you think about just before sleep. Prayer can be a valid spiritual therapy ordering thoughts before sleep, both for children and adults. Relaxing the entire body can help, and so can relaxing the mind by taking a mental vacation to some quiet isle; but relaxing the soul should not be overlooked or undervalued. Fix your mind on God. Think about what God is like and savor the reality of his kindness, compassion, and watchful care.[55] A meaningful verse of Scripture ("Let not your heart be troubled") or the words of a familiar hymn, such as "God Will Take Care of You," "O God, Our Help in Ages Past," and "O Love That Wilt Not Let Me Go," may actually minister in your experience. The words of Sidney Lanier's peom "The Marshes of Glynn" may speak powerfully:

> As the marsh-hen secretly builds on the watery sod,
> Behold I will build me a nest on the greatness of God:
> I will fly in the greatness of God as the marsh-hen flies
> In the freedom that fills all the space 'twixt the
>   marsh and the skies:
> By so many roots as the marsh-grass sends in the sod
> I will heartily lay me a-hold on the greatness of God:

The parable also addresses those wondering if God is working in their lives. A part of becoming a Christian and discipleship is letting God work. Sometimes it is okay to be idle in God's name, to enjoy leisure because God can be counted on to grow the seed. Becoming a Christian is not something that can be produced by gritting teeth and trying hard, but by letting go and letting God. The modern minister deserves to know in his inward being that God is working in his ministry, even when he cannot see it, that only God can give the growth that really matters.

Helmut Thielicke also links the parable to old age and warns that the person who does not know how to let go, who is a stranger to the quiet, could be a miserable creature in the latter years. He cites Count von Moltke. When he was asked what he was going to do in the quiet closing phase of his life after years of great prominence, his reply was, "I want to see a tree grow." He would not have said so had he not already found times for quiet.[56]

The parable, an actual sample of faith, glows with the conviction that the kingdom begun with the mighty ministry of Jesus will grow and reach harvest. The parable speaks personally that God's work begun is continuing imperceptibly and is moving toward harvest in individual lives and beyond history. The blade from the seed even now is visible. George Buttrick exclaimed, "The harvest song shall one day be raised in joy!"[57] Let the parable do its thing: kindle hope.

NOTES

1. This unity in diversity is recognized by Gunther Harder, "Das Gleichnis von der selbstwachsenden Saat. Mark 4, 26-29," *Theologia Viatorum*, (1948-49), 53.

2. Noted astutely by Rainer Stuhlmann, "Beobachtungen und Überlegungen zu Markus IV.26-29," *New Testament Studies*, 19:153 (1973). He notes that the kind of contrast depends on the translation of *automatē*.

3. For other surveys of representative interpretations see Harder, pp. 53-60; and C. E. B. Cranfield, "Message of Hope, Mark 4.21-32." *Interpretation*, 9:158-161 (1955).

4. According to Harder, p. 51.

5. R. C. Trench, *Notes on the Parables of Our Lord* (Grand Rapids: Baker, 1948), p. 101. This book is a "popular edition" of the original 1861 publication.

6. Karl Weiss' monograph is *Voll Zuversicht! Zur Parabel Jesu vom zuversichtlichen Sämann, Mk. 4, 26-29* (Münster: Aschendorff, 1922).

7. Weiss, "Mark 4, 26 bis 29—dennoch die Parabel vom zuversichtlichen Sämann!" *Biblische Zeitschrift*, 18:45 (1928-29).

8. Ibid., p. 64.

9. See Joseph Freundorfer, "Eine neue Auslegung der Parabel von der 'selbstwachsenden Saat' Mark 2, 26-29," *Biblische Zeitschrift*, 17:51-62 (1925-26); and "Replik," *Biblische Zeitschrift*, 18:68 (1928-1929). I am indebted largely to Harder, p. 59, who represents Freundorfer as finding Jesus' confidence more in the final success of his work. Both Weiss and Freundorfer take a rather Christological approach actually, but Freundorfer's view is more traditional and allegorical.

10. Paul Feine, *Theologie des Neuen Testaments* (Leipzig: J. C. Hinrichs'sche, 1922), pp. 88-89.

11. A. B. Bruce, *The Parabolic Teaching of Christ* (9th ed.; London: Hodder and Stoughton, 1893), p. 120.

12. Adolf Jülicher, *Die Gleichnisreden Jesu* (Darmstadt: Wissenschaftliche Buchgesellschaft, 1963; photocopied from 1910 edition), 2:544-545.

13. C. H. Dodd, *The Parables of the Kingdom*, p. 143.

14. Vincent Taylor, *The Gospel According to St. Mark* (London: Macmillan, 1959), p. 266.

15. John Crossan, *In Parables* (New York: Harper & Row, 1973), pp. 84-88.

16. Joachim Jeremias, *The Parables of Jesus*, trans. S. H. Hooke Revised Edition (New York: Scribner's, 1963), pp. 151-152. Jeremias credited Cadoux as preceding him with a similar exegesis.

17. Jeremias, *Rediscovering the Teaching of Jesus* (New York: Harper, 1967), p. 159.

Richard H. Hiers, *The Historical Jesus and the Kingdom of God* (Gainesville: University of Florida Press, 1973), p. 16, also centered in the certainty with which the final result may be expected. The parable looked to the coming of the kingdom as a still future event.

18. As reported by Harder, p. 55. In evaluating this isolation of the independence of the seed from the sower as the *tertium comparationis*, Harder noted insightfully that whereas the gradual growth emphasis understood *automatē* positively this group took it negatively as a delimitation of the sower's influence.

19. So Jacques Dupont, "La parabole de la semence qui pousse toute seule (Marc 4, 26-29)," *Recherches de Science Religeuse*, 55:378 (1967). While he recognized the contrast, he maintained a continuity between the growth and maturation as preparation for the harvest. God commenced his work with the ministry of Jesus (p. 386).

20. N. A. Dahl, "The Parables of Growth," *Studia Theologica*, (1951), 149.

21. Cranfield, pp. 160-162, plied the contrast between "seedtime and harvest." The time of Jesus was the time of sowing, but the harvest will come.

22. Part two (vv. 27-28) contains 31 words while part one needs only 8, and part three uses 14. Part two alone comprises three-fifths.

23. Also noted by Dupont, p. 378, who observed that the relative length calls attention to this part of the parable.

24. One could argue that verse 28 is a Markan parenthesis added to interpret the parable. There is a break in tense with the use of the present *karpophorei*. Crossan, p. 85, is able to marshal the gospel of Thomas 85:15-18: "Let there be among you a man of understanding; when the fruit ripened, he came quickly with his sickle in his hand, he reaped it. Whoever has ears to hear let him hear." The stress is definitely upon the reaper, but it must be noticed that the parable is severely attenuated even on Crossan's reconstruction of Mark's parable. The parable part uses only twelve Coptic words. Furthermore, the statement is overtly Christological and portrayed as a completed action. Verse 28 is overt but so is verse 27c.

25. The Bauer lexicon allows the translation of *hōs* as the temporal conjunction "when" but commends the translation as the comparative particle "as" or "in such a way." The rendering, "when" or "while," out of favor in present translations, could be related to other temporal aspects of the parable, especially the contrast of not knowing when the germination began but immediately acting when (*hotan*) the harvest arrived (v. 29). Also the temporal indications in verse 28 could be included (*prōton, eiten*). This construction could be correlated with the view of Dupont and Dahl cited previously in notes 19 and 20. It could also be related possibly to the secret of the kingdom's presence.

26. Taylor, p. 267, has pointed out that *hōs* after verbs of saying, thinking, etc., means "how." This translation is supported by Revised Standard Version, the King James Version, the *Good News Bible* in Today's English Version, the *Jerusalem Bible*, and the American Standard Version.

27. *BAG*, p. 122.

28. Feine, p. 89.

29. Stuhlmann, p. 156.

30. *Contra* Stuhlmann.

31. Dahl, p. 142. Dahl, whose article preceded Stuhlmann's, recognized much of what

Stuhlmann saw but did not press it as far. He cited as evidence Genesis 1:11; 2:9; Leviticus 26:4; Deuteronomy 11:11-17; Psalms 65:9; 85:13; 104:14; Isaiah 30:23; 45:8; 61:11.

32. The differences more nuanced are that Leviticus 25:5,11 and 2 Kings 19:29 assume a year when no planting occurred and no harvest allowed whereas our parable involves initial sowing, but *plant* growth *is* involved with the same idea of "on its own." The other three references have divine miracle more front and center than the parable, though this is compensated for somewhat by the fact that nature and God are closely associated. It is too allegorical to treat verse 28a as overt divine miracle.

33. The *autos* (v. 27c) is telling—he himself does not even know.

34. Günther Klein, "Erntedankfest. Markus 4, 26-29," *Göttinger Predigtmeditationen*, 17:320-326 (1962-63), took a similar view, according to Stuhlmann.

35. *Hotan* must be seen in the series *prōton, eiten, eiten; de* completes the series using *kai* (6x).

36. Nigel Turner, *Syntax*, Vol. III of *A Grammar of New Testament Greek* by J. H. Moulton (Edinburgh: T. & T. Clark, 1963), p. 112.

37. Many factors in verse 29 could be turned toward the Dodd-Crossan position: the climactic nature of *Hotan de*; the citation of Joel, the *euthus* suggesting immediacy and urgency, and most especially "the harvest *has* come." Earlier the textual emendation from *karpos* to *kairos* could as well, but that speculation is put to rest by G. D. Kilpatrick, "Mark IV.29," *Journal of Theological Studies*, 46:191 (1945).

38. Blass-Debrunner-Funk, *A Greek Grammar of the New Testament* (Chicago: University Press, 1961), p. 231, classified it as general contrast rather than directly contrary (*alla*). Dupont, p. 378, argued that both *de* and *euthus* signal the contrast of verse 29 to verses 27-28. The preceding period has been one of laissez faire. No longer.

39. Margaret Thrall, *Greek Particles in the New Testament* (Grand Rapids: Eerdmans, 1962), pp. 51 *ff.*, considers many Markan usages of *de* as purely continuative.

40. The parable does not inherently suggest a Joelic-Baptizer (Matt. 3:12) motif. And even the larger context of the Matt. 9:35-38 pericope, where harvest is used for the present and missioners are required to announce that the kingdom is at hand (10:7), depicts the day of judgment as clearly future (10:15). A very similar text appears in Luke 10:12 ("in that day"). In the parable of the Tares the harvest is not yet ("let both grow together *until* the harvest," 13:30; cf. 13:39). Furthermore, I wonder if one should assume uncritically that harvest in Matt. 9:37-38 means the same thing as in Joel 3 or Mark 4! The context is human need in Matt. 9, judgment on wickedness in Joel 3, the climax of growth in Mark 4. Furthermore, Jesus may well have used the same word differently in a saying and within a parable.

41. Charles Carlston, *The Parables of the Triple Tradition* (Philadelphia: Fortress Press, 1975), p. 204.

42. As impressively Eduard Lohse, "Die Gottesherrschaft in den Gleichnissen Jesu," *Evangelische Theologie*, 18:148 (1958).

43. Eduard Schweizer, *The Good News According to Mark*, trans. D. Madvig (Richmond: John Knox Press, 1970), p. 103.

44. William Lane, *The Gospel According to Mark* (Grand Rapids: Eerdmans, 1974), p. 170n, insists that there is no reflection on the element of patience within the text.

45. George Buttrick, *The Parables of Jesus* (Grand Rapids: Baker Book House, 1973, reprint of 1928 publication), p. 21.

46. From William Barclay, *And Jesus Said: A Handbook on the Parables of Jesus* (Philadelphia: Westminster, 1970), p. 32.

47. Helmut Thielicke, *The Waiting Father: Sermons on the Parables of Jesus*, trans. John W. Doberstein (New York: Harper, 1959), p. 90.

48. Theodore Bovet, *Have Time and Be Free*, trans. A. J. Ungersma (Richmond: John Knox, 1964), p. 42.

49. Robertson, *Sermons*, Fifth Series (London: Kegan Paul, Trench, Trübner, 1905), p. 74.

50. See Jacques Ellul, *The Technological Society*, trans. John Wilkinson (New York: Vintage Books, 1964). For a more hopeful view see Alvin Toffler, *The Third Wave* (William Morrow, 1980).

51. Barclay, p. 34.

52. A. M. Hunter, *The Parables Then and Now* (Philadelphia: Westminster, 1971), p. 40.

53. Buttrick, p. 16.

54. As John Claypool, *The Preaching Event* (Waco, Texas: Word, 1980), pp. 9-20.

55. Norman Vincent Peale, *A Guide to Confident Living* (Carmel, New York: Guideposts Associates, 1948), p. 78.

56. Thielicke, p. 86.

57. Buttrick, p. 19.

Part II

The Crisis of the Coming Kingdom

7 The Parable of the Barren Fig Tree

John the Baptizer had exploded like a bombshell on the first-century scene. He had the audacity to invite religious professionals and lay people alike to repent. He addressed the entire nation and appealed for response. John reached back in Jewish history to those moments of greatness when repentance movements swept the country. He sounded a strangely familiar note that stirred the people's moral sensibilities. He was a catalyst, who set a great repentance movement in motion, but it cost him his life.

Jesus then came announcing the coming of the kingdom of God and inviting repentance. He had participated openly in the baptismal movement and stood squarely in the tradition of the Baptist, knowing full well how such a course might well eventuate. Jesus dared to share spontaneously his story of a barren fig tree and in the process to introduce tension after the manner of a prophet. This stern, very prophetic parable of his was remarkably reminiscent of the Baptizer, though with crucial difference. It was a parable of the times and a fierce one at that. It conveyed the passionate kind of authentic patriotism of a Jeremiah. To share the horticultural story about a figless tree was no safe parlor game. Jesus was creatively aggressive because the stakes were high, and he loved his people profoundly. So he sought to awaken with a crisis parable before it was too late.

Setting

Historical (Luke 13:1-5). Unidentified persons reported to Jesus a religious tragedy in Jerusalem. Galilean pilgrims to Jerusalem met death at the hands of Pilate within the Temple precincts. Their blood had been mingled with the blood of their sacrifices. This political crisis seemed to demand a theological explanation, and they apparently required one from Jesus.

The motive of the messengers reporting death in the Temple is not easily ascertained, but it is fascinating to speculate. Could it be that they hoped to rouse Jesus to lead a revolt against Rome by reporting an unspeakable instance of religious persecution? Surely Jesus the Galilean would be inflamed by Pilate's cruel repression. Jesus' response that the victims were not worse sinners (v. 3) does mean that he defended the slain to a degree and refused to provide a theological justification of Pilate's executions. Indeed, here is a situation in which Jesus did not affirm the act of his government. Nevertheless Jesus did not build upon the incident to inflame nationalistic feelings. So any intent to sway Jesus to a Zealotic mission of the sword against Rome failed as Jesus seized the teachable moment to restate his fundamental mission of calling all to repentance.

Another possible explanation of motive is that the ones reporting the incident sought to trap Jesus. If he uttered any deprecations of Pilate, it could be used as evidence of sedition and treason. If so, Jesus said nothing unambiguously damaging. Indeed, could it be that they were throwing the incident up to Jesus because he hailed from Galilee? They would tar Jesus with the same brush or dissuade him from Jerusalem. Galilee was seen as a hotbed of revolutionary sentiment. Josephus, the famous Jewish historian, depicted some Galileans a generation later as "ever craving for revolution, by temperament addicted to change and delighting in sedition . . ." (*The Life*, 17). If the harbingers intended to indict Jesus the Galilean, his parallel incident involving the death of eighteen Judeans (v. 4) would have neutralized the Galilean issue. Could it be that they merely wished to dissuade Jesus from his Jerusalem journey else he meet a similar fate?

All these intriguing reconstructions are possible, but lack of further detail in the text or secular history makes certainty impossible. Neither of the two incidents, the atrocity or the accident, can be corroborated and illumined by secular history.[1] The massacre of the Galileans in Jerusalem by Pilate was certainly in character, however, since Josephus recorded several massacres (*Antiquities* 17.9.3; 18.3.1; 20.5.3; *Jewish War* 2.3.3.9; 5.1.5), and Philo summarized the enormities of Pilate's administration (*The Embassy to Gaius* 38). I suspect that the number of Galileans involved in this Passover murder was very small, reducing it in time to a minor incident.

As the text stands, perhaps the best deduction from fragmentary evidence is that a simple causal connection was being forged between harsh death and personal sin. After all, it was a religious catastrophe, happening as it did in the environs of the Temple. Like Job's friends, the reporters inferred that calamity came as punishment for sin (Job 4:7; 8:20). They might have been Pharisees or others influenced by popular theology (as John 9:2) and by disdain of unorthodox Galileans. This is clear from the fact that Jesus marshaled a second example featuring accidental death of Judeans in Jerusalem. Neither these Galileans nor the eighteen Judeans were guilty of any extraordinary sin that caused their death. This is especially apparent from the causal clause in verse 2 rendered "because they suffered thus." They were arguing backward from the severe suffering to severe sinning. Like the Book of Job, Jesus rejected out of hand such superficial theology. Jesus answered his own rhetorical question twice with emphatic negation of the unhealthy theology.[2] "No, I tell you . . . ."

So Jesus banished superstitious theology with a sovereign declaration, yet he soberly recognized that sin does cause destruction for all if not remedied. He warned of all perishing similarly unless they repented. This "conditional prophecy," so like Old Testament prophets, hinges ultimate outcome upon response. The same conditional factor appears also in the "parable of the extra year" (Luke 13:6-9), connecting setting and story. Both are announcements of judgment urging timely repentance. As in the case of certain other parables, the Barren Fig Tree story is integrally related to the preceding "unless you repent" as a kind of midrashic comment.[3]

Literary. The setting in Luke (*Sitz im Buch*) is first of all in a section (12:49 to 13:9) focused on interpreting the present hour. Jesus upbraided the multitudes because of alarming inconsistency. They were eagerly attentive to the signs of changing weather in the sky, but they did not know how to interpret the present time (12:56). The section as a whole carries the urgency and rebuke of the "this generation" sayings that challenged unresponsiveness,[4] sayings and parables that belonged to a prophetic critique from within Judaism, not an outside bombardment. The evangelist has placed the parable in this realized eschatology section as a part of the journey to Jerusalem. The Lukan Christ announces a messianic visitation.

The thirteenth chapter of Luke itself has a great interest in Jerusalem. Jerusalem rejects her Messiah and brings destruction upon herself (13:34). Jesus will suffer a prophet's death in Jerusalem (13:33). Luke 13:1-9 is a call of repentance to the Jews. So Luke 13 connects with Luke 19:41-44 and 21:20-24.[5] For the evangelist, however, the message is no longer merely for Jerusalem but is a dire warning to the Christian community. The invitation for all to repent (Luke 13:3,5) referred originally to Jewish hearers, but for the evangelist it meant every reader as well.[6] The evangelist preached through this section his message of judgment and repentance, aware of its relevance for other generations (as Rom. 11:22).

The Picture Part

Jesus moved aggressively from his urgent appeal in the setting to a brief specific situation parable. As in so many parables, direct discourse carries the action and communicates the meaning, as a simple exchange or dialogue comprises most of the parable.[7] There is as usual internal juxtaposition present in the stances taken by the two speakers with the final speech climactic.

The owner of the vineyard defines the situation by arriving for the third time, seeking fresh figs only to find none. He announces that he has sought fruit three years in a row and gathered none. He orders the tree cut down and asks rhetorically why it should clutter the vineyard. The vinedresser requests one more year and promises special treatment of digging and dunging.

The picture comports well with actual practice.[8] Fig trees often were planted in vineyards. The fig trees could grow to thirty-five feet in height with large, palmate leaves and might produce three crops of figs in a single year. There were delicious summer figs in June (Isa. 28:4; Jer. 24:2; Hos. 9:10), green or winter figs (Song of Songs 2:13), and late or autumn figs (Jer. 8:13; 29:17). Incidentally, figs were eaten fresh or dried and made into tasty cakes (1 Sam. 25:18; 30:12) and even used medicinally (Isa. 38:21). Vineyards were located on hillsides normally, and figs flourished even in stony soil. Large landowners rented out vineyards to tenants (Song of Songs 8:11; Matt. 21:33-43) as in the parable.

The three years of bearing no fruit probably referred to the third, fourth, and fifth year of life if the tree were a new one.[9] Fig trees do not bear in the first two years normally but would be expected to produce in the third year, as is the case with so many fruit trees. After three years a tree could be presumed barren and might lawfully be cut down.[10] There was very little hope after three years without fruit, but the vinedresser in the parable wants one more chance. He desires to make one last big effort.

The Object Part

Allegorical Possibilities. Though allegorical interpretation has been dubbed dubious during the twentieth century, nearly every scholar finds one or more details of this parable too enticing to pass up. Even Jeremias allows that the disciples would see Jesus in the figure of the vinedresser.[11] Recognition of allegorical pointers in parables is not necessarily inappropriate if the allegorical interpretation is grounded in the historical situation and subordinated to the primary point.

The vineyard in the parable may well refer to Israel. The Song of the Vineyard (Isa. 5:1-7) portrays an ideal vineyard painstakingly cared for with high expectations. Prize grapes were planted, but wild grapes resulted. The owner became so chagrined that he willfully neglected the vineyard and let it grow up in weeds as judgment. Explicitly Israel is identified as the vineyard: "The vineyard of the Lord of Hosts is Israel, and the men of Judah are the plant he cherished" (Isa. 5:7, NEB). Fruitlessness and judgment are two themes shared by the parable and the song. It could well be that Jesus had the song in mind and intended the vineyard to suggest Israel to his hearers. Indeed, he may have had Psalm 80 in mind as well when he portrayed the vinedresser's plea for another chance: "O God of Hosts, once more look down from heaven, take thought for this vine and tend it" (v. 14, NEB).

The question still remains whether the fig tree had particular symbolic reference. In the Old Testament, figs as the fruit of the land could suggest prosperity in Israel but could also be prophecies of impending national distress (Jer. 5:17; 8:13; Joel 1:7,12; Amos 4:9). The fig tree could be used on occasion as a symbol for Israel (Hos. 9:10). Numerous students have ventured the more specific connection of the fig tree to the city of Jerusalem,[12] making the parable a more explicit anticipation of the destruction of Jerusalem. The fact that both incidents in the setting (Luke 13:1-5) had to do with destruction and death in Jerusalem may be an indirect pointer to Jerusalem, as well as the entirety of Luke 13, but the connection to Jerusalem must remain uncertain if very possible.[13] It cannot be ruled out that the tree is simply symbolic of an individual, as in Luke 6:43-45, or of the religious leadership.

The reference to three years in the parable to refer to the owner's trips to his fig tree has challenged the most intrepid interpreters. Theodore of Mopsuestia, affectionately known as "Teddy the Mop," took it to refer to the whole time from Abraham to Jesus. Augustine applied the three years to the three dispensations of natural law, written law, and grace, though the third year could scarcely refer to an era of grace. Luther allowed that the years pointed literally to the calendar years of Christ's activity, though his scheme makes a fourth year awkward. It is best to take it realistically in the picture part and referring to repeated divine efforts. The one more year surely points generally to the great messianic visitation of Jesus and possibly to the journey to Jerusalem.

Basic Point. The basic thrust of the parable appears in the tension between the judgment of the owner's speech (v. 7) and the plea for mercy of the vinedresser's speech (vv. 8-9). The second speech, with its request for one more year, is climactic and takes its distinctive character over against the owner's reasonable decision to remove the fruitless fig tree. The vinedresser's alternative did not contradict since he allowed for a cutting down a year hence. The parable is exceedingly open-ended, the presumption being that the vinedresser's counter suggestion carried the day for one more season with the eventual outcome still in the balance. This conditional aspect to coming judgment finds parallel in Joel:

> Turn back to the Lord your God;
> for he is gracious and compassionate,
> long-suffering and ever constant,
> always ready to repent of the threatened evil.
> (2:13, NEB)

So an announcement of judgment becomes a cry for repentance. Jesus, apparently going beyond the Baptizer (Luke 3:9), sounded not only the note of the imminence of catastrophe but also a year of grace. "Jesus is conscious of giving Israel a last opportunity of repentance," as William Manson put it.[14] This awakening parable sought to evoke an immediate response. The urgency of the moment cannot be exaggerated. There must be an end to indecision. The parable invites a positive decision to repent.

It is interesting to compare the parable at this point with a previous parable in "The Story of Ahikar":

O my boy! thou art like the tree which was fruitless beside the water, and its master was fain to cut it down, and it said to him, "Remove me to another place, and if I do not bear fruit, cut me down." And its master said to it, "Thou being beside the water hast not borne fruit, how shalt thou bear fruit when thou art in another place?"[15]

If Jesus had this old story in mind, he made telling changes. He not only deleted the talking tree. His parable advocated another chance while the former parable pessimistically predicted continual failure. For Jesus it was late, but not too late. Jesus still held out hope for his people.

The nature of the repentance expected is reasonably clear from the Gospel parable. Repentance means turning from a course that leads to disaster. Therefore, it involves awakening to a new understanding of the time. One must see the peril in which Israel stands. One must recognize the uniqueness of the hour. One must respond to the mission of the Teller of the parable. "To judge the time rightly is to acknowledge it as the time of Jesus the Messiah, whose presence is the most significant ingredient of the time since he is the bearer of the message of God's final judgment."[16]

More specifically repentance means turning from inauthentic, fruitless existence to authentic, fruitful existence. Presuming upon religious connections to Abraham will not suffice (Matt. 3:9). Jesus expected the nation and individuals, as the case may be, to bear fruit. Indeed, good works are a test of the genuineness of repentance (Matt. 3:8), signs by which one's inner nature is known (Matt. 7:15-20), "a decisive standard for divine judgment" (Matt. 3:10).[17] Repentance for Jesus involved a conversion to his proclamation of the kingdom (Mark 1:15, Matt. 18:3), total surrender and commitment to the will of God. In practical terms the Baptizer applied repentance to compassionate sharing of food and clothing and to just relationships (Luke 3:10-14). The dual warnings in the setting and in this parable of the times invite, as it were, redirection to an authentic existence in the kingdom.

Hermeneutical Exploration

This fierce parable of judgment lit by grace fairly begs application to new situations. Surely the evangelist Luke provided the clue that the parable could be applied to individuals and to the church and to questions of theodicy—God's dealing with the world.

The Strange Sovereignty of God. Jesus took some of the fuzziness away concerning providence and God's will. It was not God's will that those Galileans were executed. It was not God's will that those Judeans died from a crashing tower. Nor is it God's will that a DC-10 carry hundreds to instant death! Jesus made no mistake about it. He cast aside superstitious religion and warped theology. Sin did not cause these deaths. God did not back up Pilate's legions. There was no divine cause involved in the atrocity or the accident. The Johannine Christ also made it absolutely clear that a man born blind did not bring blindness upon himself by his sin nor did his parents cause the blindness by their sin (John 9:2). So God is not behind every tragedy, punishing. God allows accidents out of his permissive will.

Then is God in charge? Yes, because only real omnipotence can create persons free. Omnipotent love bypasses the need to dominate. Yet God is still at the helm because his strange sovereignty overrules secular history. Julius Caesar intended a personal empire but provided instead the political setting for the church. Bitter wars between Protestants and Catholics led ultimately to a new world order demanding more toleration.[18]

The parable comes back into the picture to speak further of God's strange sovereignty. The barren fig tree falls unless there is change. While God did not cause the atrocity perpetrated by Pilate nor the accident of the tower, he will not ignore the barren fig tree indefinitely. He will do something about it. Indeed, in this case, we can read history's fatal finish to the parable. The parable ended asking for another year. The year came and went. Tragically Israel did not repent. In AD 70, Jerusalem was utterly destroyed by the Roman legions as the historian Josephus recorded in *The Jewish War* (7.1.1). God acted in salvation history through a secular force. The fig tree was cut down. Titus, general of the Roman army, put Jerusalem to the torch. Three towers and a lone western wall were left. Today the Titus arch still stands in the ancient forum of old Rome, commemorating military victory over the rebellious Jews and the spoils of war.

Not forever is a barren fig tree permitted to cumber the ground! There is a limit, an irrevocable limit. God gives nations and individuals over to the destructive consequences of their rebellion. Forty years after the utterance of the parable of the Barren Fig Tree Jerusalem lay in ruins. God's sovereignty is strange, but sovereign it is. God is a God of *agape* but not "sloppy *agape*."

The Prophetic Word of God. This parable is very much like the preaching of prophets. It seems to portray a national crisis and implies a national ministry. Clearly Jesus functioned like Jeremiah and Isaiah, as a courageous forthteller for his beloved nation. Jesus was reluctant to believe that Israel's final answer would be negative. His final journey to Jerusalem was one last loving attempt to win Israel. Like the great prophets, Jesus dared to challenge his own nation and to invite the whole populace to join the repentance movement. He sought to arrest the course of his country. Jesus spoke like a prophet.

A certain convenient heresy of the twentieth century must be exposed and jettisoned as contrary to the New Testament. Some have glibly spoken of a comfortable distinction between a New Testament evangelist and an Old Testament prophet. This comfortable theory permits the modern Christian to ignore the tough, unread message of the prophets and to concentrate only upon select themes of the New Testament. This flounders on the rude fact that Jesus himself was a prophet. It would be necessary to take Jesus out of the New Testament. Reverence for Jesus Christ and the integrity of his person and message require Christians to take seriously the whole Bible, including the Old Testament Jesus loved so well.

So Christology is informed indirectly by the parable. The conception of Jesus as a prophet, a favorite model for certain American liberals, cannot be written off as irresponsible thinking unfounded upon the Scriptures. The truth is that Jesus as prophet is founded profoundly upon the Scriptures (Luke 13:33). Jesus was a prophet and that realization throws a flood of light upon the historical Jesus. On the other hand, Jesus as prophet is by no means a sufficient Christology. He was the greatest prophet, but he was far more. He was Son and called the Father "Abba."

The Prophet had a prophetic edge to his message that named sin without apology. In the midst of the Watergate scandal, some named the unlawful entry and subsequent cover-up as "stupid" and evaporated all the moral content from the matter. There was a glaring need in our permissive society to name the problem as "sin" and face up to reality. Karl Menninger, noted psychiatrist and founder of the Menninger clinic, invites thinking people to rediscover the reality of sin. He has written a bell-ringing book, *Whatever Became of Sin?*, in which as a psychiatrist he provides an eyewitness account of "the disappearance of sin." He writes provocatively:

Is no one any longer guilty of anything? Guilty perhaps of a sin that could be repented and repaired or atoned for? Is it only that someone may be stupid or sick or criminal—or asleep? Wrong things are being done, we know; tares are being sown in the wheat field at night. But is no one responsible, no one answerable for these acts? Anxiety and depression we all acknowledge, and even vague guilt feelings; but has no one committed any sins?[19]

These searching, probing questions urge reconsideration of the prophetic naming of sin and call for repentance in contemporary Christianity. The call to repentance has given way to an invitation to accept Christ.

The prophetic warning against barren fig trees should be noted by churches. W. A. Visser't Hooft reminds that two great church groups of past church history have gone completely defunct and have passed out of existence. They were the Church of North Africa and the Nestorian Church of Central Asia. He traced the cause of death in both cases to the same factors: 1) institutional egocentricity, 2) the lack of any real sense of evangelism, and 3) an unwillingness to let the institution be led by the Holy Spirit.[20] The parable constantly calls churches to repentance before it is too late. Uselessness is invitation to disaster. There is danger in false security (1 Cor. 20:12-13).

The Pitying Grace of God. This prophetic word of God is not brittle and harsh but lit with grace. The owner of the vineyard was himself patient inasmuch as he came back three successive years. His decision to remove the barren tree did not constitute an impetuous act. The vinedresser went even further by interceding on the tree's behalf in favor of one more season. He offered to give the tree unusual attention in one final effort to bring it to its natural function of bearing fruit. The spirit of the dialogue is captured in a sermon by the famous Baptist John Bunyan:

Barren fig-tree! dost thou hear what a striving there is between the vinedresser and the husbandman for thy life? "Cut it down," says one; "Lord, spare it," saith the other. "It is a cumberground," saith the Father. "One year longer," prays the Son. "Let it alone this year also."[21]

So the parable ends on the note of another chance; hence "the parable of the extra year." Isn't it just like God to give another chance?

Jesus specialized in second chances. His disciple Peter crumbled under pressure after all his previous bluster. Three times he put distance between himself and Jesus (Matt. 26:60-75). He renounced his friendship and disowned his discipleship in a dramatic display of fear and failure, but Jesus would not let failure have the last word. While he would not look over the breakdown, neither would he write off Simon. He gave him another chance; "Simon, son of John, do you love me above all?" (John 21:15).

Saul of Tarsus received another chance after his unthinkable support for the murder of a martyr. He held coats while stones bludgeoned Stephen to death (Acts 7:58-60). God still did not give up on him but provided another chance.

Nor does God give up on failures today. Christ lifts beaten men and women to their feet again. It is not all over because of a major blunder. God gives an extra year. Rather than being abandoned, there is special interest. God refuses to write off the man in the gray flannel suit who serves time for business crime, the woman who gives up her Christian friends for another set, the dropout from church who has joined that horde of "alumni," or the Christian once full of promise who has borne little fruit.

The parable is unquestionably stern. Not forever will God allow a barren tree to cumber the ground. The parable of the Barren Fig Tree unmistakably bespeaks judgment, but it is lit with grace. Isn't it just like God to give another chance?

NOTES

1. The insurrection under Judas of Gamala happened too many years previous to fit into Pilate's procuratorship (AD 26-36). Nor would the slaughter of the Samaritan pilgrims on Mount Gerizim (AD 36), which cost Pilate his position, suit a Jerusalem execution of Galileans. See Josephus, *Antiquities*, 18.4.1.

2. Reiling and Swellengrebel, *A Translator's Handbook on the Gospel of Luke*, p. 500,

point out that the Greek construction *ouchi, lego humin* (No, I tell you) is emphatic and rejects what has been intimated rather than merely introduces what follows.

3. Cf. W. R. Farmer, "Notes on a Literary and Form-Critical Analysis of Some of the Synoptic Material Peculiar to Luke," *New Testament Studies*, 8:310 (1962), who sees a *chreia* or general principle followed by a parable. This he parallels to the Greek rhetoricians.

4. As others have pointed out correctly, the fourteen "this generation" sayings do not refer to the Jewish race or to a future, final day but to the Israel of Jesus' day.

5. H. Flender, *St. Luke, Theologian of Redemptive History*, trans. R. H. and I. Fuller (Philadelphia: Fortress Press, 1967), pp. 108-110.

6. Ibid., p. 111.

7. Of ten lines, seven involve direct discourse; or to put it otherwise, fifty of seventy-seven words in the parable proper belong to the two speeches. The actual count depends upon which text is followed, of course, as there are minor textual problems.

8. I am indebted to J. C. Trever, "Fig Tree, Fig," *IDB*, E-J:267 (1962); J. F. Ross, "Vine, Vineyard," *IDB*, R-Z:785 (1962); and W. Corswant, *A Dictionary of Life in Bible Times*, trans. Arthur Heathcote (Suffolk: Hodder and Stoughton, 1960), p. 118.

9. C-H. Hunzinger, "*sukē*," *TDNT*, 7:755n (1971), raises the interesting possibility that the tree in question was an older one that had once been fruitful. He credits the sixth edition of Joachim Jeremias with the idea, but it does not seem to be present there. Rather Jeremias, *Parables*, p. 170, seems to think of six years.

10. So Derrett, "Fig Trees in the New Testament," *Heythrop Journal*, 14:260 (1973). In *Baba Bathra* 2:13 are found these words: "Abba Saul says: All trees that bear no fruit may be cut away according to the plumb line's measure." Note Deuteronomy 20:20. F. W. Danker, "The Shape of Luke's Gospel in Lectionaries," *Interpretation*, 30:345 (1976), calls attention to the theme of divine patience in Tobit 13:6-13 and the Wisdom of Solomon 11:26 to 12:10 as parallel.

11. Jeremias, *Parables*, p. 171.

12. Such as Zahn, Grundmann, and Bornhäuser. Heinz Giesen, "Der verdorrte Feigenbaum—eine symbolische Aussage: zu Mark 11,12-14, 20f," *Biblische Zeitschrift*, 20:95-111 (1976), following Münderlein insists that nowhere in the OT does the fig tree portray a city. J. G. Kahn, "La Parabole du figuier stérile et les arbes récalcitrants de la Genése," *Novum Testamentum*, 13:38-45 (1971), following Flusser and Lindsey, points back to the trees of Genesis 1:11,12 and considers the parable midrashic.

13. J. M. Creed, *The Gospel According to St. Luke*, p. 181, went so far as to say, "The fall of the tower in Siloam is an anticipation of the greater destruction which threatens the whole city." Furthermore, the potential cutting down in the parable is not the end of the vineyard or history as it were, but rather takes place within history. See G. Stahlin, "*ekkoptō*," *TDNT*, 3: 859 (1965).

14. T. W. Manson, *The Gospel of Luke* (London: Hodder and Stoughton, 1930), p. 163.

15. The Story of Ahikar 8:30 in R. H. Charles (ed.), *The Apocrypha and Pseudepigrapha of the Old Testament in English* (Oxford: Clarendon Press, 1913), 2: 775.

16. F. W. Young, "Luke 13:1-9," *Interpretation*, 31:62 (1977).

17. F. Hauck, "*karpos*," *TDNT*, 3:615 (1965).

18. See Eric Rust, *Towards a Theological Understanding of History* (New York: Oxford University Press, 1963), pp. 145,169-173.

19. Karl Menninger, *Whatever Became of Sin?* (New York: Hawthorn Books, 1973), p. 13.

20. Cited by A. Leonard Griffith, *God and His People* (Nashville: Abingdon Press, 1960), p. 13.

21. John Bunyan, "The Barren Fig Tree," *20 Centuries of Great Preaching*, ed. Clyde Fant and William Pinson (Waco, Texas: Word, 1971), 2: 332. Bunyan was dangerously close to stereotyping the Father as judgment and the Son as grace.

8 The Parable of the Rich Fool

Will it matter that I was? That personal question tolls our being and sets us to thinking. Is my expression of life making any difference? The question itself assumes what the observation of common sense notices—that some lives matter much and that others seem to matter little. Of course, some lives are writ large in public, and others are lived out in modest privacy. They will be measured accordingly by newspapers, but obituary columns lack the transcendent valuation.

Jesus, that millionaire of language, queries our personal existence and commitments in such a fashion as to shake the foundations. He exhibited an enormous concern about life. He saw its intrinsic value, its Source, its potential. He interpreted life from the transcendent perspective of the kingdom of God. He did not content himself merely to discovering the meaning of life and the way to joy. He was compelled by a vision to awaken others. He took risks. He spoke with astounding certainty. He recognized that some expenditures of life were meaningless and unworthy and unexamined. He knew an expenditure of life expressed as trusting God which provided lasting joy. He invited others to commit to the things that matter and the things that last.

His parable of the Rich Fool is a stern warning against greed, but it is far more. It carries an exposure of inauthentic existence, a life wrapped up in possessions and pleasures yet nevertheless unprotected and surprisingly vulnerable. To study this far from harmless story is to have one's own life interrogated. Analysis may actually cause change (*metanoia*) and lead to a life worth living.

Context

Luke 12. A helpful beginning of an analysis is to see the parable in its several contexts, including its position in Luke. The parable ap-

127

pears only in this one Gospel and is similar to numerous other Lukan texts that sound the alarm regarding the peril of riches. Several figures in the sociological spectrum of Luke's Gospel are wealthy, and the ethic of abundance and sensitivity to poverty are consciously linked by the evangelist. The segment of the Gospel in which chapter 12 is set comprises a loose collection of pointed teachings on a variety of themes. Some are directed to disciples (12:1,4,22,32) and some to the general crowd (12:15,54). Warning and judgment feature in several of the paragraphs. It is more significant that the parable is situated beside the poetic call to a life of faith in God not exhausted by anxiety (Luke 12:22-34). This latter passage maintains continuity with the parable, but a positive directive as well. To the insight that life is not a matter of possessions (v. 15) is added that life is more than food (v. 23). Both are a kind of lesson in values. Giving is commended (v. 33) rather than hoarding.

Immediate Precipitant. In Luke 12:13-15, a family conflict surfaces as a brother, probably the younger, requests that Jesus as a rabbi intervene on his behalf and order a partition of the family property held by the older brother. Apparently the younger brother chafed at the advantages enjoyed by the first-born son in Jewish law and tradition. Ordinarily the eldest retained control of the family property and most of the liquid assets (Deut. 21:17). It is possible that the younger expected more than customary, or perhaps his older brother neglected to implement a disposition made by the father during his lifetime.[1] The young man, in any event, was not contending for personal maintenance but property partition. In his demand, he stood over against Psalm 133, a psalm given over entirely to the beatitude of brothers living in unity. Perhaps both brothers were determined by an unhealthy concern or covetousness.[2]

Jesus responded by rejecting the function of divider foisted upon him. He would not perform as rabbi or new Moses, but rather insisted upon his special mission and displayed once again his will to do one thing. The retort by Jesus did signal that the man's request was inappropriate, that, indeed, he failed to understand life, a far greater issue than a partition of land. The young man was far more valuable than he knew. He was not in touch with his own value and the possibility of frittering it away.

Jesus seized the teachable moment by means of a striking pronouncement. He did not merely cite precedent or verse but virtually created a new Scripture verse on the spot with impressive authority: "Look out for and be on guard against every kind of greediness because a person's life does not consist in the abundance of his possessions" (v. 15).[3] Jesus warned about the desire to have more, that inevitable appetite that distorts living. Greed of any variety is outrageously hazardous.[4]

The parable of the Rich Fool expands on the great warning against greediness. Thus the parable and pronouncement interpret one another. It is possible chronologically that the historical incident (Luke 12:13-15) occurred on a separate occasion than that of the parable, inasmuch as it makes sense alone,[5] but it is probable that the two belong together.[6] After all, both the brother in the context and the principal in the parable expected too much of land. They imagined land provided security.

Literary Analysis

The parable itself is composed of an interior soliloquy (vv. 17-19) and the intrusion of God (v. 20). It is presented as a past event, though vibrant with its use of future tenses like "I will pull down my barns" (v. 18). The story narrates a specific situation about a particular rich man who experienced an unusual bumper crop.[7]

The narrative moves almost entirely on the vehicle of direct discourse. The mode of direct discourse actually sets up the situation and names the dilemma, outlines the strategy, and daydreams beyond. The private thoughts revealed allow the hearer to know the personal motives behind the outward actions, a procedure appropriate incidentally to the ethic of Jesus which tracks sin to its lair in the human heart. The interior soliloquy is naturally unguarded because it is private. His self-centeredness need not be disguised. The parable concludes with a climactic speech spoken assertively and a penetrating rhetorical end (v. 20).[8]

It is fascinating to compare the different record of the parable in the gospel of Thomas:

Jesus said: There was a rich man who had much money. He said: I will use my money that I may sow and reap and plant and fill my storehouse with fruit so that I lack nothing. This was what he thought in his heart. And that night he died. Whoever has ears let him hear (92:3-9).

The two parables stand apart. In the gospel of Thomas, there is a stress on money as such, the money is to buy a successful crop that has not yet happened, death only and not God is mentioned, and the subtle dialogue of Luke's Gospel is missing. Did you notice though that both stressed "what he thought in his heart"? Direct discourse is prominent in both. A strategy for lacking nothing is established in each. False security is exposed.[9]

The comparison of the two heightens one's sense of the content and character of Luke's parable. Did you notice other distinctives of the two accounts?

Possible Antecedents

There are some striking antecedents to the parable that may have influenced it or at least provided potential guidance for the wealthy farmer. One downright eerie parallel is from the book of Sirach:

> What time he saith: I have found rest,
> And now I will enjoy my goods—
> He knoweth not what lot shall befall
> He shall leave them to others and die (11:19).

There the notion of foolish confidence appears as in the parable, and this passage surely belongs to background influence.[10]

Two Old Testament passages demand notice. Psalm 49 is quite impressive with its warning against "men who trust in their wealth" (v. 6), but who must "leave their wealth to others" (v. 10) because of the nature of death. Ecclesiastes 2:14-26 contains several of the subtleties present in the parable:

There is nothing better for a man to do than to eat and drink and enjoy himself in return for his labours. And yet I saw that this comes from the hand of God. For without him who can enjoy his food, or who can be anxious? God gives wisdom and knowledge and joy to the man who pleases him, while to the sinner is given the trouble of gathering and amassing wealth only to hand it over to someone else who pleases God. This too is emptiness and chasing the wind (NEB).

Whether Jesus had this passage in mind, it too points out that joy belongs to the life oriented to God (theonomous), and it reminds that amassing wealth only means it must be passed to others. The rich fool was just chasing the wind!

The Story Itself

The only human character in the parable is portrayed as already wealthy before his bumper crop (12:16). His farm would have been located in the open country.[11] He faced a severe storage and surplus problem and began to talk to himself (v. 17). He faced the logistical problem of housing his corn after it was threshed into grain. The mention in the text of his dialogue with himself could suggest "a misguided contrivance of some kind,"[12] but it is more likely a genuine perplexity at first. The parable pictures a debate within himself. The man was not malignant to begin with, his dilemma was quite real, and he underwent a genuine struggle. The problem, as we shall see, lies in his resolution. The assessing of the dilemma does not reveal the core of his being (v. 17). Indeed, the being he chose to become may have been unsettled before this moment of truth. It was a soul-searching experience. The uncertainty and resolution stand out in the soliloquy.

"What shall I do?" (v. 17)
"This I will do." (v. 18)

He galvanized his perplexity into a plan.

His resolution called for the pulling down of old barns and erecting larger ones.[13] The expected result was surplus for the foreseeable future and an economic platform for complete leisure and constant festive merriment. The farmer, overwhelmed with good fortune and apparent security, imagined that he could in effect throw a feast that would last for years and remain merry. He projected physical well-being and cheer, a kind of secular joy.[14] There is a contrast to secular joy in Psalm 19:8 where it is stated that genuine joy is found in God's will. In a sense, the parable has to do with how to find genuine joy in the use of abundance.

The soliloquy becomes a dialogue as God intervenes with a divine assessment of aggressive self-centeredness. "Tonight you must die." The man hears the summons that cannot be disregarded. Earthly stories have heavenly meaning. Eduard Schweizer points out that life is a loan and that the farmer is responsible for the life that God has given him and must one day present it to God for judgment.[15] The self-sufficient farmer is accosted as a "fool," likely in the same sense of a life lived without reference to God (Ps. 14:1). Literally the verse reads, "This very night *they* are demanding from you your soul" (v. 20). The

third person plural "they" is surprising. It may be a rabbinic circum-
locution for God[16] or even a reference to angels.[17] Frank Stagg makes
the creative suggestion that "they" refers to the material possessions.[18]
The man certainly is possessed with what his possessions can do for
him selfishly, especially his new abundance. These barns which he had
constructed with such effort, who will possess them now? It seems he
made a bad investment.

Portrait of Inauthentic Existence

Presumption. The secular farmer, dazzled by a stroke of good
luck, presumes that he possessed his possessions and could die in his
own good time. This grand presumption can be documented textually
by all the uses of "my" and by all the future tenses. In three verses he
spoke of "my crops" (v. 17), "my barns" (v. 18), "all my grain and my
goods" (v. 18), and even "my soul" (v. 19). He reckons in pipe dream
fashion how he will enlarge his agricultural empire and then enjoy a
gay old age. There is an unmistakable atmosphere of vaulting eupho-
ria: "Man, you have plenty of good things laid by, enough for many
years: take life easy, eat, drink, and enjoy yourself" (Luke 12:19,
NEB). So he imagined that he had secured his life. So "a man spends
his last day on earth planning a long future."[19] His presumption is that
life is his to command, that he is the architect of his own destiny. He
glibly spoke of "many years." One of his misinterpretations of abundance is that it secures life.

Self-Indulgence. A second misunderstanding of abundance was
the farmer's use of it to buy "the good life." It was not that he enjoyed
counting his money or purring over his deeds or exercising economic
clout. Rather he equated the good life with leisure and immoderation
in drinking and eating. He saw joy in constant privilege, gratifying
one's own desires incessantly. He made the wrong use of *excess*. The
excess of crop posed a problem. He chose to resolve it with *excessive*
self-gratification. Greed can become idolatry (Col. 3:5). He did not see
the stewardship of abundance.

His commitment to self-indulgence and indolence issued in a
hoarding instinct. He had rather fill empty barns than empty
stomachs. He treasured up grain rather than gold. The contemporary
community at Qumran expressed its "everlasting hatred for all the
men of the Pit because of their spirit of hoarding."[20] There was much

physical need in a poor country that went unmet while a privileged few indulged themselves.

The fortunate farmer, inundated with abundance, acted out an inauthentic existence because he had a wrong notion of the good life, a wrong notion of joy, and a limited notion of the possibilities of abundance.

Practical Atheism. The farmer became a hollow man because he lived as if God did not exist. Conceivably he accepted theoretical theism, but in actual values he functioned as a thorough secularist. The big issues like the meaning of life went unexamined. He reckoned with death at best at a great distance. He failed to see his dependency on God. His life was not God oriented (theonomous) but self oriented (autonomous). His practical atheism kept him from comprehending his stewardship. The ground yielded an exceptional crop, a lavish gift of the earth, but it did not dawn on him that it was grace. He misunderstood his abundance as what he deserved or earned. "Heaven rained on him so he naively thanked himself and dammed it up."[21] He raised the right question ("What shall I do?"), but he gave the wrong answer.

Exposure of Inauthentic Existence

Internal Juxtaposition. The secularism often touted as tough realism turned out to be flimsy illusion in the parable. The juxtaposition of "many years" anticipated (v. 19) and "this night" announced (v. 20) lays bare the thrust of this awakening parable. The opinions of people are not the same as the judgments of God! And it is not merely the frustration of an untimely death. God addresses him to explain not only the jarring fact of unwanted, immediate death but also the folly of his life and values. The desperate farmer experiences the recognition of a wasted life when it is too late to render it otherwise. The parable, thus, becomes a call to others for whom death summons have not yet come to build different kinds of barns and throw different kinds of parties (Luke 14:12-14).

The moment the parable pictures is more than an isolated incident. It is a negative moment of truth (*chairos*). It captures the intent of an existence. The juxtaposition exposes a presumptuous stance of self-indulgence.

Crisis of Death. The story is a parable of crisis in several senses, but primarily it takes its urgency from unwanted death. The gentle-man farmer faced a crop crisis when he found himself deluged with more than he could house. He evaluated the crisis and acted decisively but wrongly. He failed to see the potentialities inherent in a crisis of abundance. Central, however, is the shock effect of sudden death, forcing a painful awareness of the truth. For the hearer the parable became a personal event (a language event), creating a crisis and im-plicitly inviting the response of repentance/conversion.

Professor Jeremias is quite right that the parable goes beyond the ancient maxim, "Death comes suddenly upon man."[22] It is not merely death but the divine Presence implying that the indulgent farmer had only been chasing the wind.

This kingdom parable assumes that God is sovereign Lord and that humanity is responsible.[23] God's judgment exposes inauthentic existence.

Suggestion Toward Authentic Existence

The parable by implication would commend an unselfish "stew-ardship of abundance," arising from a life rooted and grounded in God. Authentic existence may be experienced by participation in the kingdom of God as one accepts God's sovereignty and the values of the kingdom. Freedom from possessions and selfishness can be acted out by giving. The story of the Widow's Mite (Luke 21:1-4) illustrates that one can have authentic existence without abundance of posses-sions. Indeed, one free to share even out of her necessities exemplifies a genuine personhood.

Both the generalizing conclusion after the parable (v. 21) and the next passage provide positive content to the truly good life. "This is how it is with the one who treasures for himself but is not wealthy toward God." The hoarding, selfish style is alluded to in contrast to the style of laying up treasures in heaven, making an impressive con-nection to the parable and suggesting an alternative.[24] Luke 12:33 is critical because it says that the one who can sell possessions and give is actually wealthy. Spiritual treasure comes by giving rather than by getting or keeping. In other parables, Jesus pointed to compassion for the wounded (Luke 10:25-37) and for the hungry (Matt. 25:35).

The adjacent passage shows the way decisively. Life is more than food (v. 23). So life has higher purposes than eating and drinking

(12:19). Anxious care about clothing, height, or rich attire is misguided. The inner core of authentic existence or joyful living is rather trusting in God (v. 24), a theonomous life.

Christological Penetration

Jesus' identity or mission comes up indirectly when he firmly refused to be a divider or judge (v. 14), yet went on to assert far-reaching teaching. He did not presume the prerogative of a local rabbi to make a judicial decision, but he did presume a greater theological authority. Jesus took his role quite seriously and sought to correct a misconception. Interestingly Moses sought the role of judge and was resisted by some of his countrymen (Ex. 2:13). Jesus was sought by a countryman for the role and he resisted. Moses actually handled an inheritance problem (Num. 27:1-7; 36:2-10), but Jesus saw his mission quite differently.[25] Was Jesus intentionally distinguishing his ministry from that of Moses?

The outspoken young man in the crowd made a Christological error. He imagined that the finest gift Jesus could bestow was a legal decision in his favor. Jesus responded by tendering the gift of life through a startling parable. He corrected a secular assumption. He acted with breathtaking authority as Spokesman for God. He spoke in God's name (v. 20). He functioned as Creator of Scripture. He acted as Definer of existence. He became teacher and prophet and evangelist. He saw himself able to read the inner personal motivations. He comes across as a self-directed religious figure not to be dominated, a person maintaining control of his life. Most importantly Jesus' own personal existence was not predicated upon possessions, but upon God. Jesus' death did not embarrass the memory of his previous life but displayed it in all its grandeur. His authority and assurance are clues to his identity.

Contemporary Significance

Proofs of Spiritual Poverty. A person of some spiritual depth knows that she or he is not self-sufficient but dependent, relying on others and God. The rich fool sought to secure his independence. He knew of no joy except secular festivity. He had not found the deeper joys or gotten beyond presumption to the securing of life in God. His assumptions and intentions belong to the secularism of any era. As in his case, the secularism many style tough realism turns out to be flimsy illusion.

The good life he devoutly pined for reminds us of the modern aspiration for a share in the "good life" action. One American game of some educational merit implies that the most successful life leads to a millionaire's house situated on Golf Course Lane. Glance at an airline magazine and observe its message of the content of the good life. Note the advertisements and its overall impression of the good life.

John Reid has named eloquently the proofs of the rich fool's poverty:

1) The lack of thanksgiving.
   Never a thought of God as the giver of increase enters his mind.
2) The lack of helpful service.
   His was a resolve to "stow" rather than to "bestow." He has no idea of giving, only of getting.
3) The lack of any worthy outlook for the future.
   He worked with no higher vision than the ambition to be a glutton and a winebibber.
4) In what he leaves behind him and takes with him.
   He left no imperishable monument in deeds of kindness. His treasures were of the earth, and the earth kept them.[26]

Such clarifying analysis should alert the church to secularism in its own values and within its membership, but it should not escape notice that Jesus expressed concern for the spiritual welfare of a thoroughly secular person. He sought to awaken secular humanity. The church should not content itself with internal analysis and ministry but should move beyond maintenance to mission. Christians must find ways to invite secularists to a life better than "the good life" and to a joy lastingly merrier than secular joy. Spiritual poverty calls for evangelistic caring. The original parable was addressed not to disciples but to the crowds, not merely to the church then but to those outside. The church today needs to make contact with the "unchurched American."

The Gravity of Greed. The actual alarm about greed (Luke 12:15) surprises because then greed holds far more danger and evil and misuse of life than suspected. Has greed become a socially acceptable sin, a minor misdemeanor, understandable and naturally pardonable? Yet greed damages nature, can distort free enterprise, can dilute a Christian witness, can destroy community in an office, can lead to war, and can deny the sovereignty of God.

Greediness damages the greedy person. David Redding said of the rich fool, "He had deliberately blown out his candle with the whirlwind of his greed."[27] Greediness is the enemy of our own well-being. There is an introverted life-style aggressively self-centered which has made ultimate commitments to transitory realities. Greed can produce an inauthentic existence.

The Vantage of Death. Death came into the parable in a sovereign fashion, not at the behest of the wealthy man but at the word of God. It arrived at the height of the man's self-assurance. There is a brutal irony in the leisurely life projected and death at short notice. And his projections of leisure were not from the panic of last minute pleasure before impending death but the fundamental failure to reckon with death. At the very least, he failed "to reckon with the possibility of sudden and swift crisis."[28]

In the parable and in human experience, death exposes apparent shrewdness as ultimate foolishness. Had the farmer pondered his own death more reflectively and realistically he would have interpreted life and abundance differently. He lived the unexamined life, which Socrates believed was not worth living. The vantage of death can be a very helpful friend rather than merely a morbid trip or scare tactic. Death contains positive potentialities because the expectation of death can bring urgency and responsibility into life and can expose the superficiality of many of the concerns on which we spend our precious allotment of time.[29] The threat of death can propel Christians to get on with lasting achievements before the night falls. Death is a helpful interpreter of life, a kind of hermeneutic of existence. It can be a correcting perspective revealing better expressions of life than hoarding and self-indulgence. Robert Browning in his poem "What Makes Life Live?" wrote, "You will never know, what life means till you die:/ Even throughout life 'tis death that makes life live,/Give it whatever the significance." The vantage of death sharply improves perspective.

In a reflection called "Reading Your Own Obituary," Robert Raines reports the unusual experience of Nobel, "the dynamite King." Nobel, the inventor of dynamite, spent his life gathering a vast fortune from the manufacture of weapons of destruction. One morning in 1888 he awoke to read his own obituary. An error had been made.

Alfred's brother had died, and the reporter confused the names. Anyone would have been disturbed to read his own obituary, but the experience was severely stunning for Alfred Nobel. He saw himself as seen by his contemporaries as "the dynamite King." As far as the public knew, this was the full extent of the purpose of his life. None of his personal intentions to break down barriers that separated people and ideas were recognized. He would be remembered simply as the merchant of death. As he read with horror, he made a new resolution. He would make clear to the world the true purpose of his life. He decided to express his life's ideals through his last will and testament. Of course, the result was the Nobel Peace Prize, the most valued of awards given to those who have done most for the cause of world peace.[30]

A funeral is often a brief moment when other people center on the life of the deceased. It frankly comprises a rather intense scrutiny for a life to endure. Thoughtful people see the life whole, observe the broad contours more readily, consider what were the primary investments. A funeral or a death experience can be a moment of truth when family and friends in serious sadness think hard. Lives can be jolted into repentance or awakened to claim a religious kinship or heritage with the deceased. Sometimes a change of job or emergency surgery or a graduation similarly becomes the occasion of a heightened awareness of the course of an individual's life.

The vantage of death offers fresh alternatives to the question What shall I do with excess, with life, and with God? The implication for the Christian is to be committed to the things that matter and the things that last. Kenneth Bailey reminds that in the parable the goods are first *given*, then *stored*, and the same goods are *left*.[31] Both his life and goods were on loan.

Ruminations on Retirement. The parable indirectly may be quarried towards a better foundation for approaching retirement. It challenges some popular misconceptions. It is imagined that the quality of retirement turns upon the stocking up of abundance. Of course, poverty in the golden years cannot be idealized when many still suffer severely economically while in failing health, nor should a person with opportunity neglect provision for life after work. Nevertheless the parable warns that the good life in retirement does not consist either in abundance or self-indulgent leisure. Retirement may last too long for ease and immoderation to sustain and satisfy.

Rather, retirement invites more stretching and growing than ever before and sometimes more time to care about others and find true happiness. Some retired persons who are Christians are discovering the joy of ministering and giving more extensively than previously.

The parable realistically conveys the implication that everyone cannot expect a great many retiring years. Life before retirement should be lived. One may pour the best energies into stockpiling for a lively old age and miss the chance to know children and spouse and friends.

The parable can actually make a quantitative difference, if heeded, in retirement and life itself. "Let anyone who has ears to hear, hear." It can matter that you were.

NOTES

1. Rules of inheritance are given in detail in the *Mishnah* in *Baba Bathra* 8-9. There appear the categories both of actual inheritance and of maintenance. It was understood that the firstborn son received a double portion (8:5). Interestingly, a father could apportion in such a way as to make others equal with the firstborn. There was paternalistic provision for younger sons at the point of maintenance. However, this system intended the retention of the family ground in one piece. J. D. M. Derrett, "The Rich Fool: A Parable of Jesus Concerning Inheritance," *Heythrop Journal*, 18: 139 (2, 1977), rejects the relevance of these instructions however. He does argue that the younger man may not be better off with a partition because in some instances a person receiving that apparently favorable decision wound up in poverty (p. 133). Bailey, *Through Peasant Eyes* (Grand Rapids: Eerdmans, 1980), pp. 58-59, points out that the brother essentially demands an exegetical decision from Jesus the rabbi.

2. So G. Eichholz, *Einführung in die Gleichnisse* (Neukirchen-Vluyn: Neukirchen Verlag, 1973), p. 180. He goes on to identify this anxiety as not other than that of every person, a universal-existential application. On "economic anxiety" as related to the context, see the keen observations of Wayne Oates, *Anxiety in Christian Experience* (Philadelphia: Westminster Press, 1954), pp. 24-25.

3. The passage is notoriously difficult to translate. See C. C. Tarelli, "A Note on Luke XII.15," *Journal of Theological Studies*, 41:260-262 (1940), who connects *huparchontōn* with *perisseuein*.

4. In general, the Dead Sea community at Qumran would have applauded the pronouncement and the parable. The covenanters held a contempt for riches and those who were scampering after possessions.

5. Several considerations favor separation. One major possibility is that the immediate

reference in 12:13-15 is to covetousness in the usual sense of desiring the possessions of another. Also the introduction and the parable stand separately in the gospel of Thomas at 94:1-5 (72) and 92:2-9 (63), but the introduction there lacks the pronouncement and has been turned to other purposes.

6. In favor of connecting the two, observe (1) that the pronouncement is a strong warning and that the story functions as a warning parable; (2) that the essence of life is at stake in both; (3) that both center upon inheritance and abundance; and (4) that verse 15 is a chreia or dominical dictum followed by a parable parallel to Luke 13:5. Eichholz, pp. 179-181, places the setting and parable together in the original source, but he labels both verse 15 and verse 21 as Lukan. Bailey, p. 59, out of his lengthy, recent experience points out how land remains the most sensitive issue in the Middle East.

7. Eta Linnemann, *Jesus of the Parables*, p. 4, is surely right that the Rich Fool is an illustration, but I believe she has overstated the difference between it and a parable proper or specific situation. It is surely an awakening parable as well and contains typical characteristics, including internal juxtaposition. The parable acts as an interpretation or even a midrash on verse 15 but within the usual parabolic boundaries.

8. Other characteristics of the parable include a "crack in reality" (Wilder) in the divine intervention. The overtly theological language is also unusual, though often enough in Luke.

9. J. N. Birdsall, "Luke XII,16ff, and the Gospel of Thomas," *Journal of Theological Studies*, 13:332-336 (1962), concludes negatively for any connection with the Thomas tradition.

10. Derrett, p. 145, is convinced that the Sirach passage is a direct influence. He also holds that the author of the parable was an artist who linked Sirach 11:19 with Isaiah 22:13; 56:12; 57:11. However, the Isaiah 22:13 passage reckons with death in a way alien to the parable. Attention should also be given to 1 Enoch 97:8-10, though there wealth is gained unrighteously.

11. The word rendered "farm" is *chōra*, which means "open country" or a region removed from cities. Incidentally it is the same word used to speak of the far country (Luke 15:13). In context land or farm is likely.

12. So Derrett, p. 143. He is able to show that the word *dialogizomai* has negative implications in the LXX and in the New Testament. He does admit that in the papyri the word means "disputed, debated." Certainly the resolution in the parable is of a calculated sort. A text like Mark 2:6-8 suggests a malevolent intent, but Luke 3:15 pictures people genuinely searching. G. Schrenk, "*dialogizomai*," *TDNT*, 2:96 (1964), takes it to mean here "to ponder" or "to consider."

13. Derrett, p. 144, suggests an intentional allusion to 2 Chronicles 31 within the parable. His argument is ingenious but precarious. The parallel is more verbal than substantial. The generous giving of tithes in 2 Chronicles was not because of an unusual harvest but an unusual king. The issue is not abundance of harvest but an abundance of tithes for the cultus. Certainly there was a storage problem in both cases. Derrett, that master of detail, has seized upon the issue of abundance in the parable rightly, but he may be influenced by his own social setting unduly.

14. Often festive joy as Judith 12:13,17 and 3 Maccabees 5:17,36. R. Bultmann, "*euphrainō*," *TDNT*, 2:774 (1964), portrays secular joy as "the most to which the worldling who forgets God can aspire, hoping to secure it by his possessions."

15. Eduard Schweizer, *"Psuchē" TDNT*, 9:647 (1974).

16. A. R. C. Leaney, *The Gospel According to St. Luke* (New York: Harper, 1958), p. 87, paralleling to Luke 12:48 and 6:38. There is a significant textual variant in 12:20 in any event. A few important manuscripts prefer *aitousin* rather than *apaitousin*.

17. R. C. Lenski, *The Interpretation of St. Luke's Gospel* (Columbus: Wartbury Press, 1946), p. 686, quoting Burnaud and citing Job 33:22 and Luke 16:23.

18. Frank Stagg, *Studies in Luke's Gospel* (Nashville: Convention Press, 1965), pp. 90-91.

19. John Crossan, *In Parables*, p. 85.

20. *Rule* 9:22. Jesus is different in that he seeks to awaken the rich rather than despise them.

21. David Redding, *The Parables He Told* (New York: Harper and Row, 1962), p. 129.

22. Joachim Jeremias, *The Parables of Jesus*, p. 165. His insistence that Jesus had in mind the approaching eschatological catastrophe is unconvincing. His crisis category, so brilliantly explored, is too narrowed. I will not rule it out entirely because the young man from the crowd did not know who Jesus was nor what time it was.

23. F. Buchsel, *"krinō," TDNT*, 3:938 (1965) states, "If there is no judgment of God as Jesus bears witness, then Jesus and His preaching can have only a constantly diminishing historical significance."

24. There are slight textual problems with the inclusion of verse 21, but far more debate whether it belonged originally with the parable or represents a comment by the evangelist. Many scholars believe it is an editorial remark. One cannot be dogmatic, but it seems tailored to the parable. It is the thrust beyond the story to generalize about any who elect a similar commitment.

25. For further speculation see Derrett, p. 133f.

26. John Reid, "The Poor Rich Fool," *Expository Times*, 13:567-68 (1901-2).

27. Redding. On the "having mode of existence" see Erich Fromm, *To Have or to Be?* (New York: Harper, 1967), especially pp. 108-110.

28. I. H. Marshall, *Commentary on Luke* (Grand Rapids: Wm. B. Eerdmans, 1978), p. 524. Jülicher, *Die Gleichnisreden Jesu*, 2:616 (1910), generalized that even the richest of men is at every moment wholly dependent upon the power and mercy of God.

29. So John Macquarrie, "Death and Eternal Life," *Expository Times*, 89:46 (1977).

30. Raines, *Creative Brooding* (New York: Macmillan, 1968), p. 121.

31. Bailey, p. 58.

9 The Parable of the Six Brothers

Outraged righteousness blazes forth in the parable usually dubbed the Rich Man and Lazarus. The Teller delivers the punch only an otherworldly perspective can command. He offers no sugarcoated gospel. He refuses to placate the comfortable and presumptuous but rather serves up an inimitable example of the radicality of the kingdom of God. He reckons with the absolute necessity to respond in the time of decision.

Before plunging further into interpretation, illuminating considerations, such as possible sources and the actual nature of the story and background, rightfully claim first attention.

Possible Sources

The teachings of Jesus relate to the Old Testament and go beyond, and this is the case in this instance. Behind Luke 16:19-31 stands Psalm 49.[1] The parallels are interesting and illuminating. Surely Jesus had these earlier sentiments in mind, as perhaps did some hearers. The psalm sounds the resounding note of the inevitability of death and the loss of wealth and pomp. Man is like the animals who perish: "Man cannot abide in his pomp, he is like the beasts that perish" (49:12,20, RSV). The focus of the psalm is on the rich and the claims of Sheol. Confidence in pomp is foolish.

Obviously, the parable does not owe its story form to the psalm. Could it be a kind of illustrating text of Psalm 49? In any event, Luke 16 goes beyond and speaks to the demand for a sign. It is equally likely that the greatest commandment belongs to the background. It is most necessary to love God and neighbor (Mark 12:33). You shall love your neighbor as yourself (Lev. 19:18) just as Moses commanded (Luke 16:29).

142

A further fascinating possibility is that an Egyptian story lies in the general background. The story, having many variations, recounts a journey to the underworld by one Si-Osiris, who returns with the startling revelation of unexpected reversals.[2] Possibly Jews from Alexandria, Egypt, brought the story to Palestine. One version tells of a poor scholar and a rich tax collector whose destinies were reversed.[3] As many as seven rabbinic versions have been found as well.[4] At most, however, only the situation part of Jesus' story (Luke 16:19-23) bears a resemblance. This in turn points up again that the dialogue part (Luke 16:24-31) of a parable carries the distinctive twist, but the original hearers did hear the story out of a particular background that influenced the way they responded.

Nature of the Story

Some insist that the story in Luke 16 is not a parable. There may be theological reasons for this position, but the supporting literary argument runs along several lines. It is argued that Luke 16:19-31 reflects an actual event, a true story, and is not a fictional parable. It is true that the text does not say anywhere that it is a parable. More importantly, proper names do not appear in parables ordinarily, and the personal name Lazarus is used in this passage. Famous early Christians like Tertullian and Ambrose questioned whether the story was a parable.[5]

It can be demonstrated by literary analysis, however, that the pericopé is a parable, though it remains possible that behind the narrative there may have been a recent incident of the death of a poor man by the name of Lazarus. Through form, the story belies that it is a narrative parable like others Jesus told and Luke narrated. It is a classic "specific situation" with the telltale beginning "a certain man. . . ." This introductory formula (*anthropos de tis*) is a dead giveaway! And notice position in the Gospel (*Sitz im Buch*). This section of Luke is chock-full of parables. The very chapter begins with a parable (Luke 16:1-8), and the preceding chapter contains three parables. There are other parables in Luke 18. The presumption is quite strong that the evangelist grouped parables in this segment of his Gospel. If, furthermore, it were merely a true story of something that actually happened, then it would be most unusual. It would be an unexplained interruption in a series of stories about Jesus or from Jesus.

There are other parable clues. Notice the juxtaposition of the rich man and the beggar. This is an antithesis of two types as in other parables like the Pharisee and the Tax Collector. Also the name Lazarus means "God helps," which adds to the meaning of the parable. The extensive dialogue (16:24-31), which has been shown to be so characteristic of parables, leaves no real doubt that from literary analysis the form is that of the narrative parable.

The parable depicts clearly two movements: one, the earthly condition of a very wealthy individual and the relative condition of the beggar Lazarus; two, the otherworldly condition of each reversed. The greater length, a clue to emphasis, is given over to the otherworldly dialogue. There is no conversation in the earthly scene that establishes the situation, but there is an elaborate dialogue of three full exchanges in the second scene. If reversal were the only point, the second segment (esp. v. 27 *ff.*) would be superfluous. More is going on.

There are explicit theological terms within the parable, two in particular. The word "Hades" appears (v. 23) as does "repenting" (v. 30). This signals the fact that it is not merely an earthly story with a heavenly meaning, nor is it merely a secular story with a religious meaning. Rather it is an otherworldly or apocalyptic parable with a this-worldly significance! Furthermore, observe the constant usage of the term "father" for Abraham (vv. 24,27,30) and the reference to the rich man as "son" (v. 25). This signals the important fact that the rich man is self-consciously Jewish, a literary observation that points to a purpose of the parable.

This long parable contains a hidden unity. The two, Lazarus and the rich man, are connected/separated by a table throughout. In the first division, the banquet table belongs to the rich man; but in the second, Lazarus sits at table with Abraham in a heavenly banquet. The story begins with those alive on earth, follows them beyond death, but is reflecting on the living at the end (v. 28). Some scholars too flippantly say that "the second part which is launched on the basis of the first has very little connexion with it."[6] It is also inappropriate to assign one or both halves to early church proclamation because of the organic interdependency of the two parts and the characteristic dialogue following upon a narrative explanation that sets up a situation.[7] After all, the reversal may be seen as the first scene portrays Lazarus begging and the second presents the rich man begging.

Background Notes

A few select background notes further advance understanding. For example, references to the poor in the Psalms usually indicate the "pious poor," persons depending on God despite their lot. G. D. Kilpatrick points out that the poor man in the Psalms typically is oppressed by a stronger neighbor and looks for God to free him and vindicate.[8] The poor man, furthermore, is a sympathetic figure as in the case of Nathan's parable wherein the poor man is idealized and the rich man's seizure of the poor man's only lamb is castigated (2 Sam. 12). While the rich man in Luke's parable did not mistreat the desperate cripple, neither did he respond with compassion out of his superfluity.

The luxury of the rich man's attire and banquet deserves comment. He wore a mantle of purple wool and linen underwear imported from Egypt. He had no necessity for daily work. One can picture crystal drinking glasses at table filled with undiluted wine.[9] The destitute Lazarus desired the droppings from the banquet table (v. 21a). This does not refer to crumbs but chunks of thrown-away bread. Montefiore described it graphically:

What fell from the table were the big bits of bread which were used to clean or dry the hands after the eaters had dipped them, for example, in a dish full of bits of meat and gravy. Napkins were not used for the hands. The guests wiped their hands on bits of bread, and then threw the pieces under the table.[10]

So the beggar waited for soiled bread, not for a gift of food.

Another detail is the revolting description of the dogs licking the beggar's wounds (v. 21). Some have seen the reference to the dogs as a sign that they were kinder to the prostrate cripple than the rich man. They were not inactive as the rich man but rather salved his wounds. While this is possible and gives added point, dogs were mainly mongrel and were despised scavengers. Full-grown dogs were rarely kept except occasionally as watchdogs.[11] More likely the picture of the despised mongrels licking his sores was intended to heighten the sense of utter helplessness and the incredible degree of neglect. What a horrible human experience to find street dogs looming over one's powerless body. He experienced the rape of human dignity and received no asylum or comfort. Lazarus is abandoned to canine mongrels. This was his torment (cf. v. 24). So the parable portrays a derelict and a dereliction. One was abandoned, deserted, forsaken. The other was abandoning, deserting, forsaking. The rich man was derelict in his duty to be his brother's keeper.

It is also possible that Lazarus experienced deprivation even after death. Though the parable mentions the burial of the rich man, there is no parallel comment about the poor man. The silence may betoken one last disgrace.

To lack burial counted as the greatest deprivation. This fate was decreed fitting only for the condemned and those under a curse. Lack of burial brought severe injury to the deceased; the soul's peace was jeopardized; it was constrained to roam restlessly about.[12]

In any event there must have been quite a contrast between burials.

One other background issue concerns the audience. Did Jesus address the parable to Pharisees? The context does not really settle the issue. Indeed, the historian Josephus reports, "The Pharisees simplify their standard of living, making no concession to luxury" (*Antiquities*, 18,12). T. W. Manson has captured the imagination with the fresh suggestion that the hearers to whom the parable was directed were Sadducees.[13] This is a highly suggestive conjecture since the story would be so appropriate to those of the upper stratum who did not believe in the afterlife. From this standpoint the parable takes on the added point that it refers to the religious rich, a thought enhanced by the thrice repeated reference to Abraham as father.

Certain problems appear. Would the Sadducees reject the reference to torment out of hand? Had it been addressed to Sadducees, would both Moses *and the prophets* have been called forward when Sadducees accepted only the books of Moses as scriptural? They also rejected the reality of angels (Acts 23:8). These issues are not sufficient to discredit but to question Manson's speculation. Is it not also possible, however, that the rich man called to mind a tax collector as in the Egyptian parallel? In attempting to answer the question of audience, students have centered on the issue of selfish wealth without sufficient attention to the question of what group characteristically demanded a sign and who presumed automatic election. The demand seems to have arisen ordinarily in scribal circles (Mark 8:11; Matt. 12:38; Luke 11:29), though not to the exclusion of Sadducees (Matt. 16:1). Jesus did joust with the Sadducees about the resurrection in one Jerusalem conflict story (Mark 12:18-27). On balance, the Sadducees remain the most likely audience, but Pharisees and tax collectors are also possibilities.

Incidentally, the rich man is popularly called "Dives," not because he has a name in the Greek text, but because Dives was the Latin translation in the Vulgate (*Homo quidam erat dives*) for the Greek word (*ho plousios*) referring to a rich person. Interestingly, a very ancient manuscript of Luke (P[75]) contains the mention of Neves as the name of the rich man (*onomati Neuēs*).[14]

Interpretation

The Name Lazarus. It is noteworthy that the proper name Lazarus appears at all as mentioned, but the generalization that this is the only instance of a proper name in any parable must be modified to recognize another proper name, Abram (hereafter Abraham), in this very parable. The meaning of Lazarus' name is almost certainly a key to interpretation, and scholars have ransacked a vast array of possibilities including the following interesting options:

1) Conflation with the Johannine Lazarus story (John 11). The name Lazarus came from this famous story of death and resurrection[15] (but the Lazarus in John was not penniless or bereft, and Luke 16:31 stands in some tension).

2) A literary device for narrative convenience. The name was added because the following dialogue would flow more smoothly if he were provided a name (but this theory suffers from the fact that the rich man is not named, and Christians retelling the story have tended to supply the Latin name *Dives* so both lead characters would have names).

3) Etymological clue. The name rescues the parable from the possible interpretation that the poor man went to Paradise simply because he was poor. Helmut Gollwitzer actually entitles this parable "Lazarus, the one called 'God helps.' "[16]

4) Connection to Eliezer. The name Lazarus should be connected with the Old Testament figure Eliezer, Abraham's servant (Gen. 15:2). (A check in the LXX shows that the Greek in Genesis 15:2 is *Eliezer* while Luke 16:20 has *Lazaros*. However, this may be a rabbinic abbreviation). It has been suggested that at the time of Jesus, Eliezer-Lazarus was among the common Jewish folk a type of an

humble but zealous and God-fearing man of the lower stratum, fit to be borne on angels' wings to Abraham's bosom, to serve him as it were in Paradise as he had served him on earth.[17]

Of these fascinating alternatives, (1) and (2) are unconvincing, (4) deserves further reflection, and (3) is compelling, but with one important comment. The name Lazarus is clearly a Jewish name. The poor man then was Jewish. The rich man was Jewish. Thus, there is an incident of unbrotherliness, a denial of covenantal obligations, and a deep identification by the Teller of the parable with the Jewish poor. Thus, the name is the exegetical clue correcting the one dimensional idea of reversal and implying Lazarus' trust in God's grace, though this is not the primary thrust of the parable. If the parable were teaching that the poor were automatically blessed in the afterlife, there would be no need for the specific name Lazarus.[18]

It is often carelessly said that Lazarus is an incidental figure in the story.[19] Clearly he is secondary, but he is not incidental. He is named and his name is appropriate to the parable. Furthermore, his destitute condition is described more lengthily than is the luxury of the rich man. There is some marked empathy and understanding for him. He enjoyed the heavenly banquet at the table of Abraham and was a true son. Furthermore, it is not really true that he disappears after the first scene. Assuredly he never speaks, but notice that Lazarus as messenger figures in every step of the dialogue. Send him on an errand of mercy (v. 24). Send him on an errand of witness (vv. 27-28).

Perhaps the spirit of Lazarus was like that of the psalmist:

> Turn to me, Lord, and answer;
> I am downtrodden and poor.
> Guard me, for I am constant and true;
> Save thy servant who puts his trust in thee
> (Ps. 86:1-2, NEB).

The Great Reversal. The reader is smitten by the dramatic reversal in the story. A beggar with no earthly pretensions finds fulfillment beyond death; a man fabled for his wealth is met with disaster in Hades. The rich became poor and the poor became rich. The extent of the reversal is best seen by dividing the parable into two begging scenes: Lazarus begging (16:19-21); Rich man begging (16:22*b*-31).

When you read the parable as two begging scenes, the contrasts become heightened. The basic contrast may be stated as follows:

a wealthy man (v. 19) with the good things (v. 25) is in anguish (v. 23)

a poor man (v. 20) with the bad things (v. 25) is comforted (v. 22)

Lazarus, once sick and hungry, is comforted at Abraham's side. The rich man, once wealthy and healthy, swelters in Hades. The rich man sees Lazarus comforted as once Lazarus had been spectator of the rich man's life of ease. B. T. D. Smith acutely observed, "The rich man now longs for a drop of water from the finger of Lazarus as formerly Lazarus had longed for the crumbs from his table."[20] The reversal is complete. Things are not as they seem. The opinions of men are not always the same as the judgment of God. The parable intends to shock and to awaken.

The firmness of the reversal is furthermore established by the two denials to the two requests. First the rich man requested water for his parched tongue (v. 24). Abraham turned down the request with unhinging words: "Remember that you in your lifetime received your good things, and Lazarus in like manner evil things; but now he is comforted here, but you are in anguish" (v. 25). It is both inappropriate (v. 25) and impossible (v. 26) to send Lazarus. In the second request, the rich man urged Abraham to send a messenger to alert his five living brothers (v. 27). Abraham denied the request on the grounds that the brothers have had already ample exposure to God's truth through Moses and the prophets. Lazarus is disallowed from ministering in Hades or witnessing on earth. There will be no sign. Internal juxtaposition is seen then in the rich man/poor man reversal and the request/refusal exchange in the dialogue.

As a great reversal, the parable stands in the apocalyptic tradition that characteristically promises vindication and a great divine reversal to harassed and downtrodden believers. The parable implicitly controverts the popular theology that wealth is a sign of blessing and illness a sign of divine displeasure. It is a contradiction of cheap grace and presumption upon election. The reversal had severe meaning for the rich man because he presumed upon his family connection to Abraham.

Careful reading of the parable finds three appeals to Abraham, which consistently address him as "father" in each instance (vv. 24,27,30)! This is of crucial importance for the original historical context. It is apparent from this natural appellation of Abraham as father that the rich man is a Jew. He had relied not only upon wealth but also upon birth. He imagined that he enjoyed religious security. His heredity claim collapsed through the development of the story. In the Mishnaic tractate *Sanhedrin* may be found the claim, "All Israelites have a share in the world to come" (10:1). It was even said that Abraham was stationed at the gates of Gehenna to turn back any Jew who might have found his way there.

The challenge of the parable to such automatic election recalls the preaching of the Baptizer. There stands in Q (Matt. 3:9; Luke 3:8) a saying of John claiming that God is capable of raising children of Abraham from inanimate objects if need be. This fierce assertion, derived from a scriptural injunction (Isa. 51:1-2), rejected the dogma that salvation depends on pure lineage.[21] The Baptizer's corrective came as a retort to the smugness, "We have father Abraham" (Matt. 3:9). This kind of smugness is upended by the reversal in the parable as well. The parable is a significant continuity with the proclamation of the Baptizer. The truly elect are those who have responded to the call of God.

With the issue of presumption the matter of culpability comes into view.

Culpability of the Rich Man? It is quite true that the parable "does not say" that the rich man mistreated the poor man or went to Hades because of his relationship to him, but it is imperative to observe that the two were connected in destiny. The poor man was deposited at the rich man's gate (v. 20). He was not across town in the squalor of some ghetto constituting the "invisible poor." He belonged to the highly visible destitute. There followed a prolonged ignoring of the poor man who was continuously at his gate. The rich man knew the poor man's name and requested that he do something for him that he had not done for Lazarus during his lifetime (v. 24). He requested what he had not bestowed. Abraham's refusal to allow Lazarus to cool his tongue (v. 25) implies that the rich man had not gone out to the poor man.

The degree of Lazarus' destitution heightens the picture of callousness. Observe the poor man's plight as derived from the brief but informative description. He suffered from illness, lameness, and hunger. He experienced the misery of being covered with sores. He apparently was a cripple since he seems to have been brought there and left. He was reduced to begging and was content if only he could receive the castoffs. The climax of his misery came in the form of street dogs who continuously licked his abscesses. Furthermore, he may not have been given even the soiled bread. Jeremias points out that verse 21 should read, "He would gladly (if he could) have filled himself."[22]

Contiguous to such human deprivation stood equally exceptional human privilege. The point is not that the rich man was simply a lover of money. He was not a miser hoarding his gold. Rather he was self-indulgent. Apparently he did not work. He made merry over a feast constantly. The operative words are "daily" and "sumptuously" (v. 19). Such feasting did not belong only to the odd occasion. There was constant pandering to his stomach. How could he justify such a ravenous appetite when hunger camped at his gate? Did the beggar die of hunger or a hunger-related disease within twenty yards of a sumptuous table? The rich man's heart seems to have been as hard as anthracite.

Furthermore, the rich man took no active part to help. He made no effort to stave off the street dogs. There is an astounding lack of compassion parallel to that of the priest and Levite in the parable of the Compassionate Samaritan (Luke 10:31-32). Duncan Derrett put it well, "He was a flagrant wrongdoer though passive in his wrongdoing."[23] Jesus believed that the greatest commandment, the basis for one's being, was love of God and neighbor. Moses taught it. The compassionate Samaritan practiced it. Jesus held persons responsible for it. Lazarus was a Jewish brother, a part of the covenantal responsibility (Lev. 19:18). The implication of verse 31 is that the rich man himself refused to hear Moses and repent. Could it be that the rich man broke the law of hospitality? When Jesus spoke of feasts, he commended quite a radical redirection. The dominical direction for a guest list counseled against merely inviting friends and family and in favor of inclusion of the poor, maimed, lame, or blind (Luke 14:13).

In summary, the rich man is blameworthy, not because of active mistreatment nor mere wealth, but because he failed to brother a person in desperate condition lying prostrate at his gate. He broke the greatest commandment and failed to be his brother's keeper. Apparently "feasting together with Lazarus is beyond his comprehension."[24]

Call to Decision. The rich man in Hades was quite insistent, however, that his brothers would repent if they received a visit from the dead (v. 30). Abraham explained that his brothers possessed sufficient witness already through the Scriptures written by Moses and the prophets (as Isa. 58:7-9), but the rich man adamantly pressed his case. He insisted that his siblings would respond if exposed to such a manifest witness as an apparition from the dead. This attitude represented by the rich man corresponds to the demand for a sign characteristic of the generation to which Jesus spoke (Mark 8:11).

The demand for a sign requires some kind of unequivocal divine indication. The rich man, in effect, downplayed the witness of the Scriptures and presumed to set his own standard. This dialogue demonstrates that Jesus not only understood the mentality behind a demand for a sign but also that he recognized the implicit evasion, the impenitence, the rationalization, and the plain rejection of the sovereignty of the Scriptures (cf. 1 Cor. 1:22-24; 2 Cor. 4:6,10-13). The plea amounts to a practical repudiation of the sovereignty of God. Just as Jesus refused to give a sign when confronted in his ministry,[25] so Abraham refused. He did not merely refuse. He made the value judgment that if the brothers' intransigence is so set that they will ignore the clear witness of Moses and the prophets, then they will scoff at a returning Lazarus as well. "No sign will be given," wrote Charles Smith, "because no sign would avail."[26] The problem is not an inadequate revelation but an inadequate response. Thus the parable forcefully refuses to offer or honor a sign,[27] a purpose of the parable that once more illustrates how the person and ministry of Jesus indirectly were involved in his parabolic defenses. The historical demand was that Jesus substantiate his ministry. The parable answered the demand and assertively invited a reorientation by responding to the proclamation of the Parabolist. Jesus struggled with the question of signs in his temptations quite decisively and was personally faced by it again on the cross (Mark 15:31-32).

A positive possibility lurks within the refusal. The five living brothers may choose to hear the word (as Rom. 10:17). The parable as a whole is heavy with judgment, and the sense of hopelessness threatens to dominate. There is an unmistakable "too late" conveyed by the parable.[28] However, as one looks at stages of the parable, it appears that while it is too late for the rich man after his death it is not too late for his brothers. They may be on the same trajectory as he. Presumably they are like him in attitude and life. While what happens here and now is decisive, it remains to be seen what the five living brothers will choose. It must have been an electrifying final touch for the original hearers. It became existentially real to the living listeners. They found themselves in the parable in startling fashion. So in a highly creative fashion, Jeremias has suggested that the narrative be called the parable of the Six Brothers. He explained his insight in this manner:

The surviving brothers, who have their counterpart in the men of the Flood generation, living a careless life, heedless of the rumble of the approaching flood (Matt. 24:37-39 par.), are men of this world, like their dead brother. Like him they live in selfish luxury, deaf to God's word, in the belief that death ends all (v. 28).[29]

This keen observation about the living brothers brings the message alive. The parable ceases immediately to be a curious story about the lives of a very rich man and a very poor man and the way their lives eventuated. It becomes a call to decision. It is not yet too late. The vantage of the afterlife offers new urgency and interpretation to the present.

The implicit invitation is to repentance. Notice the prominence of thoughts like hearing Moses and the prophets (v. 29), repenting (v. 30), and being persuaded (v. 31). The need is for the living brothers to hear and be persuaded and repent. Such a repentance involves a radical reorientation of life around the will of God, and that will of God is given definition by the love commandment and the proclamation of Jesus. If they would hear the word, if they would hear the parable, repentance would occur. In short, *Jesus responded to the demand for a sign with the sign of Jonah through the parable.*

This evangelistic parable calls to decision. It is bold. It not only retorts but it proclaims as well. Options are still open. The moment of existence is now. Hearers must be redeemed from greed and freed for compassion. The possibility of a decisive encounter with the Teller of the parable exists. The parable makes plain that whoever desires to save his or her life will lose it (Mark 8:35) and dramatizes the truth inherent in the question, "What shall it profit a person to gain the whole world and suffer loss with respect to his soul?" (Mark 8:36) The parable's overall impact is to underscore the cruciality of this life in the light of the Beyond and to demand choice. Our here will determine our hereafter.

Word for Today

Existential. This narrative parable leads to a "disclosure situation." It exposes a self-defeating life-style. It discloses a form of inauthentic existence. The story lays bare the possibility of an incredible insensitivity to human need when one's life is aggressively self-centered. The rich man's life was as hollow as a Ping-Pong ball. He was "too calloused to care." The parable reveals that authentic existence is not possible if one predicates life on creature comforts and studied indifference to hurt. Radical selfishness can lead to unthinkable insensitivity. Rich persons in any era can be so wrapped up in a portfolio of stocks and bonds and debentures and so oriented to gourmet diets that they are grandly oblivious to the nearby human on the rubbish heap.

The parable reaches to the water table of our common existence. It is not that all of us possess such uncommon wealth or can choose to party daily, but some of us may have constructed houses without windows to the world. We may be so self-oriented that the "hurting other" remains outside our circle. Those in touch with authentic existence know that "everybody's beautiful in their own way"—including old beggars. Not to know that is not to know life.

The truth is that life in the kingdom is authentic existence; life outside the kingdom is inauthentic existence; and Jesus of Nazareth is the clue to the nature both of the kingdom and authentic existence. A Christian is someone who loves the things that Jesus loved, who values the things that Jesus valued, and who opposes the things Jesus opposed. To accept Christ means not only to be pure in heart but "a man for others." To accept the lordship of Christ means to identify with his convictions and let him be the center of our being. In Christ is authentic existence. For Paul, life was Christ (Phil. 1:21).

Eschatological. The revised perspective created by the parable derives from the life beyond. For example, beggars are important to God; each person has a personal eschatology, a life beyond death; no one can live as if God did not count and get away with it; God will make all things right; and life must be lived in the light of life after death.

The parable, like some others, is a kind of theodicy. Observation of life leads thoughtful persons to ponder why the innocent suffer and the wicked prosper (Jer. 12:1). The eschatological vantage of the afterlife illumines the question to the extent that God wills compassion for the suffering, both by persons who come in contact and by loving inclusion in the future life.

Marxists have attacked the irrelevant otherworldliness of "pie in the sky by and by when you die." They have characterized religion as the opiate of the people because it shifts focus and responsibility away from the injustices of this world. Some Christians certainly have given up on this world as hopeless, suffering from what Nietzsche called "the eternity corruption," but the parable itself rather demonstrates the contemporary relevance of the eschatological perspective. There is no blessing of or blinking at social wrong. Such callous rich as the principal character face a severe comeuppance, indeed. Furthermore, religion does not legitimate the social order. The popular notion that the poor experience the misery of impoverishment because of their sins, a comfortable theory for the successful, is countered by the parable.[30] Most decisively the parable is focused on this world and is a call for repentance to the living brothers. It is not merely an announcement about the afterlife or mere encouragement to the destitute after death. The parable is unmistakenly addressed to the living: Turn from self-indulgence and lack of compassion or face the consequences. It is then *a catalyst for social change*. The vantage from the afterlife illumines social injustice and names it for what it is.

Our personal lives cannot be the same once confronted by the life to come. Otherworldly perspectives, overly discredited, can in fact prove enormously relevant. The view from beyond can redeem people from lives that do not matter. One can be so heavenly minded that he or she is of no earthly use, but one should not be so mesmerized by that corrective to forget the more critical obverse side—one can be so earthly minded that she or he is of no heavenly use!

Ethical. This parable is also an excellent paradigm for the relationship of the social and evangelical gospels because the two concerns intersect. One cannot opt for one or the other as too many Christians do. Neither can one merely take a middle-of-the-road stance and call for balance. Rather the parable conveys a holistic perspective, a unitive understanding of the whole person. The parable calls for repentance which has social consequences. To recover the importance of repentance as expressed in the parables is to reestablish the ethical aspect, too long in eclipse. Lorenzen is quite right when he speaks of eternity, social concern, and sins of omission: "There are situations through which God calls for our help, and, if we don't help, nobody will. And the sins of omission with their 'too late' will be with us into eternity."[31]

From a social perspective, there are revolutionary impulses inherent in the story. George Buttrick offers personal comment by way of further extrapolation.

The story offers no support to the glib assumption that Dives would have fulfilled all duty had he dressed Lazarus' sores and fed his hunger. True charity is more than flinging a coin to a beggar; it is not spasmodic or superficial. Ameliorations such as food and medicine are necessary but there is a more fundamental neighborliness.[32]

So a modern reader may recognize the need for social action, as well as social work. Social systems often fail to give all segments an opportunity. One of Shakespeare's famous sentences speaks, "The fault, dear Brutus, is not in ourselves, but in our systems that we are miserable." There is something wrong with a system that allows vulgar luxury and pathetic poverty. Both personal and social repentance are needed. Richard Rohrbaugh spanks preachers who have published sermons on the parable and settled for individualistic moralizing.[33]

Concern for world hunger, a cause whose time has come, is also addressed by the parable. Lazarus was hungering to the point of desperation. The rich man was feasting to the point of dissipation. The mental picture of a glutton of rotund proportions, an Oriental merchant with a Santa Claus figure emerges. Even so, there are enclaves of poverty in our midst, continents of hunger around us. Helmut Gollwitzer opens his volatile volume, a book that bears the provocative title *The Rich Christians and Poor Lazarus*, with a question whose answer stings:

Who are we? Answer: We are the rich man. That is, incontestably, the most exact description of us. 'We belong to that third of humanity which is concerned with slimming cures, while the other two-thirds are concerned with hunger.' And this third consists for the most part of baptized Christians, the other two-thirds of unbaptized persons.[34]

Our global village desperately needs compassionate response from rich Christians. Jesus portrayed the judgment of the nations when the Son of man will give unstinting blessing to those who gave food when he was hungry, drink when he was thirsty (Matt. 25:35). So our Lord identified with the world's hungry, and the New Testament expresses frequent care for the poor (1 Thess. 4:12; Eph. 4:28; 1 Tim. 6:17-19; Jas. 1:27; 2:14-17; 1 John 3:17). *Seeds*, a magazine with a message for our times, is devoted to arousing Christian concern and conviction about world hunger.[35]

An unprecedented breakthrough for aiding the hungry could take place in the last quarter of the century. A growing conscience and a growing technological sophistication could conspire to provide subsistence for every human being on earth, and the parable can help it happen. A tithe of Christian leaders has caught the vision, and actual efforts have made stunning advances.

Other ethical implications arise, such as concern for medical missions. The famished beggar put up with lameness and skin disease without benefit of doctor or clinic. There is an implicit missionary call residing in the Word for today. There is furthermore the call for local churches to fashion weekday ministries to express concern for those "at the gate."

A response to the challenge of the parable must include personal life-styles. We experience a multiplication of artificial necessities and the unremitting temptation to spend. James Denney spoke realistically to the connection between the call to charity and self-indulgence:

All works of love, from Christian missions down, are carried on under the pressure of a perpetual deficit. When people say they have not anything to give for such causes, they are as a rule telling the truth. They have nothing to give because they have already spent everything. But the true moral of this is that the call for charity is often also a call for self-denial and thrift. No one will ever have anything to give who has not learned to save, and no one learns to save without checking the impulse to spend his money for things which it would no doubt be pleasant enough to have, but which he can quite well do without.[36]

Denney's comment is down to earth. Daily feasting is a little much alongside daily misery.

These ethical implications should not be misused by any who would generalize about all rich persons. Some attacks on the rich are green-eyed criticisms. Some rich Christians put their money in the service of the kingdom as do some widows on modest income.

Evangelistic. The word for today is incomplete without strong reference to the evangelistic inference in the parable. For one thing, the desperate may trust God. Lazarus could offer nothing, but God's grace reached out on angels' wings. The poor are good enough, worthwhile enough to receive spiritual blessings. They can become Christians. Some unintentionally take dignity away from the poor by imagining that they only need social help.

For a second thing, the pulpit must challenge false security. Some want to accept the gift of grace but not the cost of discipleship. As did the rich man, some presume on connections to a Christian family or church and make no change in life or in heart. So religion is wounded in the house of its friends by the heresy of nominal Christianity. Discipleship must become a constitutive component of evangelism. Furthermore, the call to repentance must touch the life of every person with its insistence on reorientation and change. And there are some, seemingly immune to ignition, who do not want to be convinced and so stubbornly refuse because they have seen no sign or reason to believe. Some are temporarily anesthetized by a comfortably secure life and need confrontation by a word from beyond.

Once the crucial importance of the five *living* brothers has been discovered and transference made to the presently living, the evangelistic call to decision comes forward. For those still alive, now is the moment of existence; now is the moment for decision. There is still time. It is not yet too late. The parable sounds an opening reveille. In *Man in God's World*, Thielicke put it memorably:

And these five brothers—they are you and me! *We* still have the decision to make, *we* are still living in the here and now when we should be hearing his voice and not hardening our hearts. So the theme of this parable which says so much about the beyond is my life and your life. It is as if every spotlight in the house were focused on that stage where you and I live out our lives/are still living out our lives—the place where we must decide about eternity.[37]

Postscript on the Afterlife

Now a final word about the intimations of the worlds beyond death is in order. The parable surely does not intend a literal description of the temperature of hell nor the furniture of heaven. Indeed, it does not speak of hell and heaven. The parable speaks of Hades. It does speak of a destiny to be avoided and, by implication, of one to seek. The language of the parable is apocalyptic, like the last book of the New Testament and hence is symbolic. Thus it is wooden to literalize.

Sometimes the parable is read too hurriedly. Hell or Gehenna is often assumed when, in fact, the parable uses neither word and does, in fact, name the rich man's new abode as Hades. The New Testament makes a distinction between Gehenna and Hades. Gehenna is the final abode of the wicked.[38] Hades on the other hand refers to the realm of all the dead (as Acts 2:27,31). Hades appears ten times in the New Testament. It is pictured as lying within the earth (Matt. 11:34; Luke 10:15). In Revelation 20:14, it is actually stated that ultimately Hades will be cast into the lake of fire (Gehenna), thus indicating distinction between Hades and Gehenna and the limited duration of Hades. Hades is the place of death. In Revelation, death and Hades are used in correlation (Rev. 1:18; 20:13,14).

In the LXX, Hades refers to the Jewish Sheol. In texts where the Hebrew Old Testament speaks of Sheol, the Greek texts normally have Hades. Life in Sheol was a shadowy existence. It was thought of as the realm of the dead beneath the ocean (Job 26:5), as the dark region (Job 10:21 f.) in which everyone dwelled (Ps. 89:49). The conviction grew that the land of the shades would not last forever. Isaiah saw that the oppressed righteous will arise from the dust of death while their dead overlords will remain in Sheol (26:13-19). A psalmist saw a coming destruction of the wicked and reward that awaits the righteous (73:2-24). So there were visionaries that saw somewhat beyond the traditional theology, but Sheol in the Old Testament remained basically the abode of the dead.

In the time of Jesus, the Pharisees believed that both the righteous and the ungodly are in Hades.[39] Josephus reported further that Pharisees taught that "there are rewards and punishments under the earth for those who have led lives of virtue or vice" (*Antiquities*, 18, 14). Thus the parable of Jesus fits well enough the Pharisaic expectation of rewards and punishments, though the application most likely startled.

By far the most intriguing connections lie in the intertestamental literature. Interestingly in 2 Esdras the righteous get a foretaste of the blessedness that will come full force after the resurrection, and the unrighteous get a foretaste of the punishment that awaits them at the last judgment (7:78-100).[40] The most informative text, however, is surely in Ethiopic Enoch 22! There Enoch, along with the angel Raphael, sees four hollow places beneath a mountain created for the purpose of housing all the souls of people.

Interest heightens as details of Enoch 22 relate to the parable. For example, voices can go forth to heaven and make suit (v. 5). And there is a separation. The spirits of the righteous have a separate compartment replete with a bright spring of water (v. 9). On the other hand, sinners who went scot free of judgment in life suffer in great pain (v. 10). Sinners who suffered for their sins during life suffer less in their chamber (vv. 12-13).

This apocalyptic vision illuminates the background from which some may have heard the parable. Could it be that the rich man's request that Lazarus bring water assumes the bright spring of water in the hollow place for the righteous?[41] In both the parable and in Enoch 22, blessing and punishment begin in Hades after death.

Now care and caution are important. The notions of background documents should not be read into the parable. Neither should improper deductions be drawn from the parable itself. The parable's primary purpose is not to describe the afterlife but to impact on the present world. However, the impact depends for its force on a view of the life to come. Some implications may be carefully drawn.

For one thing, it can be surmised from the parable that there is an immediate arrival in a life beyond. After all, the five brothers are alive when the rich man speaks in Hades. This comports well with the saying to the penitent thief on the cross (Luke 23:43) and such Pauline texts as Philippians 1:21-23. The bliss enjoyed by Lazarus is not dwelt upon but put succinctly that he was "in the bosom of Abraham" (Luke 16:22-23).

Actually Jewish writings speak of "the bosom of Abraham."[42] This idiomatic expression often refers to rest. It was understood as the dwelling place of the righteous. Primarily two ideas predominated, and both are present in the parable. One is intimate fellowship and the other is a banquet. It could refer to blissful fellowship enjoyed with the patriarch (as 4 Macc. 13:17). The fact that the rich man is described as spotting Abraham a long way off and Lazarus as near to

Abraham as physically possible (Luke 16:23) suggests the meaning of loving fellowship. Moreover, the privilege of reclining beside the host denoted a place of honor (John 13:23). Surely the reference then is to Abraham's table as well. Both scenes in the parable are, after all, feasting scenes. The banquet imagery evokes intimations of the great messianic banquet (Matt. 8:11). It was the feast of the blessed, and Lazarus enjoyed the place of honor.[43] So loving table fellowship symbolizes the quality of existence in the coming bliss.

Other issues are less certain but equally interesting. The primary one concerns the question whether Hades here is an intermediate state. It has already been observed that Revelation 20:14 sees Hades as a state preceding Gehenna. Furthermore, the afterlife portrayed in Enoch is explicitly delimited as an interim place until the day of judgment (22:4). A further judgment of the wicked is anticipated when they will be bound forever in an ultimate annihilation (22:7, 10). The sheer fact that the word *Hades* appears in the parable rather than Gehenna tends to favor the idea of a temporary condition, as does the fact that the condition is immediately at death. Though an intermediate state is probably presumed, it is not a purgatory. There is explicitly no going from one place to another because of the great gulf fixed (Luke 16:26).[44]

Still other questions deserving further reflection remain. Does the parable teach that memory belongs to the experience beyond death? Abraham requires the rich man to remember his and Lazarus' prior condition on earth (Luke 16:25). Is memory part of the experience of anguish?

Think further. The ball is now in the reader's court.

NOTES

1. Hans-Joachim Kraus, *Psalmen*. Vol. 15/1 of *Biblischer Kommentar Altes Testament* (Neukirchen: Neukirchener, 1961), pp. 368-369, supports Psalm 49 as a background source for the parable because of the reversal theme. Some scholars have favored Deuteronomy 24:6 *ff*. C. H. Cave. "Lazarus and the Lukan Deuteronomy," *New Testament Studies*, 15:325 (1969), argues for Isaiah 1:5 with Genesis 15 in mind and read at Shabuoth.

2. Most scholars who report this parallel refer back to H. Gressmann, *Vom Reichen*

Mann und Armen Lazarus (Berlin: Verlag der Konigl., 1918), p. 205, who did the original research. For a good summary see Thorwald Lorenzen, "A Biblical Meditation on Luke 16:19-31," *Expository Times*, 87:41 (1975). The differences between the two stories include the fact that the Egyptian story predicates the salvation of the abject, poor individual upon a life in which good deeds outweighed sins. This is in sharp contrast to the radical grace of fetching angels. Equally important is the fact that the Egyptians, father and son, visit the realm of the dead (Amnte) and return to the living while the parable rejects this solution in favor of the Word. It should be registered that not all scholars support the hypothesis of an Egyptian source. O. Glombitza, "Der reiche Mann und der arme Lazarus; Luk. XVI: 19-31," *Novum Testamentum*, 12:166-167 (1970), notes that while Jeremias, Rengstorf, and Grundmann follow Gressmann, Schlatter and Bultmann see a Jewish background.

3. So Joachim Jeremias, *The Parables of Jesus*, p. 183.

4. So Frank Beare, *The Earliest Records of Jesus* (Nashville: Abingdon Press, 1963), p. 182.

5. H. G. Lang, *The Parabolic Teaching of Scripture* (Grand Rapids, Michigan: Eerdmans, 1955), p. 261, represents this view. So also Tertullian, *de Anima*, 7; Ambrose, *Expositio Evangelii secondam Lucam*.

6. C. F. Evans, "Uncomfortable Words—V (Luke 16:31)," *Expository Times*, 81:229 (1970).

7. This has been caused by the influence of verse 31, which sounds like early missionary experience. Recently Crossan, *In Parables*, pp. 66-67, has identified the entire second half of the parable as early church reflecting on Easter faith and betraying strong ties to Luke 24. More attention to the function of direct discourse would possibly lead to reassessment.

8. Kilpatrick in a lecture at The Southern Baptist Theological Seminary in Louisville, Kentucky, during the fall of 1976. He based his notions on the LXX.

9. Jeremias, *Jerusalem in the Time of Jesus*, trans. F. H. and C. H. Cave (Philadelphia: Fortress Press, 1969), p. 92.

10. C. Montefiore, *The Synoptic Gospels*, Second Edition (London: Macmillan, 1927), 2:1003.

11. A. C. Bouquet, *Everyday Life in New Testament Times* (New York: Scribner's Sons, 1953), p. 143, entertains the possibility that the dogs were kinder. He is cautious, however, and reminds that while children had small puppies, full-grown dogs were not kept domestically. Also note that the diminutive form for dog is not utilized. Also the pattern of Lazarus begging and no aid and Dives begging and no aid would best be kept intact by seeing the reference to the licking dogs as a part of the "bad things" he experienced on earth (*ta kaka*, v. 25). Lorenzen, p. 39, points out that the fact that dogs were considered unclean placed the poor man by association outside the religious realm.

12. Rudolf Kittel, *The Religion of the People of Israel* (New York: Macmillan, 1925), p. 102.

13. T. W. Manson, "The Sayings of Jesus," in *The Mission and Message of Jesus* (New York: E. P. Dutton, 1938), pp. 588-89. Thus the model for the rich man could be a wealthy aristocrat in Jerusalem and suggests that the parable was spoken nearing or even upon entering the Holy City. I. H. Marshall, *Commentary on Luke*, "The New International Greek Testament Commentary" (Grand Rapids: Wm. Eerdmans, 1978),

p. 625, provides evidence for the avarice of Pharisees.

14. Cf. K. Grobel, ". . . Whose Name Was Neves," *New Testament Studies*, 10:381-382 (1964), who speculated that the name *Neves* in P75 represented a shortening of Ninive, which means "Nobody." Grobel related the parable very much to its Egyptian heritage. See also H. J. Cadbury, "A Proper Name for Dives," *Journal of Biblical Literature*, 81:399-402 (1962), who accepts the date for the Bodmer Papyrus of Luke as between AD 175 and 225 and reports its relative completeness (6:10-18:18, 22:4-24:53), but is cautious about any premature conclusions. See also B. Metzger, *A Textual Commentary on the Greek New Testament*, pp. 165-166, who reports the later names of Phineas and Finees as other unlikely candidates.

15. So R. Dunkerley, "Lazarus," *New Testament Studies*, 5:321-327 (1959), who argues that both the parable and the raising belong to the Perean ministry. His reconstructed *Sitz im Leben Jesu* places the parable previous to the miracle at a time when disciples wanted him to help Lazarus who was ill and to create a favorable sensation for their cause.

16. Gollwitzer, *Die Freude Gottes: Einfuhrung in das Lukas-evangelium* (Berlin: Burckhardthaus Verlag, 1952), p. 186.

17. So Israel Abrahams, *Studies in Pharisaism and the Gospels* (New York: KTAV, 1967 from 1924 edition), 2:203, citing the research of A. Geiger. J. Duncan Derrett, "Dives and Lazarus and the Preceding Sayings," *New Testament Studies*, 7:371 (1961), also connects Lazarus to Abraham's steward Eliezer. Presumably Eliezer was the one sent to find a wife for Isaac (Gen. 24:2 *ff.*), which in turn could possibly relate to the potential messenger role presumed in the dialogue of the parable. H. H. Guthrie, "Eliezer," *IDB*, E-J: 87-88 (1962), indicates that Eliezer also means "my God is my help."

18. So Glombitza, p. 178. E. Bammel, "*ptochos*," *TDNT*, 6:906 (1968), who thinks the parable is intrinsically pre-New Testement, takes the position that the issue is poor and rich as such. All rich men are alienated from the sphere of God. There is felicity because Lazarus is a poor person. This view flounders on verse 31.

19. As J. Creed, *The Gospel According to St. Luke* (London: Macmillan, 1930), p. 209.

20. B. T. D. Smith, *The Parables of the Synoptic Gospels* (Cambridge: University Press, 1937), p. 137.

21. So J. Jeremias, "*lithos*," *TDNT*, 4:271 (1967). The further connection to Luke 3:8-11 is uncanny.

22. Jeremias, *The Parables*, p. 184. He documents the fact that *epithumein* with the infinitive in Luke always points to an unfulfilled desire.

23. Derrett, p. 373.

24. Eugene Wehrli, "Luke 16:19-31," *Interpretation*, 31:279 (1977).

25. The only sign Jesus proffered was the sign of Jonah. See K. Rengstorf, "*sēmeion*," *TDNT*, 7:233 (1971); R. A. Edwards, *The Sign of Jonah*, No. 18 of "Studies in Biblical Theology," Second Series (Naperville: Alec R. Allenson, 1970) provides a careful redaction criticism of the gospel traditions.

26. C. W. F. Smith, *The Jesus of the Parables*, Revised Edition, (Philadelphia: Pilgrim Press, 1975), p. 167.

27. Cf. N. Rimmer, "Parable of Dives and Lazarus," *Expository Times*, 66:216 (1955), who argues that the only point of the parable is the refusal to give a sign. He sees the parable as a harmonious whole "when we regard verses 19-28 as the 'scaffolding' on

which the one point of the Parable, contained in verses 29-31, is built." He is right in seizing upon the importance of the refusal but may underestimate the tendency of Jesus to go beyond defense. In the refusal itself, there is the implicit possibility of hearing the word.

28. See Glombitza, pp. 173-175, 179. The fact that Lazarus, a Jew, was saved makes it difficult to identify Israel in any very broad sense with the rich man.

29. Jeremias, *The Parables*, p. 186. P. Trudinger, "A 'Lazarus Motif' in Primitive Christian Preaching," *Andover Newton Quarterly*, 7:29 (1966), makes the novel suggestion from a redactional vantage that Luke 16:31 was intended to correct the earliest *kerygma*, that centered upon the resurrection, in favor of a focus upon the cross. This is unlikely from the standpoint of Lukan theology in which there is precious little *theologia crucis*. Also the repeated reference to Moses and the prophets is decidedly early. It is doubtful that resurrection was primary in the original parable. Some mss. have the simpler idea of going from the dead.

30. So Richard Rohrbaugh, *The Biblical Interpreter: An Agrarian Bible in an Industrial Age* (Philadelphia: Fortress, 1978), pp. 79 ff.

31. Lorenzen, p. 42.

32. Buttrick, *The Parables of Jesus*, p. 143.

33. Rohrbaugh, pp. 79-85. I would register reservations about his strictures of Buttrick and would fault him for ignoring Weatherhead's remarks, especially on the rich fool in *In Quest of a Kingdom*, pp. 175-177. In a sense, the preacher does bear more responsibility even than the academic interpreter of texts because the preacher must allow the text to become word of God in a new setting of needs.

34. Helmut Gollwitzer, *The Rich Christians and Poor Lazarus*, trans. David Cairns (Edinburgh: St. Andrews Press, 1970), p. 1. See also his remarks on "Repentance: Solidarity in Colonial Guilt" (pp. 6-10) and "The Inadequacy of Traditional Charity" (pp. 11-17).

35. *Seeds*, Gary Gunderson and Andy Loving coeditors, is committed to enabling Christians to respond to the poor both with charity and justice. Its editorial address is c/o Oakhurst Baptist Church, 222 East Lake Dr., Decatur, Georgia 30030.

36. James Denney, *The Way Everlasting* (1911), pp. 173 f. Quoted by J. Baillie, *A Diary of Readings* (Nashville: Abingdon, 1955), p. 293.

37. Thielicke, *Man in God's World*, trans. John Doberstein (New York: Harper, 1963), pp. 64-65.

38. See T. H. Gaster, "Gehenna," *IDB*, E-J: 361-362 (1962); who points out that Gehenna is portrayed as a punitive conflagration (Deut. 32:22; Isa. 33:14), a blazing hell (Dan. 7:10; Enoch 18:11-16; 27:1-3; 90:26; 2 Esd. 7:36; IQS 3.4, 13; and IQH 3.29).

39. See Jeremias, "Hades," *TDNT*, 1:146-149 (1964), for a good treatment of the views during the time of Jesus both of Pharisees and of Josephus. He also provides a neat scheme of the development in viewpoint after the exile. He seems to press the evidence regarding the personal view of Josephus inasmuch as the primary text is a hortatory warning against suicide.

40. Cited by H. Bietenhard, "Hades," *Dictionary of New Testament Theology*, 2:207 (1976). See also G. W. E. Nickelsburg, "Future Life in Intertestamental Literature," *IDB*, S: 348-351 (1976). He points out Enoch 92-105 where in the context of oppression of the

poor by the rich the seer writes of reward for the righteous and punishment for sinners who have prospered.

41. So A. O. Standen, "The Parable of Dives and Lazarus, and Enoch 22," *Expository Times*, 33:523 (1921-22).

42. See *Test. of Abraham*, 20. See also Strack-Billerbeck, 2:226.

43. See R. Meyer, "*kolpos*," *TDNT*, 3:826 (1965) who reports the guess that the parable may suggest a sponsorship rite upon entrance.

44. E. F. Bishop, "A Yawning Chasm," *Evangelical Quarterly*, 45:3-5 (1973), points out that *chasma* denotes something like *wadi* and refers metaphorically to a great ravine. He sees it implying depth more than width. As a matter of possible importance, it should also be recorded that Ecclesiasticus 41:4 may preclude any correction of life in Hades.

Part III

The Grace and Repentance of the Kingdom

10

Luke 15

Parables of the Lost Sheep, the Lost Coin, and the Compassionate Father and Angry Brother

The most famous parable chapter depicts in gripping fashion incidents of a lost sheep, a lost coin, and a lost boy. Each story is deeply emotional in a heartwarming fashion, so much so that E. Earle Ellis writes of the seeking shepherd, the weeping woman, and the waiting father.[1] These vivid images are not at bottom a deluge of words and a drizzle of thought but a powerful portrayal of a "Hound of Heaven" sort of God and a mini-portrait of the ministry of Jesus. The modern Christian invariably feels that through Luke 15 Jesus proclaimed the gospel, especially the good news about his heavenly Father. Jesus' own love for sinners shines through unmistakably in a winsome fashion, indeed. Even familiarity fails to dull the chapter's appeal, and close study enhances it.

Luke 15 belongs to that segment of the Lukan travel narrative that focuses upon "the gospel of the Messiah" (14:1 to 17:10). This significant section displays a gospel concerned for the despised (14:1-24: the lame, the blind, the poor) and the lost (15:1-32). Furthermore, this gospel of the Messiah is shot through with the burning note of crisis (16:1 to 17:10). Luke 15 then is nestled within the midst of an extended block of teaching material and has a very close correlation to the theme of Luke: "The Son of Man came to seek and to save the lost" (19:10).[2]

168

Setting and Structure

Table Fellowship (*15:1-2*). The setting is classic. The tax collectors and sinners were attracted to the side of Jesus, provoking the criticism of certain fastidious Pharisees. One of the most startling dimensions of the historical ministry of Jesus was this association with sinners (as Mark 2:15-17).[3] The term "sinner," however, did not simply refer to those immoral but also to those in a dishonorable vocation (donkey drivers, tanners, shepherds, peddlers). A sinner was one who could not or would not follow the scruples of the Pharisees. Some sinners chose a life of unrighteousness, but others were so tagged because their very vocations made it impossible to maintain ritual purity and their livelihood at the same time. These people of the land were called the *Am-ha-ares*. Furthermore, a sinner could be simply a Gentile who by definition was thought to be immoral (as Gal. 2:15).[4] So the word *sinner* did not merely mean "immoral" but might include social outcasts like tax collectors.

Table fellowship was the eye of the storm. When Jesus welcomed, perhaps hosted, sinners through the fellowship of a meal, the Pharisees' criticism rose to the level of a formal complaint: "This one *receives* sinners and eats with them" (Luke 15:2b). In fairness, their religious sensitivities were offended. They held a lofty view of the table as an altar and a meal as something that should not degenerate into mere eating and drinking.[5] Some of the Pharisees had organized themselves into religious fellowships (called *havurah*) and brought the rules of ritual purity expected in the Temple into their common meals. They compared themselves to Temple priests at the altar when they ate together only with those who kept the law.[6] Casual banqueting with sinners and possibly eating non-kosher food would have been genuinely and emotionally objectionable, and the fact that Jesus had accepted the disciplined fellowship of a Pharisaic meal (Luke 14) may have exacerbated the situation in their eyes.

Though the Pharisees interpreted the meals with sinners negatively, Jesus instigated these festive fellowships for a positive purpose. These meaningful meals with outcasts were themselves parabolic, "prophetic signs, more significant than words, silent proclamations that the Messianic Age is here, the Age of forgiveness."[7] After all, the Old Testament anticipated a future shepherd who would feed the sheep of God (Ezek. 34:23-24; Mic. 5:2-4) and spoke of a great messianic banquet (Isa. 25:6-12; 49:8-13). Jesus would have agreed with the Pharisees that table fellowship is, indeed, socially binding and has religious meaning, but more and other than they imagined. The very essence of Jesus' ministry and mission can be identified in his determined association with sinners from his baptism to his crucifixion between thieves. He opened up a new chapter in religious history with his attitude toward sinners, but his eating with sinners added up to more than a social misdemeanor to the Pharisees. It may have cost Jesus his life. While the immediate precipitant of his crucifixion occurred when he cleansed the Temple, the issue that put electricity in the air and made his violent death inevitable was his fellowship with sinners. Each of the three parables of Luke 15 places Jesus' positive interpretation on the meals and contrasts heaven's response and that of the Pharisees to the table fellowship.

Structure and Stress. The entire chapter functions as an artistic unity that portrays three parabolic responses to criticism. If one is to see the chapter whole, it is particularly necessary to connect the opening two verses (15:1-2) and the closing eight verses. The episode concerning the elder son (15:25-32) is then seen rightly as a rejoinder to the criticism of the Pharisees and scribes and as an invitation to join the festivity of the kingdom.

A striking pattern of response can be detected among all three parables despite their individuality. One thrice-repeated note is the *sharing* of joy found in every parable (15:6,9,23). Another is the circumstance of lost and found (15:6,9,24,32). Still another remarkable theme unifying the chapter stressed by the evangelist is the repenting of the sinner (15:7,10,17-21). Above all then, the reader senses "the invitation to *share in joy* over the conversion of sinners"[8] pulsing all the way through. The spirit of the joy and invitation of the returned shepherds and the woman with her recovered coin and the father spontaneously ordering a celebration is downright contagious. The Lukan Christ invites every reader to "rejoice with me."

The three parables do fall into two distinct parts however. The chapter is like a *diptych,* a pair of paintings on two hinged panels.[9] The first panel contains the companion parables of a lost sheep and a lost coin. These first two parables are introduced by an interlocking, rhetorical question ("what man among you," v. 4),[10] are general situation, and reflect considerable verbal parallel (cf. vv. 6-7,9-10). In each, the lost object is sought. The second panel contains specific situation ("a certain man," v. 11) and focuses upon receiving the sinner rather than searching for the sinner.

Recovering the Lost (15:3-10)

Recovering the Lost Sheep (15:3-7). Jesus invited listening and involved hearers when he engaged the immediate audience in his upcoming comparison with a rhetorical question: "What man of you having a hundred sheep . . ." (v. 4). He posed the dilemma of the owner of a flock of a hundred having one sheep who has strayed, "fallen behind during a night journey" or "lost on pathless regions while out at pasture."[11] Would he not leave the ninety-nine in the wilderness and seek the lost one until he found it?[12] Many students here insist that the shepherd left the flock safely in a sheepfold[13] while others are adamant that the drama is dissipated unless the picture of the ninety-nine left alone is retained,[14] but probably other shepherds cared for the flock. A famous and fascinating first-person account of the accidental finding of the Dead Sea Scrolls by Muhammed ahd-Dhib in 1947 provides a likely parallel.

> . . . I was tending a flock of fifty-five head in the wilderness, with two shepherds besides myself. Each one had his own flock. The three of us were sleeping in the wilderness; and in accordance with custom each one of us would count his flock of an evening. By chance I had not counted my flock for a couple of days. It was on the third day at nearly 11 o'clock that I counted my flock, and found one goat lost. I came to my companions and said to them: "I want to leave my flock with you, and I want to go search for the lost goat." I left them and went to look for the goat. I was forced to go down wadis; and I got very far from the two shepherds. . . .[15]

This modern experience of an Arab shepherd evokes something of the actual situation of the parable.

The shepherd left the flock in any instance and kept on searching until he found the one lost sheep. Since a straying sheep would often lie down helpless and refuse to stand up, it was necessary for the overjoyed shepherd to lift him to his strong shoulders for the return.[16] He called together his circle of friends for them to share his joy, possibly welcoming to a feast. Here the direct discourse is used: "Rejoice with me because I have found my lost sheep" (v. 6c), calling special attention to the invitation to rejoice.

The boundless joy in heaven at the bringing back of the lost is revealed as the application of the parable (v. 7). As often in the Old Testament and in Luke, salvation and joy are combined. It is a redemptive or soteriological joy.[17] So far so good, but several bumps in the road stand in the way of further understanding. Does Jesus teach that some do not need to repent? Does the parable itself illustrate repentance anyway? Neither question is answered easily and glib interpretations are unsatisfying.

Certainly the story depicts the lost sheep as altogether passive, but just possibly repentance is included in the simple thought of *return* and restoration. Repentance then is not merely human agency but is itself aided by divine involvement.[18] Certainly Luke-Acts is a constant call to repentance, and repentance is vividly portrayed in the third parable of Luke 15 (vv. 17-21).[19]

The first question, whether Jesus excepted some from repentance appears answerable as a resounding no (as Luke 13:3). The summation of his proclamation expects universal repentance (Mark 1:15), the parable of the Pharisee and the Publican leaves the self-righteous Pharisee unjustified (Luke 18:9-14), the parable of the Two Sons suggests that apparent obedience can be actual disobedience (Mt. 21:28-32), and numerous sayings expose self-righteousness and pride (Matt. 6:1 *ff*; 23:5 *ff*). The call to repentance is "addressed to all without distinction and presented with unmitigated severity," Behm explains, "in order to indicate the only way of salvation there is."[20] When Jesus referred to those not needing a physician (Mark 2:17) he spoke with irony using the term *righteous* at face value as used in rabbinic parlance,—righteous from a legal standpoint. Probably the same kind of subtle thrust, an *ad hominem* argument, is present then in Luke 15:7. The shape of repentance needed by those such as the Pharisees was perhaps not so much moral reformation as the swallowing of pride, entering the kingdom, loosening up enough to rejoice, and accepting the grace of the God of the ungodly.

The key to further understanding of the parable is definitely Ezekiel 34. Luke 15 and Ezekiel 34 play similar roles in their respective testaments. Recall that the Old Testament speaks often of God or Yahweh as the Shepherd of Israel (Gen. 49:24; Ps. 23:1) who goes before the flock (Ps. 68:7; Jer. 50:19) and of Israel as needing a shepherd (1 Kings 22:17; Num. 27:17). Ezekiel 34:1-10 attacks bad shepherds who only care for themselves and fail in responsibility to the lost and injured. The nature of God is one who cares for his sheep and searches for them (34:11-12). James Mays sums up the essence, "Through it the Lord appears as the God who is moved by the harassed and helpless."[21] Ezekiel 34 is even messianic and eschatological as it anticipates David becoming the shepherd who will care for Israel (vv. 23-25).

In this light, it appears that the Pharisees had forgotten their reason for being, had ceased to relate their role to the nature and purpose of God, and could even accost as irreligious someone who cared for the lost. There also lurks the strong possibility that Ezekiel 34 influenced Jesus as one messianic model, that he saw himself as Shepherd of Israel and saw his ministry to sinners as an eschatological fulfillment. Certainly the rest of the New Testament named him Good Shepherd (John 10), Great Shepherd (Heb. 13:20), Chief Shepherd (1 Pet. 5:4), and Shepherd of souls (1 Pet. 2:25). And very early Christian art in the catacombs from the third century portrays Jesus as a radiantly youthful figure with a sheep on his shoulders.[22]

A gospel song captures the appeal of the parable:

> None of the ransomed ever knew
> How deep were the waters crossed;
> Nor how dark was the night that the Lord passed thro'
> Ere He found His sheep that was lost.

Recovering the Lost Coin (Luke 15:8-10). A companion parable addressed a typical domestic experience and involved a feminine experience to complement the masculine experience of the first one. Man and woman combinations appear throughout the Gospel of Luke, reminding the readers of Jesus' inclusion of women and Luke's special sensitivities. Possibly Jesus jarred the critical hearers sociologically both with his illustration of a shepherd and of a woman! Shepherds for example, were a proscribed trade suffering under a social stigma established by Pharisaic opinion and were deprived of civil rights.[23] The shepherding function which Pharisees loathed, Jesus lionized as a positive model! Woman disdained as inferior, Jesus depicted as admirable.

The domestic scene envisioned is one of a windowless dwelling with a low door and a packed earth floor. If a woman lost one of her ten Greek silver coins, Jesus asked, would she not light a flickering earthenware lamp and sweep the floor with a palm twig? The hearers of the parable would have nodded easily perhaps because they know how sentimentally special that drachma was. The lost coin may have fallen from her necklace or veil and may have even belonged to her dowry.[24] She keeps on looking until she finds it and then invites her woman friends and neighbors to share her jubilation. "Finding creates boundless joy" and the joy is not completely realized until it is shared with others.[25] Here is spontaneous exhilaration. The direct discourse (v. 9) invited others to join the joy caused by finding a valued lost coin and functioned as a veiled invitation to Pharisees with ears to hear.

Then Jesus spoke for God because "He knows God well enough to know what will make him happy."[26] There will be joy in the very court of heaven at the recovery of a single sinner. Recovery of the lost has cosmic significance. It is important to note that both verses 7 and 10 represent kingdom of God *valuations* because they claim to speak of what heaven values and also because of their testimony to the value of one lost sinner. These simple sayings have helped to humanize societies and to evangelize the world. The ratios of ninety-nine to one and ten to one are effective devices that convey that one lost sheep or one coin matters. So Jesus put a new perspective on his activities. In fairness to his critics, they had not seen the issue in this light. Jesus interpreted his befriending of sinners in such a manner as *to aid the critics* who had only thought of immoral associations. In the process, he involved his critics personally.

These two parables indirectly reveal "the fetching of sinners home"[27] as Jesus' self-understanding of his mission. Do they not also express the intense joy Jesus personally experienced in seeking and finding the lost? Jesus clarified for his critics and disciples the nature of his mission through these parables, explaining his fellowship with sinners more than merely defending, but contrasting heaven's valuation with those of his critics. Jesus also spoke not only of heaven's valuation of every lost sinner but also metaphorically of God as housekeeper and shepherd and so used a feminine picture of God along the way. These parables exemplify how Jesus transformed an intimidating challenge to his very integrity into a teachable moment to encourage sinners, to interpret his actions theologically for Pharisees, and in the process maintain the respect of his disciples.[28]

Receiving the Lost (15:11-32)

The paragon of the parables strikes the depths of common existence with its tale of a young man who left home and the family dynamics that developed in response to his return. This longest and best known of the parables Geraint V. Jones characterized as "infused with a transforming vision."[29] Not only has this great short story been titled traditionally "The Prodigal Son" but Jeremias has refered to it as the parable of the Father's love.[30] Helmut Thielicke captivated multitudes with his compelling picture of the waiting Father: "He will wait for him and never stop watching for him."[31] All these portraits are telling, but exegetically it is better to name it the parable of the Compassionate Father and the Angry Brother because it compares two ways of receiving the lost.

The Key Role of Direct Discourse. No less than twenty-eight lines or parts of lines out of the parable's forty-seven contain direct discourse. The degree to which conversation dominates this specific situation narrative is remarkable. For example, the first movement (15:11-24) is punctuated by three speeches from the younger son, including a request; a decisive, interior monologue; and a confession. The only person to speak in both movements is the father, who speaks with authority at the climax of each.[32] The servants obey him and accept his interpretation of the prodigal's return. The only dialogue is the exchange between the father and the older son.

The speeches should be marked in one's text and may be set out as follows:

Part 1 (15:11-24)
    Request of the Younger Son (v. 12*b*)
    Interior Monologue Within the Younger Son (vv. 17*b*-19)
    Confession of the Younger Son (v. 21*b*)
    Directive of the Father (vv. 22*b*-24)
Part 2 (15:25-32)
    Explanation of the Servant (v. 27*b*)
    Outburst of the Older Son (vv. 29*b*-30)
    Explanation of the Father (vv. 31*b*-32)

These speeches carry most of the narrative freight for the parable and fairly invite interpretation.

Part 1 (15:11-24). A man of some means[33] had two sons, the younger of whom requested his part of the inheritance. The younger son was probably a single, older teenager eager to emigrate. Palestine was a poor country visited by famine and foreign troops, and many young Jewish men who wanted to get on in the world had a better chance in the trading cities beyond Palestine where millions of Jews lived in Diaspora. As a junior son he could expect a far more modest portion than the senior son.[34] The fact that he was the second son absolutely must not be relegated to insignificance. The fact that the first son remained is all too understandable. Interpreters are divided on the question whether the young man sinned in his request. Some urge that his request really amounted to a desire for his father to die while others set it in the cultural context of normal emigration.[35] At the very least, his leave-taking reads like careless haste (v. 13*a*).

The certain sin he committed was squandering his inheritance in loose living. It amounted to more than wasting money. It was quite serious for a Jewish male to waste his inheritance. He apparently lived extravagantly until his resources were depleted. The characterization of his new life-style as "reckless living" refers minimally to his being carefree and a spendthrift[36] but may very well imply sexual immorality (Titus 1:6), drunkenness (Eph. 5:18), and generally reckless dissipation (1 Pet. 4:4). Just at the point in his personal story when he found himself broke, as the narrative would have it, a famine struck. Mark well the young man's circumstances—a Jewish alien penniless in a strange land. Survival was at stake, food at a premium in a famine, and jobs for foreigners not plentiful in hard times.

In desperation, the young man became a pig herder, the very last job a Jew would accept. To herd swine, after all, meant contact with unclean animals (Lev. 11:7). He had become a Gentile. The rabbis taught that "none may rear swine anywhere" (*Baba Kamma* 7:7). A Jewish curse ran, "Cursed be the man who keeps swine" (*Baba Kamma* 82*b*). He was so famished he was eager to eat carobs, the swine fodder. These pods were probably the wild carobs, which were black, bitter berries growing on low shrubs and containing very little nutritional value.[37]

The misery of unrelenting hunger was definitely in the picture, and no one showed compassion upon this Jewish alien. No one treated him like family. His circumstances must be measured, not spiritual- ized. He was lonely, alienated from his heritage and the culture of the far country, estranged from his environment. Degraded psycholog- ically by his job and deprived of dignity by hunger, hard times were crushing him. However, there was a Jewish proverb that said, "When the Israelites stand in need of carob-beans, then they return to God."[38] Stomach pains should not be underestimated! It dawned on him that at home even servants enjoyed an abundance of bread.

The beautiful aspect of the story is that the young man did come to himself. His pain was creative. A moment of truth arrived. The penny dropped. Dan Via calls the awakening experience a great recog- nition scene,[39] and William Barclay described it as the most compli- mentary thing ever said about sinning mankind.[40] It was a *great awakening*, a penetrating recognition and resolution that often comes in direst circumstances. Pride took a beating, truth had an inning. The text announces that "he came to his senses" (TEV, NEB), which Jere- mias has shown to be an expression of repentance in Hebrew and Aramaic.[41]

In a very revealing interior soliloquy, the young man talked to himself without shame and with realism. He saw what his own choices had done and took responsibility for his sin against God (personal im- morality?) and against his father (squandering inheritance?). He re- solved to make a clean breast of it and return to the father's house as a hired servant.

Equally winsome stands the graphic picture of the waiting father, glimpsing his lost boy while he was still a long way off. His spon- taneous response was compassion (v. 20). It was undignified for an old man to break stride and run, but this father discarded dignity like a mother did in the story of Tobit.[42] He ran all the way to his son. Before the first word of explanation, he flung his arms around his boy's neck and kissed him. In the Old Testament, members of a family commonly kissed one another, including a man kissing his son (2 Sam. 14:33); and an embrace was a classic expression of reunion (Gen. 29:11,13; 33:4; 45:14).[43] It must have been an overwhelming experi- ence of forgiveness and affection between two men, captured unfor- gettably in stone by the sculptor Rodin.

Then the father issued sweeping directives to the servants for a proper reception. They put the best robe about him, the sign of the honored guest; they placed a signet ring on his hand, the bestowal of authority (Gen. 41:42; Esther 8:2: 1 Macc. 6:15);[44] they put shoes on his feet, a luxury worn by free men; and they killed the fatted calf, a sign of extravagant hospitality in the Old Testament (Gen. 18:1-21).[45] So the father "set jubilation afoot through his household" as they began to make merry with a feast. After famine came a feast. The father more than met his son's hunger and put aside his request to be a servant and restored him to sonship.[46] I suspect that the essence of sonship gets established by artful contrast to servanthood. It is sometimes said that this shower of gifts really belonged to the elder brother, but even if the father had made a disposition of the farm to the elder son, the *usufrucht* or produce legally belonged to the father for life.[47]

Part 2 (15:25-32). The euphoric feelings evoked by the first part are dispelled by the second. Indeed, some have felt that the elder brother episode is a literary blemish or later addition, but proper exegesis in fact can demonstrate organic wholeness.[48] The narrative places the industrious first son coming in from work in the fields. The dance of the men must already have begun so that the rejoicing and the din could be heard outside. He inquired of a servant the reason for the party, and he is informed that his long-lost brother has returned, and they have killed the fatted calf in his honor.

The elder brother bristled and protested the party by refusing to join it (v. 28a). His indignant anger took the shape of stiff protest. Strikingly, the father went out to the elder brother as he had gone out to the younger, twice outside the house in a single day to express fatherly love. The father loved both sons and personally invited his first son to come to the party. The fatted calf killed for the younger son symbolized favoritism to the older son and activated his envy and sibling rivalry. In a revealing outburst, he verbalized his anger at the apparent unfairness. A life of virtue has been left without reward. A life of dissipation has been celebrated with a feast. The real point, the thing that really upset his notion of things, was that they were feasting in honor of a sinner. He preferred to eat with his own circle of friends (v. 29a).

The father affirmed him but invited him to join the joy caused by a lost boy found. The father's positive explanation climaxes the second part as his parallel speech did the first part. But the elder brother is left glaring at the festivities, enjoying his own whipped-up despair.

The Point of Comparison. While it is sometimes suggested that the parable has two parts with different meanings, its point appears when the interpreter searches for the internal juxtaposition within the parable. The key to interpretation is the discovery of the intentional contrast between the father's response of compassion (v. 20) and the elder brother's response of indignant anger (v. 28).[49] The parable has to do with two responses to a prodigal's return or two ways of receiving sinners. Furthermore, the father's attitude of compassion is displayed both in his directive to his servants (vv. 22b-30) and in his explanation to his first son (vv. 31b-32). The angry speech of the elder brother (vv. 29b-30) fairly invites comparison with its sour self-centeredness in contrast to the father's contagious joy. Note specifically that the father "owned" his sinful son (v. 24) and that the servant (v. 27) and the father (v. 32) identified the returning son as the elder brother's brother, but the elder brother disowned him and identified him as the father's son (v. 30). In terms of body language, the father ran to his son even before he arrived and embraced him emotionally while the elder brother refused to enter at all and stood stiffly apart, smoldering with anger.

This interpretation fits the historical situation hinted at in Luke 15:1-2.[50] Jesus took pleasure in the tax collectors and sinners and feasted with them. The scribes and Pharisees criticized Jesus for feasting with sinners. The parable *explains* the ministry of Jesus to sinners and *exposes* the legalistic hardness of his critics, but more it is proclamation to his entire audience. Perhaps the segment on the repentance of the sinner was particularly illuminating to the Pharisees who may have had no awareness that any of these sinners at Jesus' table had repented. Perhaps, as Jesus put a new face on the shared meals, the Pharisees began to see the despised sinners in a more winsome light.

The sinners in the audience may have felt drawn to Jesus when he reflected in such a highly sympathetic fashion the plight of sinners in bondage and the glory and possibility of change. To some not yet decided, it may have been a proclamation of grace: "Come home, come home, You who are weary, come home" (as Jer. 3:7,12,14,22).

Jesus also showed great sensitivity putting himself into the Pharisees' sandals. He understood how they felt about his eating with sinners. They felt like the elder brother who stood aghast outside a feast. Their tempers flared at the seeming impropriety of the meals with sinners. The speech Jesus put in the elder brother's mouth (vv. 29b-30) reveals empathic capacities. The father in the parable loved both his sons, and Jesus loved Pharisees as well as sinners. He invited them to join the festive meal, accept the sinner, and a God of extravagant grace. He sought to awaken them by showing them themselves. He offered them a better existence than they had known. He offered greater happiness.

Jesus left unsettled whether the elder brother swallowed his pride and came in on dancing feet. Through the parable, he invited Pharisees to enter the kingdom. As Schrenk has put it, "He shows both groups the Father who opens his doors to the guilty and seeks to overcome legalistic hardness."[51] Jesus hoped that his opponents would "abandon their resistance to the gospel." The parable called for decision.

So the parable does speak of the Heavenly Father's love in a compelling fashion (as Jer. 3; 31:20; Isa. 63:7). The parable functions as a kind of metaphor of God's love.[52] It declares that the way to the heart of God the Father is open even to the greatest sinner.[53] However, it is not just the Father's love but specifically the Father's compassion for a returning sinner. Well might the disciples pray the "Our Father" to such a gracious, compassionate God! By using the parable as a defense of his own ministry, it is apparent that Jesus believed that he was doing the very work of God. He identified his own attitude and ministry to sinners with that of the Father's. So some indirect expression of the purpose or self-understanding of Jesus breaks through. His ministry enacted and conveyed the Father's will.

The "being with" of a fellowship meal is prominent in the context and parable. The elder brother preferred a banquet with his own circle rather than a party given by his father for his brother. Furthermore, he thought he had his brother's number, knew who he was altogether when he associated him with the sorority of shame (v. 20). He was harshly critical of anyone who enjoyed fellowship with sinners. Yet meals make fellowship and the New Testament views a person as decisively determined by his being with others.[54]

The Portrait of Repentance. The great parables of God's grace and love are also calls to repentance. In this parable, the point of comparison falls upon two responses to a returning sinner, and so the parable portrays a moving experience of actual repentance of one kind and calls for another. The nature of repentance appears in several stages. First, repentance is *a great awakening* (v. 17). The prodigal's circumstances were crowding him. He was battling with what his sins had done to him. He was aroused by a sudden awareness that his father's servants were better off. His crisis brought an acute recognition of reality. The description of him, that he came to his senses, is a probing depiction of the actual character of repentance.[55] His motives were surely mixed, including the survival instinct.

Second, repentance is a *returning to the Father* (v. 18a). The younger son resolved to arise, leave the far country behind, and move toward the father's house. In fact, the father is the one who makes repentance appealing. Joachim Jeremias puts it poetically, "Repentance means learning to say *Abba* again, putting one's whole trust in the heavenly Father, returning to the Father's house and the Father's arms."[56] Among the prophets repentance often meant "to go back again" or to return.[57]

Third, repentance is *a confessing of sin* (vv. 18b-19, 21). The son took responsibility for his actions and his guilt when he confessed, "Father, I have sinned against heaven and against you." The prodigal had experienced, furthermore, a loss of the sense of worthiness because of his sin, his hunger, and his pig-herding. He felt worthless until his father revealed his enormous worthwhileness. In the act of returning and confessing, he threw himself upon his father's mercy much as the praying publican (Luke 18:13). The understanding of the nature of sin is that sin is simultaneously vertical and horizontal, as Exodus 10:16.

It should be noted in passing the good such repentance did. A self-destructive life-style was reversed. Alienation was overcome by the father's joy. Self-respect was regained. A cleansing by the catharsis of confession took place. The parable is, indeed, good news.

Perhaps there is also a call to repentance[58] and a further clue to the nature of repentance within that invitation. It has already been pointed out that the father invited the elder brother personally but that he stiffened into self-pity and self-righteousness. Furthermore, the narrative is highly significant in its description of the older as angry and refusing to enter. This is one of the refusal parables and like the parable of the Marriage Feast (Matt. 22:3) has to do with refusal to enter a very special party. There is conflict between petty self-will and the father's will. The father did not take no for an answer but reassured his first son and invited him again. The senior son's initial reaction is altogether natural and understandable, but the father wanted him to get beyond it, to swallow his pride, and to banish his envy. The explicit nature of the repentance the father required takes the shape of joining the joy of the kingdom and discovering a joyful existence. Repentance then is also *entering the joy of the kingdom.*

The Relevance of the Parable. It remains to think about the application of this extraordinary parable of grace. Assuredly, it displays the radical nature of grace. The kingdom community appears as quite exclusive. It is "for sinners only." The God it reveals is incredibly better than expectation. "Like the Father of the Prodigal Son," Dorothy Sayers explains, "God can see repentance coming a great way off and is there to meet it."[59] The parable shows not only the kind of repentance the Father responds to but also the way the Father responds to repentance! As shocking as grace appears to elder brothers and sisters, it is the very character of God and the only basis of divine acceptance.

Grace is the most radical and revolutionary idea known, and it becomes a word of judgment upon any censorious attitude or cynicism about the repentant. Indeed, the motives of the prodigal were not perfectly altruistic, but the father welcomed him lovingly. James Price is quite right that the parable becomes a call to the church to welcome repentant sinners "without reserve as brothers and sisters and so gladden their homecoming."[60] After all, the church is in its very essence a community of grace called into being by the love of Christ. It is a new kind of community.

The revelation of God coming through the parable can overcome the modern feeling of cosmic lostness. Many ordinary folk feel they are unimportant and do not matter. Many are hypnotized by an overwhelming feeling of personal insignificance in the light of the vastness of the universe. Many can identify with the prodigal's estrangement. He was estranged from his past, from his old world at home, and his newfound world as well. He was estranged from his environment, from himself, from society, and from God.[61] The parable proclaims, however, that humanity is not alone in the dark forest of life. Rather, behind the immensities of space and the disappointments of human experience reigns One who cares. Jesus shared his faith through the parable that "this is my father's world." The parable rejects Camus's notion of the benign indifference of the universe.

The parable discloses how sensitively God loves, especially when we need it most. Of course, "God loves each one of us as if there were only one of us to love" (Augustine), but God's love reaches out especially to a hurting, lost, confused daughter or son. Bishop Roy Nichols tells about a young woman who went to see a psychiatrist. His story becomes a kind of modern parable. The doctor determined early in the interview that she was a wife and mother of three children. As a critical start he asked, "Which of your three children do you love the most?"

Immediately she responded, "I love all three of my children the same."

He waited a moment. The answer seemed to come too quickly. He probed further: "Come now, you love all three children the same?"

"Yes, that's right," she answered, "I love all of them the same."

Assertively he reacted, "Come off it now! It is psychologically impossible for anyone to regard any three human beings exactly the same. If you're not willing to level with me, we'll have to terminate this session."

The young woman broke up and cried. "All right, I do not love all three of my children the same," she admitted. "When one of my three children is sick, I love that child more. When one of my three children is confused, I love that child more. When one of my children is in pain, or lost, I love that child more. And when one of my children is bad—I don't mean naughty, I mean really bad—I love that child more." Then she concluded, "But except for those exceptions I do love all three of my children about the same."[62] The Father of the Lord Jesus Christ loves all, but especially when there is hurt or sin.

The parable also calls the church to evangelism in the light of what C. H. Dodd called Jesus' "unprecedented concern for the 'lost.' "[63] The church is invited to preach the love of God for sinners and to extend active concern and missionary effort toward the growing numbers of non-Christians in the world. Some Christians who were born on the right side of the spiritual tracks imagine themselves advanced when freed psychologically from any concern for the lost. The liberal spirit rather may be seen in the compassionate father.

This evangelistic mission should call both kinds of sinners, reputable sinners and disreputable. A. M. Hunter says that "if the younger son was lost in the 'far country,' the elder was equally lost behind a barricade of self-righteousness."[64] It seems, does it not, that some sins are respectable, like personal envy and stuffy self-righteousness and unbrotherliness. Other sins appear disreputable, like theft, murder, adultery, and careless waste. Some are warmhearted sins and others are coldhearted sins. Jesus called both the elder son and the younger son, and Christians must call both kinds of sinners in the name and power of Jesus Christ.

The fifteenth chapter of Luke reads like Word of God with its portraits of a lost sheep, a lost coin, and a lost boy and with its correlated pictures of God as a seeking shepherd, a searching woman, and a compassionate father. A lasting impression of a gospel for the lost lingers and remains.

NOTES

1. E. Earle Ellis, *The Gospel of Luke*, "The Century Bible" (London: Nelson, 1966), pp. 196-97. This view strictly held depends upon the possibly close connection to Jeremiah 31:10-20 that describes God as a shepherd and Rachel weeping for her children and Ephraim returning to God. The theory has been advanced by H. B. Kossen, "Quelques remarques sur l' ordre des paraboles dans Luc XV et sur la structure de Matthieu XVIII 8-14," *Novum Testamentum*, 1:75-80 (1956). It must be noted that the woman does not weep in the parable.
2. See I. Howard Marshall, *Luke: Historian and Theologian* (Grand Rapids: Zondervan, 1971), p. 116.
3. Ernest Fuchs, "The Quest of the Historical Jesus," *Studies of the Historical Jesus*, No. 42 of "Studies in Biblical Theology" (London: SCM Press, 1964), p. 21, has called attention creatively to the conduct of Jesus with sinners as a telling characteristic activity. Robert Lindsay has made the arresting suggestion that Luke 15:4-10 may have belonged historically with the calling of Levi!
4. See Karl Rengstorf, *"hamartōlos,"* TDNT, 1:320-329 (1963); also Norman Perrin, *Rediscovering the Teaching of Jesus* (New York: Harper, 1967), pp. 92-94.
5. So Israel Abrahams, *Studies in Pharisaism and the Gospels* (New York: KTAV, 1967), First Series, pp. 54-60. Concerning the Lukan description of the Pharisaic grumbling (*diegonguzon*) D. Derrett, "The Rich Fool: A Parable of Jesus Concerning Inheritance," *Heythrop Journal*, 18:143 (1977) 143, points out that it almost always suggests a plot, "a misguided contrivance of some kind."
6. So Jacob Neusner, *First Century Judaism in Crisis* (Nashville: Abingdon Press, 1975), p. 36.
7. Joachim Jeremias, *Parables*, p. 227. Earl Davis, "The Significance of the Shared Meal in Luke-Acts" (Unpublished Ph.D dissertation, The Southern Baptist Theological

Seminary, 1967), p. 186, isolates mediation of forgiveness, love for the outcast, fellowship, and eschatological joy as messianic banquet themes. Some scholars believe that Jesus understood the meals as anticipation of the eschatological meal in the kingdom of God. For a cautious view, see Robert Banks, *Jesus and the Law in the Synoptic Tradition* (Cambridge: University Press, 1975), pp. 108-111. William Blevins, "The Early Church: Acts 1-5," *Review and Expositor*, 71:473 (1974), put it beautifully and succinctly, "For the Pharisees Jesus' table fellowship was a *disgrace*, but for Jesus it was an act of *grace*."

8. C. H. Giblin, "Structural and Theological Considerations on Luke 15," *Catholic Biblical Quarterly*, 24:22 (1962). The idea goes back to Bornhauser and Gollwitzer.

9. I owe this memorable image to Jean Monnier, "Sur la grâce, à propos de la parabole de la brebis perdue," *Revue d' histoire et de philosophie religieuses*, 16:192 (1936).

10. The rhetorical question is assumed for the introduction of the second parable by *hē*. This can be definitely documented by comparison to Luke 14:28,31. Clearly the evangelist saw both sets of parables as single units delivered in the same breath as it were. The *tis ex humōn* formula usually introduces general situation. Note the subjectives and futures used in the parables and *ean* in verse 8. An affirmative answer or nodding concurrence is expected.

11. Walther Eichrodt, *Ezekiel*, translated by Cosslett Quin (Philadelphia: Westminster, 1970), p. 470. I agree because of Psalm 119:126 that defines in effect a lost sheep as one strayed and because of Ezekiel 34:4,16 where lost and strayed are closely bracketed. Significantly, it also occurs in Matthew 18:12 and gospel of Thomas 107:24. The gospel of Thomas text appears to be a Gnostic misunderstanding and distortion. The parable in Matthew 18:12-14 has a different context and application and form. It stands in the Ecclesiastical Discourse and is applied pastorally to straying church members. J. Dupont, "La parabole de la brebis perdue (Matthieu 18, 12-14; Luc. 15, 4-7)," *Gregorianum*, 49:287 (1968), points out that the evangelist was preoccupied with pastoral love which results from the presence of Christian sinners in the church. The form in Matthew involves two rhetorical questions (v. 12*a,b*), two third-class conditional sentences (vv. 12*b*,13*a*), and two applications (vv. 13*b*-14). Several aspects of the Matthaean choice of words seem more primitive, such as "go astray" (3x), "does he not" (*ouchi*), "if," and "truly I say to you."

12. Jeremias, *Parables*, p. 133, identifies the flock as medium in size, suggesting a moderately well-to-do person but not a gentleman farmer. K. E. Bailey, *Poet and Peasant: A Literary Cultural Approach to the Parables in Luke* (Grand Rapids: Eerdmans, 1976), p. 148, makes the fresh suggestion that the shepherd may have been part owner along with others in the village who later joined him in rejoicing. He insists that an owner of each herd would hire a shepherd. This adds realism to the mutual rejoicing, but the most natural rendering is that he was the owner. The number of a hundred is carefully chosen for effect in the story.

13. Especially E. F. Bishop, "The Parable of the Lost or Wandering Sheep. Matthew 18. 10-14; Luke 15. 3-7," *Anglican Theological Review*, 44:45 (1962), who points out that the shepherd would have counted his sheep at dusk as he let them into the sheepfold. How else would the shepherd know there were ninety-nine unless he had just counted? Hence he agrees with the evangelistic hymn in its words, "There were ninety and nine that safely lay in the shelter of the fold." In reading Bishop's article, you smell the sheep

and the shepherd and visualize crumbling cliffs and uncultivated land. However, the absence of any mention of a sheepfold and the fact that the text speaks of living in the wilderness weaken probability.

14. So Linnemann, *Parables*, p. 65; Dupont, p. 281, favors abandonment because it underscores the statement of the more value of the one repentant in a picturesque and paradoxical sense. However, the formal characteristics of a general situation parable constitute a significant literary argument against a radical break with ordinary practice.

15. Reported by W. H. Brownlee and quoted by Bishop, p. 57, For a similar view see Bailey, p. 149.

16. So Jeremias, *Parables*, p. 134. Bishop, p. 48, also points out that sheep are not as surefooted as goats and would be in far greater danger.

17. See E. G. Gulin, *Die Freude im Neuen Testament* (Helsinki: Finnish Literature, 1932), pp. 99-105, who stressed the special Lukan emphasis on soteriological joy and its connection to the doxological note.

18. See G. Bornkamm, *Jesus of Nazareth*, Irene and Fraser McLuskey (New York: Harper, 1960), p. 82.

19. It is well known that Luke stressed repentance even more than the other evangelists. Matthew (3:8,11) and Mark (1:4) use *metanoia* only vis-à-vis John the Baptizer while Luke used it not only of John (3:3,8) but also Jesus (5:32; 15:7) and significantly for the risen Christ in a kerygmatic context (24:47) in relation to forgiveness of sins (as Acts 5:31). The verb *metanoeō* is likewise more prominent in Luke (9x) than in Mark (2x) or Matthew (5x). Strikingly, only Luke spoke explicitly of repentance in the calling of Levi (Luke 5:27-31; Mark 2:13-17; Matt. 9:9-13). Luke also showed some tendency to use explicit theological terms and to draw out doctrinal significance. Jeremias, "Tradition und Redaktion in Lukas 15," *Zeitschrift für die Neutestamentliche Wissenschaft*, 62:183-184 (1971), argues that verse 7*a,b* goes back to an underlying Aramaic alliteration but that 7*c* is redacted.

20. J. Behm, "*metan.*, "*TDNT* 4:1002 (1967). Perhaps the most explicit passage is on the Baptist (Matt. 3:7 *ff*). K. Rengstorf, pp. 331-32, calls particular attention to the egotistical nature of self-righteousness and to Matthew 23 as a prophetic call to repentance. On Matthew 23, see the fine monograph by David Garland, *The Intention of Matthew*—23, No. 52 of Supplements to *Novum Testamentum* (Leiden: E. J. Brill, 1979).

21. Mays, *Ezekiel, Second Isaiah*, "Proclamation Commentaries" (Philadelphia: Fortress Press, 1978), p. 44. The Christian reader is reminded of Matthew 9:36-38.

22. Jeremias, "*poimēn*," *TDNT*, 6:497 (1968).

23. Ibid., pp. 488-489. On the status of women see Jeremias, *Jerusalem*, pp. 359-76.

24. Bailey, p. 157, makes distinction between Bedouin women who customarily wear their dowry in the form of coins hanging from a veil and village women who wear coins on necklaces. However, there is a striking rabbinic parallel of a *man* losing a coin, lighting lamps, and searching until he found it. The application is to the search after words of Torah. See Strack-Billerbeck, 2, 212.

25. Linnemann, p. 66.

26. C. B. Caird, *Saint Luke*, "The Pelican New Testament Commentaries" (Baltimore: Penguin Books, 1963), p. 181. See A. J. Walls, "In the Presence of the Angels," *Novum Testamentum*, 3:315 (1959), p. 315, who wonders if the proper picture is not that of

God rejoicing and the angels standing around like friends and neighbors entering into the joy.
27. Jeremias, *"poimēn,"* p. 492.
28. The attack would have tended to discredit Jesus before his disciples. Interestingly, A. Jülicher, *Die Gleichnisreden Jesu,* 2, 331-33, recognized a long time ago that the parable had significance for three audiences and hence avoided the tendency to reduce purpose to consolation alone (as Bultmann) or polemic (as Jeremias). The fact that the sinners drew near to Jesus *to hear him* (15:1) indicates a desire for his teaching as well as his camaraderie and opens the possibility textually that these parables also had them in mind. See 16:31 where the meaning of *akouō* is "heed."
29. Jones, *The Art and Truth of the Parables,* p. 167.
30. Jeremias, *The Parables of Jesus,* p. 128.
31. Helmut Thielicke, *The Waiting Father,* p. 22.
32. It is interesting to reflect on Robert Funk's depiction of the father as the determiner (D) and the sons as two responses (R1 and R2) in "Structure in the Narrative Parables of Jesus," *Semeia,* 2:62 (1974). My stress on the position of the father's speech at the climax of each movement comports well with his theory, but dramatically it is preferable to make the prodigal willy-nilly D and the father R1 and the elder brother R2.
33. It is interesting sociologically that he not only had a herd from which the fatted calf was taken but had several servants as well. So the three parables in Luke 15 appealed sociologically to different strata. They drew from the experience of a middle-class sheep owner, a peasant woman, and possibly a rural aristocrat.
34. The legal situation is not entirely clear but Deuteronomy 21:17 indicates that the elder son received a double portion in virtually any conceivable circumstance. Indeed, it is probable that the younger son was given only a third of the disposable property while the farm with all that belonged to it passed to the elder son. There could scarcely have been a sell-off of real estate in the few days indicated. Bailey, p. 169, admits that a sale of property ordinarily dragged on for months, though he considers the parable situation an exception.
35. Ecclesiasticus 33:19-23 actually recommends that the owner not make a settlement until he was dying, but it is thereby implied that some did settle up while the father was living. The Mishnaic tractate *Baba Bathra* 8:7 reckons with willing before death. However, Bailey, pp. 164-69, is especially insistent that the son was crassly insensitive. Via, *The Parables,* p. 169, takes a similar position. Jeremias, *The Parables of Jesus,* p. 129, places the young man's departure in the context of emigration but calls his request a demand.
36. W. Foerster, *"asōtos,"* TDNT, 1:507 (1964).
37. Bailey, pp. 171-173, provides an excellent background statement, citing Rendell Harris and W. E. Lane. He insists that the reference is not to the popular *ceratonia siliqua* but the wild fruit. He also reckons with the possibility that if the swine owner butchered, the young man would not have been able to eat the meat even if starving.
38. R. Acha, ca. 320. Cited by Strack-Billerbeck, 2:214.
39. Via, *The Parables,* p. 168.
40. William Barclay, *The Gospel of Luke,* "The Daily Study Bible" (Philadelphia: Westminster, 1956), p. 212.
41. Jeremias, *The Parables of Jesus,* p. 130. C. E. Carlston, "Reminiscence and

Redaction in Luke 15:11-32," *Journal of Biblical Literature*, 94:381 (1975), points out that in Greek idiom it means "to have second thoughts" and in Hebrew "to convert."
42. Tobit 11 reflects the very close ties of a devout Jewish Family. "Now Anna sat looking intently down the road for her son" (v. 5), and "Then Anna ran to meet them and embraced her son" (v. 9, RSV).
43. See S. H. Blank, "Kiss," *IDB*, E-J: 39-40 (1962), for further detail.
44. Ingo Broer, "Das Gleichnis vom verloren Sohn und die Theologie des Lukas," *New Testament Studies*, 20:161 (1974), suggests that the ring makes him again his son, a very good suggestion because the ring did not meet any practical necessity.
45. G. D. Kilpatrick has pointed out in lecture that the verb *thusate* (v. 23) is used to mean sacrifice or "kill kosher" in the LXX, a small clue that disproves Loisy's theory that a Gentile home was as envisioned. The "fatted calf" was Abraham's best effort at hospitality when three wayfarers ventured to his tent by the oaks of Mamre (Gen. 18:1-21). A fatted calf was a delicacy enjoyed by the wealthy (Amos 6:4). Cf. 1 Samuel 28:24.
46. Contrast Deuteronomy 21:18-21. K. H. Rengstorf, *Die Re-Investitur des Verloren Sohnes in der Gleichniserzählung Jesu Luk.* 15:11-32 (Cologne-Opladen: Westdeutscher, 1967) sees the *kesasah* or "cutting off" as the background of the parable (based on *Ruth Rabbah* 7:11 on 4:7). When a person had gotten himself into incurable conflict with the interests of the tribe he was cut off in public. A jar filled with roasted grain and nuts was smashed on the street in the presence of the gathered tribe. On this reading, the father's many gifts represent a formal reinvestiture. His basic point is right whether there was a formal *kesasah* or not. For criticism see Bailey, p. 167.
47. Note the clues within the fabric of the parable: the servants respond with alacrity to the one in charge; the younger son thinks automatically of his father's servants. See *Baba Bathra* 8:7 and Jeremias, *The Parables of Jesus*, pp. 128-29.
48. J. T. Sanders, "Tradition and Redaction in Luke xv. 11-32," *New Testament Studies*, 15:433-438 (1969), argues that the elder brother segment is secondary or Lukan largely because he believes the polemic against the Pharisees extremely severe and worthier of the evangelist than Jesus. Sanders does not see the Father's love for the Pharisee and the invitation to him nor does he recognize that the two parts of the parable are a whole nor that the evangelist in fact generalizes hermeneutically at 18:9 rather than heightening. The case for the basic authenticity of both parts has been made by J. J. O'Rourke, "Some Notes on Luke xv. 11-32," *New Testament Studies*, 18:431-433 (1972); Carlston, "Reminiscence and Redaction in Luke 15:11-32"; and by Jeremias, "Tradition und Redaktion in Lukas 15."
49. H. Köster, "*splangnon,*"*TDNT*, 7:554 (1971), calls attention in a single sentence to the juxtaposition of *compassion* and *wrath*, which he sees as a technique for intensifying the awareness of the totality of mercy or wrath with which God claims man. While his remark provoked me to further thought, his emphasis is too centered in the Wicked Servant story of Matthew 18:23-35. I have for some years now espoused the notion that there exists a conscious literary parallel between the two words, both of which are First Aorist indicative passive, third singular. This is the clue to interpretation. I am pleased to note a similar line taken in passing in a recent article by James Price, "Luke 15:11-32," *Interpretation*, 31:64 (1977) though our views are arrived at independently. Cf. also Dodd, *The Parables of the Kingdom*, pp. 92-93. Observe by all means the *hoti* clauses

(24,27,32) as the consistent explanation of the joy.

50. Robert Lindsey has suggested in lecture that the parable was originally paired with the Pharisee and the Tax Collector and belongs with the account of the conversion of Zacchaeus. There certainly are connecting links between the two parables such as a similar view of repentance, a parallel between the attitude of the elder brother and the Pharisee (a contempt for sinners and a grand view of himself), radical grace, and a similar polemical situation. On such a pairing theory, the parables might fit the circumstances of Luke 15:1-2 more naturally as they would provide one story featuring sinners and another tax collectors.

51. Gottlob Schrenk, "patēr," TDNT, 5:994 (1967).

52. So Sallie McFague, Speaking in Parables, pp. 12-17.

53. Jülicher, 2:362.

54. Walter Grundmann, "sun-meta," TDNT, 7:794 (1971). Many students have made the point that the elder son was out of fellowship with the father, but Grundmann does it creatively with great sensitivity to the prepositions (meta and sun).

55. Jeremias, The Proclamation of Jesus, p. 156.

56. Jeremias.

57. E. Würthwein, "metanoeō," TDNT, 4:984 (1967).

58. Contra Carlston, "Reminiscence and Redaction in Luke 15:11:32." Carlston plays down the father's rebuke, describing it as "gentle and limited" (p. 387) at first and later as a totally positive response (p. 388). This is special pleading, albeit for a good cause. He is surely correct that the Pharisees did not play a major role in the crucifixion (p. 398). The statement "You are always with me" admittedly is open to several interpretations, but in any event the elder brother does not stand for Judaism or even for all Pharisees.

59. Dorothy Sayers, Unpopular Opinions (London: Victor Gollancz, 1946), p. 15.

60. Price, p. 69.

61. So G. V. Jones, p. 176. Jones speaks meaningfully to those who have read existential literature or the Theatre of the Absurd and/or have experienced their world as broken and their existence overrun with meaninglessness.

62. Taken from George G. Hunter, The Contagious Congregation (Nashville: Abingdon, 1979), p. 74.

63. Dodd, The Parables of the Kingdom, p. 92.

64. Hunter, The Parables Then and Now, p. 59.

11

Luke 18:9-14

The Parable of the Pharisee and the Tax Collector

The most radical idea let loose in the world came from Jesus in the way he spoke of grace. Though grace has been domesticated and tamed by pedestrian definitions and by narrowly limited applications, the unsubdued character of grace in its original import may yet be encountered in numerous parables. Such a grace perspective alters the way everything appears and injects new adventure into religion.

The parable of the Pharisee and the Tax Collector furnishes a memorable portrait of radical grace and stunning penitence. Jesus addressed the incident to those who were cocksure that they themselves were righteous and who treated everyone else with contempt. He spoke the radical word of grace to those who were so good they could hardly stand it. Perhaps those who were so bad they could hardly stand it overheard it too. The parable contrasts the attitude of two characters, as in other parables (Matt. 21:28-32; Luke 15:11-32), in one of the kinds of internal juxtaposition, and it is the exact words of each prayer that are especially compared.

The Parable

Two men went up into the Temple to pray:
> The one a Pharisee and
> the other a tax collector.

The Pharisee, having taken his position, prayed to himself:
> "O God, I give thanks to you because I am not like other men—
> > swindlers, unrighteous ones, adulterers, or as this tax collector.
> I fast twice between Sabbaths.
> I tithe on all I acquire."

But the tax collector, standing afar off, could not lift his eyes toward heaven but he kept on beating his breast, praying:
> > "O God, mercy me the sinner."

190

I say to you, this one went down to his house accepted by God rather than the other one; because everyone who exalts himself will be humbled, and he who humbles himself will be exalted.

The Pharisee's Prayer (Luke 18:11-12)

A Pharisee arrived for his daily prayer at the same time coincidentally as a tax collector. The scene was the great Herodian Temple in Jerusalem, and the time may have been the official hours of prayer, either 9:00 AM or 3:00 PM (as Acts 3:1). The Pharisee took up a prominent position, perhaps to be seen (Matt. 6:5), inasmuch as there would be many present at the official hour of prayer. He was standing for prayer, likely with his hands upward and eyes looking toward heaven, and speaking audibly but quietly. There is some uncertainty about the exact word order in the manuscript evidence.

The content of his entire prayer is cast in the form of a thanksgiving. He gave thanks to God ("I give thanks to you"), the usual beginning of prayer, but the *Berakah* (thanks) became "praise of self rather than praise of God"[1] ("I am not like the rest of men"). He is thankful *because* (*hoti*) he is not like other persons. He divides humanity into other persons and Pharisees. The prayer that follows contains no petitions, only self-congratulation and invidious comparisons of himself to the tax collector.

Moral Propriety. The Pharisee referred to other people as sinners: swindlers, unrighteous, and adulterers. The word translated "swindlers" (*harpages*) suggests a ravenous appetite (Matt. 7:15) and can be rendered simply "robber," but swindler is more precise to differentiate it from robber (*lēstēs*) as used in the parable of the Compassionate Samaritan.[2] The Pharisee may well have had the tax collectors in mind. The rabbis denied tax collectors the right to appear as witnesses in court, lumping them in the same category along with gamblers, usurers, those who flew pigeons for wages, robbers, and the violent (b. Sanh. 25b).[3] Tax collectors were associated proverbially with sinners. On the strength of the Zacchaeus story, it is evident that some practiced dishonesty in collections (Luke 19:8).

The Pharisee at prayer also cast aspersions on others as "unrighteous." The word (*adikoi*) can mean "hypocrites" in the context of the parable.[4] If so, the Pharisee expressed his rage at the very presence of the tax collector in the Temple! It is more likely, however, that the word expressed the general pharisaic dismay toward those who did not subscribe to all customs dictated by the oral tradition of the rabbis. Presumably the nearby tax collector did not bother himself with fasting and tithing, for example. This point is important for the basic interpretation of the parable.

"Other men," especially tax collectors, were also accused of adultery. Specifically the accusation assumes a man having carnal intercourse with a Jewish married women.[5] While it is probable that the tax collector was guilty of the first two accusations and possibly adultery as well, it was not known by the Pharisee. It sounds like a caricature drawn by one who never took the time to become personally acquainted with any individual tax collector. All tax collectors are tarred with the same brush. Schlatter pointed out that God alone knows the heart and can judge the tax collector.[6] The subsequent prayer of the tax collector does confirm the general accuracy of the Pharisee's superficial assessment of another person's outward righteousness.

Confident he is not like other men, the Pharisee distanced himself from sins and sinners. He likely believed genuinely what he prayed and was genuinely glad he was different.

Religious Practices. The deeply serious Pharisee practiced fasting and tithing intently. He fasted twice a week when once a year stood as the only definite mandate. The law prescribed that a religious person fast on the annual occasion of the Day of Atonement, Yom Kippur. The fast involved the entire populace in a great day of national repentance (Lev. 16:29 *ff.*; 23:27 *ff.*; Num. 29:7). While there is only one obligatory fast in the Old Testament, other fasts were encouraged in times of national emergency.[7] There are recorded some significant individual fasts, as well, such as Moses' fast of forty days neither eating nor drinking immediately previous to receiving the Ten Words (Ex. 34:28) and Daniel fasting prior to his visions (Dan. 9:3; 10:2 *f.*,12). During the Exile, voluntary fasts on other occasions became more important and unfortunately more externalized.

The picture of fasting practice during the time of Jesus is by no means certain, but it is misleading to set the parable's Pharisee merely in the context of the Old Testament. There is New Testament evidence of fasting in the time of Jesus as a more typical activity, as in the controversy when Jesus was faulted for not requiring his disciples to fast while John's disciples did so frequently (Luke 5:33). It is quite possible that many Pharisees during the Jesus era fasted twice a week, perhaps on Mondays and Thursdays.[8] *Taanith*, one of the tractates of the Mishnah and possibly reflecting traditions of the first century, sets out a procedure for fasting by individuals and congregations in time of a drought.[9]

Notice that repentance and penitence belonged to the true spirit of authentic fasting. Isaiah 58 makes this unambiguous, indeed (esp. vv. 6-7). Fasting for the Pharisee served as demonstrable proof of religious superiority.[10] Ironically, it was the tax collector who expressed the true spirit of fasting—both *mourning* and *repentance*.

The Pharisee also tithed everything *(panta) he acquired* (Luke 18:12b). The fact that he tithed everything opens up the probability that he included mint, dill, and cummin (Matt. 23:23) and rue (Luke 11:42), a meticulous observance of the law.[11] One tithing regulation ran, "A general rule have they laid down about Tithes: whatsoever is used for food and is kept watch over and grows from the soil is liable to Tithes" (*Maaseroth* 1:1). It is also possible that the Pharisee tithed not only on his herb garden but also on everything he bought, thus taking no chances.[12] The tractate *Demai* ("doubtful") labeled produce sold by "the people of the land" as "Produce Not Certainly Tithed." If the produce were purchased, it should be tithed just in case. Such guidelines inevitably put distance and suspicion between a Pharisee and a suspected nontither, such as this tax collector.[13]

Some even observed three tithes: the first or Levitic tithe which must be given to a Levite (Num. 18:21), a second or Jerusalem tithe to be eaten by the family in a worship context (Deut. 14:22), and the poor man's tithe (Deut. 14:28; 26:12).[14] Furthermore, the Pharisee may well have been a member of the urban religious communion known as "the fellowship" (*havurah*). The very basis of such societies was meticulous observance of laws of tithing.[15] The Pharisee in the parable likely found his own identity and distinctiveness in his fastidious practice of tithing.

So in moral propriety and in religious practice, the Pharisee found ample cause to thank God.[16] He imagined proudly that he existed in virtue and earned merit. This Pharisee fairly represented a typical attitude of Pharisees generally toward tax collectors and reflected the typical priority given tithing. However, not all Pharisees were like this particular one, as Jesus recognized elsewhere (Mark 12:34). One famous Jewish scholar took exception in the following manner: "Luke's Pharisee who thanked God that he was not as the Publican must have been an exceptional case, one of the weeds of ritualism, not one of its ordinary or natural fruits."[17] It is certainly true that the faults rather than the virtues of the Pharisees are better known from the New Testament because of the conflictual situation, and modern research has sought to balance the picture.[18]

It should be noted in summary fashion that the parable speaks of *a* Pharisee, not *any* Pharisee; that some of this Pharisee's attitudes are demonstrably typical of some of his contemporaries; that Jesus and the Pharisees differed sharply regarding the authority of the oral tradition; and that the burning religious issue is whether one or both of the types in the parable are accepted by God. The Pharisee in the parable was no monument to modesty so convinced as he was that there was no wrinkle in his own character.

The Tax Collector's Prayer (Luke 18:13)

The tax collector who invaded the Temple precincts for spiritual purposes is popularly referred to as a publican. He would have held a less prestigious position than Zacchaeus, who was a head tax farmer (Luke 19:2). The very mention of a tax collector entering the temple beside a Pharisee would have made the original auditors bristle as would the acceptance of a tax collector into the band of disciples (Matt. 10:3; Mark 2:14). Because of constant contact with Gentiles tax collectors were under suspicion of uncleanness.[19]

The tax collector's "body language" for prayer within the Temple is instructive. Both position and posture communicate his feelings. He obviously feels far from God (Ps. 22:1). He stood afar off from the worshiping group, expressing his alienation from God and his people.[20] It is possible that he actually remained in the court of the Gentiles, but more likely that he stood back in a remote corner of the Temple, yet within the court of the men. Furthermore, he was incapable of looking God in the eye! The fact that he did not dare raise his eyes to heaven signals his shame and guilt. The normal position for prayer involved holding up one's arms and looking upward.[21] The tax collector instead kept pummeling his chest. In the throes of spiritual struggle, he forgot where he was and lost his composure. His emotional act of beating on his breast physically expressed his inner despair.[22]

The terse word of his prayer, an outburst of contrition, expressed more of the same: "O God, mercy me *the* sinner."[23] The prayer was very much a confession. He recognized and admitted that he was a sinner, even in a class by himself. He found the honesty to name himself "sinner." He had done wrong before God. He allowed his conscience place. The prayer confesses sin *and* need. It is a plea for mercy like that of Bartimaeus (Mark 10:47), what Howard Marshall characterizes beautifully "a longing for forgiveness."[24] When the heart is stirred it speaks in telegrams.

Thus the disturbed tax collector humbled himself three ways:
    (1) by his position (*makrothen*),
    (2) by his gestures,
    (3) by his prayer.[25]
In the prayer, he prayed in the humble spirit of Psalm 51, a further clue to the meaning of the parable.

Interpretation: What It Meant

Comparison of Prayers. Since the parable speaks directly about an actual Pharisee rather than indirectly, Howard Marshall believes that it is a real story rather than a comparison.[26] This opinion calls attention to the directness both of the story and of the verdict (Luke 18:14). But is not the narrative, a specific situation parable featuring an internal juxtaposition of prayers, indeed, a comparison?

A comparison of the two prayers, rather than merely a separate characterization of each, is highly illuminating. While there is no direct dialogue between the two men and each prayer is self contained, yet their petitions clang. Each prayer is addressed to God, but they are different kinds of prayers. One is a thanksgiving and the other a petition. The thanksgiving from the Pharisee exalted himself in self-congratulation and established him as needing nothing of God. The petitionary prayer of the tax collector begged for forgiveness, as he threw himself upon the mercy of God. One prayer was a confession of sinfulness. The other was a denial of sinfulness. The Pharisee, in effect, thanked God that he was not a sinner. He did not thank God for what God had done in his life but praised himself that he was not as other men.[27] In setting the prayers alongside one another, the hearer or reader experiences religious understanding. For a brief time two seemingly unrelated people are thrown together, and the overhearing of their private prayers in a fleeting juxtaposition is a moment of truth for those with ears to hear.

The Pharisee lacked perceptive introspection. The tax collector saw his circumstances in stark and real terms. He did not fool himself. In a way, the Pharisee's religiosity and respectability misled him. He did not really know himself. Fasting and tithing can be impressive substitutes for repentance. The prophets had recognized that some used fasting as a means to manipulate God and as a substitute for real repentance. They protested "the sham holiness of external observance" (see Isa. 58; Jer. 14:12) as does the parable. The prophet Amos had warned those who place their security in sacrifice and tithing (4:4-5). Also this is another of Jesus' Temple parables, and it challenges cultic practice and loyalty as a substitute for heartfelt and genuine religion.[28] Jesus' conviction that the Temple must be a house of genuine prayer for all persons (Mark 11:17) was of immense importance to him.

The quoted prayers set side by side fairly invite response and personal application.

Verdict of Jesus. The parable is completed by a revelation of the outcome of the prayers (v. 14a). Jesus rejected the conventional assessment of tax collectors[29] and speaking for God boldly declared the penitent sinner the one heard and forgiven. Indeed, the tax collector went down the hill, on which the Temple stood, to his home in Jerusalem spiritually healed by the therapy of mercy. Jesus, in effect, pronounced a word of salvation as he did to Zacchaeus (Luke 19:9). Jesus proclaimed to the tax collector the hearing of his prayer.[30] He declared a blessing upon the poor in spirit (Matt. 5:3).

The verdict includes an exposure of the spiritual failure of the Pharisee. God's grace accepts the humble cry but rejects the proud prayer. Historically it is crucial to see that Jesus challenged the authority of the scribal tradition and as a result reduced the authority of the Pharisees among the common people. He had the audacity to invite the Pharisees to repent.

So Jesus spoke with great dominical authority and made an iconoclastic evaluation. He dared to represent the name of divine grace. By implication, Jesus acted as the Knower of the divine will and the Proclaimer of God's judgment. Surely the parable itself contributed to the repeated charge against Jesus of blasphemy (Mark 2:7; 14:64).

The verdict actually affirms and requires repentance. The Pharisee must reorient his attitudes toward himself, toward his fellow human beings, and toward God. The stirring repentance of the tax collector involved confession, prayer, contriteness, and a plea for mercy. Someone who comes to God in honest and genuine prayer from the heart will be heard. Someone who presses his or her claim upon God on the basis of personal virtue will not be accepted. Someone who confesses his or her sin and throws himself or herself on God's mercy and asks for forgiveness will receive God's grace and acceptance.[31] Incidentally one does not understand radical grace in this parable by minimizing the sinfulness of the tax collector!

In the verdict of acceptance/rejection (Luke 18:14a) and, indeed, throughout the parable, an underlying theological issue is the nature of righteousness. By the standards of outward righteousness, the Pharisee was accurate both in assessment of himself and generally of the tax collector. But by the standards of inward righteousness espoused in the Sermon on the Mount, the Pharisee was inaccurate on both counts. It could be said of the Pharisee, as Paul spoke autobiographically, "as to righteousness under the law blameless" (Phil. 3:6, RSV). The Pharisee saw himself as unlike certain other people because he kept the law. He fasted and tithed. The tax collector did neither.

Spiritually the Pharisee's problem lay in the egotistic nature of such righteousness. He was inwardly self-confident, outwardly proud (as Matt. 6:1 ff.; 23:5 ff.; Luke 14:7 ff.; 20:46; Mark 12:38 f.) and pitiless (as Matt. 23:14,23; 25:41 ff.). The verdict of Jesus displays the radical character of grace—so radical it rejects self-righteousness, so radical it accepts a penitent sinner. True righteousness must come from the heart and express itself as a creative dependency upon God (theonomous life). To those who respond with such righteousness belongs the assurance of Psalm 51:17: "The sacrifice acceptable to God is a broken spirit; a broken and contrite heart, O God, thou wilt not despise" (RSV).

The passage concludes with a paradoxical maxim or generalizing conclusion (v. 14b) that asserts that any persons who exalt themselves will be humbled and any humbling themselves will be exalted. Since the text appears in several other contexts (Matt. 18:4; 23:12; Luke 14:11), it is possible that Luke has appropriately appended the thought from Q to the end of the parable. It is a common kingdom-of-God perspective that expects an eschatological reversal of existing conditions. It should be observed, however, that each member of the maxim or *mashal* can be directly related to one of the two types in the parable. The Pharisee exalted himself and the tax collector humbled himself. It suits the verdict as well. The verdict is the decision and the maxim is the rationale. So the maxim may not only come from Jesus but also may have belonged originally with the parable.

Lukan Accent. One undeniable signature of the evangelist enlarges the historical interpretation and that is his pointed identification of the intended hearers (v. 9). Luke often prefixed a personal explanation of purpose to a parable (18:1; 19:11), adding a fascinating touch. The preacher/evangelist was concerned about the church of his day and its preaching, as well as the previous ministry of Jesus.

Several details may be put together. First, Luke bracketed two prayer parables, the first on the promise of persistent prayer (18:1-8) and the second on the peril of presumptuous prayer (vv. 9-14).[33] The opening word "also" (v. 9) may be understood as "in addition to what he had said before."[34] The evangelist created a twin lesson on prayer in order both to encourage and to challenge. One reason these stories were preserved was because they possessed coping power for dealing with later church needs.

A second factor to observe is the fact that the evangelist applied the parable hermeneutically, more broadly than merely to Pharisees, to include any of like spirit in or out of the church. This is a bold and effective transition that makes the parable word of God in new circumstances. For Luke, the parable related to any self-righteous religious person. Luke provided an essentially psychological analysis of the spiritual condition of those who place their confidence or trust in themselves rather than God and treat others with contempt rather than compassion. Thus the Lukan proclamation speaks alarm not merely to Pharisees of Palestine but admonishes church members of Rome and Antioch and elsewhere who pray in the wrong spirit and serves as an evangelic instrument to expose prideful self-righteousness on the part of non-Christians. It is possible that Luke encountered Christians who held fellow Christians in contempt and claimed superior spirituality for themselves. Self-righteousness and contempt for others are psychologically interrelated for the evangelist.

This Gospel editor also recognized that the issue throughout the parable is what constitutes true righteousness before God, as is indicated by his characterization of those who are cocksure about their personal righteousness (v. 9*a*).

Picture of God. The kind of God envisioned by the Teller of the parable may also be glimpsed. Indeed, one creative suggestion is that the intention of the parable is to win over the hearers by portraying a winsome picture of the God of freedom.[35] Actually two pictures of God stand side by side, but the one assumed by the Pharisee is false. He would take God's freedom away. After all, God could not possibly love a tax collector, and God must accept Pharisees! The tax collector, on the other hand, allows God freedom to be God.

The picture of God, obviously so crucial for the character of prayer and the style of religious life, is not merely one of freedom. The sovereignty of God emerges from the decisive verdict of Jesus regarding divine acceptance (v. 14). Even more so the picture of the God of stunning grace appears. The parable breathes the spirit of Psalm 51 with its confidence in a God of steadfast love (51:1), a God of healing forgiveness (vv. 2,7,9,10), a God who receives sinners (v. 13). Psalm 32 and 130 also come to mind.

One exciting realization is that Jesus, through the parable, offered none other than his own picture of God, a powerful portrait of freedom and grace.

The focus may now turn appropriately from historical meaning to contemporary message.

Interpretation: What It Means

Religious Pride and Concomitant Contempt. Religious haughtiness, being so good we can hardly stand it, derives from an incorrigibly good opinion of ourselves and issues in a cynicism about others. Some people have a "religious" personality like a stop sign as they swagger into worship and manage to wound religion by their spiritual arrogance. The sort of religious person who could strut sitting down communicates a distasteful spiritual pride. Any of us can fall prey to this subtle sin of the spirit. The possibility of sinning in church, even between eleven and twelve o'clock on Sunday morning, must not be brushed aside flippantly. Among other motivations people go to church (a) for help when they are hurting, but sometimes (b) for an ego trip of self-congratulation.

A proud prayer, after all, is a self-contradictory endeavor. This is especially true of spiritual primping, praying before a mirror rather than a window. Our prayers can be proud monologues preoccupied with our own ego, that "perpendicular maypole we dance around and call I." Strongly religious persons sometimes become unconscious of personal defect and indulge in presumptuous religion. We can become quite satisfied with ourselves, bask in the glow of moral pride, and be mistaken about our real nature.[36] Alfred Loisy wrote that all was well for the Pharisee in our parable if God were as content with him as the Pharisee was content with himself![37] The problem though was that "the Pharisee's virtue was so cankered by pride that it was almost rotten."[38]

Spiritual pride thrives on comparisons. It bolsters the ego to compare oneself with an irreligious scalawag. When that unwholesome taint of religious superiority makes headway then contempt for others also advances. It is not that we ever pray quite with the Pharisee's words but with his heart. Emil Brunner has reminded how truly inventive is the human heart: "I boast in not being a Pharisee like one or the other of my acquaintances. Yet as the very moment of boasting I am the Pharisee with his prayer."[39] Contempt for others often expresses a need to put others down in order to feel good about oneself. Lewis Sherrill has made the related psychological suggestion that actually an inner hostility may emerge as outward goodness and lead to a contempt of others.[40]

Religious pride is no religious misdemeanor because it causes contempt for fellow human beings and causes spiritual failure in personal worship. The gravity of pride is captured by these striking words: "Men talk about sin with a silly grin as if it only had to do with sex and swearing. Sin is rebellion against God. It is run by pride, and it ruins men. Beside pride all the frightening diseases of our day are dandruff."[41] The very essence of sin is pride, a revelation appearing in a parable featuring someone imagining during worship he was not like other men.

Confession is requisite for every worshiper. The flagrant sinner so recognized by society may know the obvious sin in her or his life.

The issue then is whether to care enough to change, to confess, to depend on God. The person engaging in arrogant religion on the other hand needs to get in touch with reality and the experience of redeeming grace. The religious are also called to an existence predicated upon grace.

"Just As I Am . . . I Come." Many are crippled by overwhelming guilt for wrongs they have done and do not know how to lay down their sins. They may not have known a human father who loves even when his children have been bad. They may not know a caring fellowship of Christians who accept and want sinners in their circle. And some today stand near the church wistfully like a hungry child peering through the window of a bakery.

There are numerous unchurched Americans troubled by a terrible sense of personal unworthiness. Some do not feel good enough to go to church or wonder if they would find welcome. They may imagine that church is for those who have it all together. They may doubt that God could possibly love them. The church can extend its ministry and share good news of a divine mercy and extend its fellowship circle in healing acceptance. The church after all is an exclusive club "for sinners only."

The grace offered sinners is costly. It is not sloppy *agape!* The parable itself is a great conversion story, and one of the ways Jesus alleviated Roman oppression was by converting tax collectors. If they refused to fleece the people because of personal reorientation to the kingdom of God, then equity could flourish. What social implications would follow if Christians could reach loan sharks and numbers racketeers who prey upon the poor and drug pushers and white collar criminals who prey upon the public. Stunning grace can bring change not merely to those who are programmed Protestants but to those indulging in blatant wrong.

Like the tax agent in the story, all alike need to lay down sins and have the courage to accept forgiveness. "The courage to be . . . is the courage to accept the forgiveness of sins, not as an abstract assertion but as the fundamental experience in the encounter with God."[42]

> Just as I am, and waiting not
> To rid my soul of one dark blot,
> To thee, whose blood can cleanse each spot,
> O Lamb of God, I come!

> Just as I am, tho tossed about
> With many a conflict, many a doubt,
> Fightings within and fear without,
> O Lamb of God, I come!
>
> Just as I am, poor, wretched, blind;
> Sight, riches, healing of the mind,
> Yea, all I need in thee to find,
> O Lamb of God, I come!

And in such confidence to lay bare our darker side, we will find acceptance.

> Just as I am, thou wilt receive,
> Wilt welcome, pardon, cleanse, relieve,
> Because thy promise I believe,
> O Lamb of God, I come!

The parable exposes the very nature of real religion (encounter with God) and authentic existence (predicated upon grace).

Leslie Weatherhead pointed to a further step: "Let us not just put down our sins; let us put down our goodness."[43] Pride and goodness keep us from God. The words of the hymn have it right, "Nothing in my hands I bring, Simply to thy cross I cling." God can be excluded by our virtues. Let us put down our religious achievements or general good character and take up his grace.

> Just as I am, without one plea,
> But that thy blood was shed for me,
> And that thou bidd'st me come to thee,
> O Lamb of God, I come!
>
> Just as I am! Thy love unknown
> Has broken ev'ry barrier down;
> Now to be thine, yea, thine alone,
> O Lamb of God, I come!

Let us put down both our sins and our goodness.

Jesus' story and his verdict require an encounter of ourselves with ourselves and with a God we cannot dupe and with a grace downright amazing.

Lessons on Prayer. The parable also reveals a great deal about prayer, both explicitly and implicitly. For example, why you go up to pray will determine how you come down from prayer. And again, the worst sinner may come to God and find forgiveness. Both neurotic guilt and appropriate guilt can find healing. And prayer can now be defined as a recognition of sin and a confession, a creative dependence upon God, an implicit belief in an approachable and merciful God.

Furthermore, real prayer does not arise from egotistic self-righteousness. Genuine prayer does not consist of empty phrases and casual cliches. Current leaders of church renewal are pointing to the rediscovery of the effervescence of natural prayer.

Also contempt spoils prayer. Those who have never known the moral slums may pray prayers that pass away like the snowflakes of yesterday when invidious comparisons become the content or spirit. A Christian can project a vanilla image of clean living and yet hold a fellow worshiper in disdain.

Does not prayer touch upon the very essence of religion and of worship? Are not some prayers an unconscious avoidance of God? We can substitute financial support for the church and abstention from alcohol for repentance and worship. The essence of religion lies not in religious activity but in encounter with God and acceptance of grace. The threat of prayer consists in its very nature to require transparency before God.

NOTES

1. Otto Michel, "telōnēs," *TDNT*, 8:105 (1972).
2. *BAG*, p. 108. (Cf. 1 Cor. 5:10 *f.*; 6:10; Titus 1:9).
3. Michel, p. 102.
4. Gottlob Schrenk, "*adikos*," *TDNT*, 1:152 (1963).
5. See Strack-Billerbeck, 1:377-380.
6. Schlatter, *Das Evangelium des Lukas*, Second Edition (Stuttgart: Calwer Verlag, 1960), p. 400.
7. See 1 Samuel 7:6; 1 Kings 21:9; Jeremiah 36:6,9; 2 Chronicles 20:3 *ff.*; Jonah 3:5 *ff.* For traditional guidelines regarding fasting during Yom Kippur see the Mishnaic tractate *Yoma*. The fast during the Day of Atonement was expanded to four days after the capture of Jerusalem (Zech. 7:3,5; 8:19).
8. One especially interesting reference after the time of Jesus comes from *Didache* 8:1, which reflects the two fasting days set aside by the new Pharisaism led by Johanan ben Zakkai. W. D. Davies, *The Setting of the Sermon on the Mount* (Cambridge: University Press, 1964), p. 284, takes the position that Monday and Thursday fasting

preceded Jamnia but fasting was on the increase after the fall of Jerusalem.

9. In *Taanith* fasting along with prayer is depicted as an appropriate response to a drought. The procedure advocated stopping of eating and starting of praying. The first three days individuals of exceptional peity would fast (1:4). That failing, the whole congregation engaged in three additional days. Nights were not included in the fast, and sabbaths and other festivals were carefully avoided.

10. For further discussion on fasting in the New Testament era, see J. Behm, "*nēstis*," *TDNT*, 4:924-935 (1967). He documents fasting as a distinguishing mark of the ideal figures of Jewish piety. He argues that the Pharisees were particularly strict in their fasts on the basis of Ps. Sol. 3:8. He seems too critical in his depiction of fasting as an exercise in virtue devoid of repentance. The *T. Jos.*, a very beautiful description of Joseph's fasting, describes the hero withdrawing for prayer and fasting in response to the Egyptian woman's advances (3:4 *ff.*). There are winsome descriptions of fasting as "they that fast for God's sake receive beauty of face" and of Joseph giving away uneaten food to the poor (3:6). There is also reference to "fasting in humility of heart" (10:2). For another treatment of fasting see Keith Main, *Prayer and Fasting: A Study in the Devotional Life of the Early Church* (New York: Carlton Press, 1971).

11. See I. Howard Marshall, *The Gospel of Luke: A Commentary on the Greek Text* (Grand Rapids: William B. Eerdmans Publishing Company, 1978), pp. 496-97, for a discussion whether the pharisaic practice of tithing went beyond the oral law as well as the Old Testament. He documents that dill (*Maaseroth* 4:5) and cummin (*Demai* 2:1) were liable to tithe, but that tithing mint and rue may not have been required.

12. So Joachim Jeremias, *The Parables of Jesus*, p. 140.

13. So O. Michel, p. 101, who reports that the tax collector is open to suspicion that he has not tithed. His work as a tax collector took from him the status of being "trustworthy." Stephen Westerholm, *Jesus and Scribal Authority*, No. 10 of New Testament Series, *Coniectanea Biblica* (Lund: CWK Gleerup, 1978), p. 56, observes that tithing had become a tangible means of distinguishing the pious from the *Am-ha-ares*. For a convenient summary on the background of tithing see his comments on pp. 53-55.

14. The third tithe took the place of the second tithe in the third and sixth years of the seven-year cycle and was intended for Levites, foreigners, orphans, and widows. In *Maaseroth* 2:2 the second tithe is portrayed as a less grave matter. The fact that the school of Shammai and the school of Hillel are very often quoted rendering different judgments could mean that the second tithe was much in contention during the days of Jesus! It was called the *Maaser Sheni*. For further discussion see Marvin Tate, "Tithing: Legalism or Benchmark," *Review and Expositor*, 70:153-162 (1973).

15. So J. Neusner, *First Century Judaism in Crisis* (Nashville: Abingdon Press, 1975), p. 36. See also his *From Politics to Piety* (Englewood Cliffs, New Jersey: Prentice Hall, 1973), p. 80.

16. H. Merklein, " 'Dieser ging als Gerechter nach Hause . . .' Das Gottesbild Jesu und die Haltung der Menschen nach Luke 18, 9-14," *Bibel und Kirche*, 32:36 (1977), cites a similar prayer out of the Babylonian Talmud (b. Ber. 28b). It is possible that the Pharisee in the parable may have thought he gained merit for himself (*Makkoth* 3:15) because he had a store of works (2 Bar. 14:12).

17. Israel Abrahams, *Studies in Pharisaism and the Gospels* (New York: KTAV, 1967 reprint), 2:57.

18. A major proponent of reassessment is surely W. D. Davies. For an introduction see his *Introduction to Pharisaism*, No. 16 of "Biblical Series" (Philadelphia: Fortress Press, 1967). I am very much in debt to this magnificent scholar and believe he will redress the balance, but his reconstruction fails to account adequately for the apparent level of conflict during the historical ministry of Jesus.

19. So O. Michel, p. 101.

20. See H. Preisker, "*makrothen*," *TDNT*, 4:373 (1967), who suggests that the reference may indeed be figurative or metaphorical to convey a sense of distance. I think there is an intentional contrast of position with that of the Pharisee.

21. Marshall, p. 680, calls attention to Luke 6:20; Mark 6:41; 7:34; John 11:41; 17:1; and Psalm 123:1 as instances of lifted eyes.

22. So Jeremias, p. 143.

23. As A. T. Robertson, *Word Pictures of the New Testament* (Nashville: Broadman Press, 1930), 2:233-234: "The Pharisees thought of others as sinners. The publican thinks of himself as the sinner, not of others at all." For a contrary opinion cf. Robert Hoerber, " 'God Be Merciful to Me a Sinner'—A Note on Luke 18:13," *Concordia Theological Monthly*, 33:283-286 (1962).

24. Marshall, p. 180.

25. W. Grundmann, "*tapeinoō*," *TDNT*, 8:16 (1972).

26. Marshall, p. 677.

27. So W. Michaelis, *Die Gleichnisse Jesu*, p. 239.

28. Schlatter, p. 399, suggested that both the negative and positive purpose of the Pharisee's ethic is cultic.

29. Jesus had quite a celebrated affair with tax collectors, attracting them to his ministry and fellowship and drawing criticism for his associations. This was a genuinely creative dimension of his ministry because he refused to follow culturally conditioned religious classifications and because in acting out his independent judgments and approach he generated newness of life on the part of tax collectors surprised by the joy of his acceptance and God's grace.

There are unflattering references to tax collectors in Matt. (5:46-47; 18:15-17). There are calls to repentance and belief (Matt. 21:31b-32; 9:11-13; Mark 2:17; Luke 5:31-32; 15:1-2). Of late, mighty debate has transpired between Brandon's radical view of Jesus as a near Zealot and the Cullmann-Hengel response. William O. Walker, "Jesus and the Tax Collectors," *Journal of Biblical Literature*, 97:221-238 (1978), argues that there is no compelling evidence to demonstrate that Jesus did not share the popular view regarding tax collectors. His intention to leave the issue open and invite further study is healthy, but it appears that he has tested a thesis helpfully but commended it unconvincingly. He places too much emphasis upon the Matthaean references; makes too little of the fact that there are *reports* of Jesus eating with tax collectors in all three Synoptics (Matt. 9:9-13; Mark 2:13-17; Luke 5:27-32; 19:1-10) confirmed as it were by *charges* from opponents who accuse Jesus of befriending tax collectors (Matt. 11:18-19a; Luke 7:33-34) by holding table fellowship; and neglects not only the revolutionary perspective of the kingdom of God generally but the intentional result of the parable of the Pharisee and the Tax Collector to shatter the popular view. Walker also raises the critically unlikely possibility that the parable arose from the early church.

30. Schlatter, p. 400.

31. Michel, p. 105, reminds that the rabbis required restitution and renunciation of vocation by tax collectors. Zacchaeus made restitution at his own initiative (Luke 19:8), and Levi may have renounced tax collecting when he became a disciple (Mark 2:14 *ff.*). Presumably neither is required in the parable. What is required by Jesus in all three instances is a reorientation of heart and life.

32. So K. H. Rengstorf, *"hamartōlos," TDNT,* 1:331 (1963).

33. See the helpful research by Michael Fink, "The Responses in the New Testament to the Practice of Fasting" (unpublished Ph.D. dissertation; Louisville: The Southern Baptist Theological Seminary, 1974), p. 175.

34. So Reiling and Swellengrebel, *A Translator's Handbook on Luke,* p. 599.

35. Merklein, pp. 38-39.

36. See the thoughtful reflections by W. Scarlett, "Two Men: A Meditation," *Christianity and Crisis,* 14:121-2 (1954).

37. A. Loisy, *L'Evangile selon Luc* (Paris: Emile Nourry, 1924), p. 443.

38. George Buttrick, *The Parables of Jesus,* p. 88.

39. Emil Brunner, *Sowing and Reaping: The Parables of Jesus,* trans. Thomas Wieser (Richmond: John Knox, 1964), p. 22.

40. Lewis Sherrill, *Guilt and Redemption* Revised Edition (Richmond: John Knox Press, 1957), pp. 106-109, so interprets the Pharisees.

41. David Redding, *The Parables He Told* (New York: Harper & Row, 1962), p. 106.

42. Paul Tillich, *The Courage to Be* (New Haven: Yale University Press, 1952), pp. 163-167. He saw legalism as the rejection of the courage to be.

43. Leslie Weatherhead, *In Quest of a Kingdom* (New York: Abingdon-Cokesbury, 1944), p. 84.

Part IV

The Character of Discipleship in the Kingdom

12 The Parable of the Unmerciful Servant

Setting (18:21-22)

A sinned-against disciple brought to Jesus a genuine dilemma. How many times should he forgive a brother who wrongs him? So Peter asked, offering a respectable answer of seven times for openers. Jesus responded first by negative clarification that his instruction had not been and would not be a practical rule of thumb. On the contrary, the distinctive injunction of Jesus redefined the appropriate stance: seventy times seven (v. 22).[1] The point clearly is an infinite number, times *without* number, a stance necessary for true forgiveness. After all,

There could be no thought of forgiveness at all if we were counting whether it was the fourth, the fifth, or even already the seventh time. We should only be saving up the sins in order to go on punishing them still when the total has been reached.[2]

So in a teachable moment when a disciple expressed a felt need for an answer, Jesus introduced a radical reorientation toward offending brothers and sisters.

The forthcoming parable would have said to Peter that forgiveness was not optional equipment for a kingdom citizen! The parable would have raised the disciple's consciousness regarding the cruciality of forgiving another. The pattern is familiar in the Synoptics wherein a genuine question out of human conflict often became the occasion for a memorable "one-liner" answer followed by an unsolicited parable on the kingdom (as Luke 12:13-21; 13:1-9). It is likely that the parable actually arose spontaneously from Peter's query.[3]

The passage enjoys a strategic position (*Sitz im Buch*) in Matthew, standing at the conclusion of the famous ecclesiastical discourse. Possibly there was conflict within Matthew's church and the pastor-evangelist called for forgiving relationships in order to restore a fractured congregation.[4] He, in effect, applied these teachings of Jesus to his divided church. After all, community is lost if forgiveness ceases. Unforgiveness could not be tolerated precisely because it destroys togetherness.[5] Throughout Matthew (9:13; 12:7) there is a particular stress upon God's requirement of mercy based on Hosea 6:6.

Unfolding of the Parabolic Drama

The parable is "a small masterpiece of dramatic choreography"[6] containing three discrete scenes or acts. Each contains an introduction and three movements.[7] There are key speeches in every scene, more or less carrying the action, and highly significant parallel pleas for mercy in the first two scenes (vv. 26b, 29b). These two pleading speeches define the issue. Internal comparison invites attention throughout, especially the contrasting responses to indebtedness (vv. 27,30). The royal speech at the finish makes the contrast of responses explicit and contains the thrust of the parable (vv. 32b-33). The contrast between the two kingly judgments of the same servant, compassion, and wrath (vv. 27a, 34a), is pivotal and stands out in the Greek text.[8] In all three scenes, imprisonment looms as a threat, and in each there is a reckoning.

A Merciful Reckoning (vv. 23-27). A king conducted a royal reckoning with his servants or ministers. The first servant may have been a high placed satrap of a province or a minister of state[9] or just possibly a revenue farmer.[10] The monarch, probably a secular king in a Gentile setting[11] such as Egypt, demanded payment of ten thousand talents, an astounding liability. A talent was the standard large weight of the time and worth in money six thousand drachmas or denarii.[12] So the king's servant owed the crown sixty million drachmas or denarii, the equivalent of sixty million working days for a day laborer! Just one talent equaled six thousand working days for a day laborer or twenty-four years of work with weekends off.

The sovereign ordered the man and his family sold into slavery and everything he possessed auctioned, a shocking and at first blush unduly harsh sentence. The severity of the punishment was due to the enormity of the debt and accepted practice of the time however. In desperation, the servant fell to his knees, his world collapsing. His body language conveyed it all. On the verge of catastrophe, he was reduced to a beggar pleading, "Delay your wrath upon me and I will repay you everything" (v. 26b). He requested an extension and frantically promised to repay an enormous debt.

The king's compassion outran the servant's request. It went beyond uncommon generosity to amazing grace. The improbable happened. He freed him from the prison fate and canceled his debt. The servant's whole existence and sense of worth and well-being had been on the brink of dissolution. Instead, undeservingly he received royal mercy. The king had been touched by the pathos of his servant's pleading and empathized to the extent of a positive stirring of pity. In the light of the remainder of the parable, it is most enlightening to observe here that the king's response of compassion (v. 27a) might well be translated as mercy along the same lines as Proverbs 12:10 and *The Testaments of the XII Patriarchs*.[13]

An Unmerciful Reckoning (vv. 28-30). That same servant sought out a fellow servant who owed him not a tithe as many denarii as he had owed talents to the king! He treated him roughly, seizing him by the throat and making peremptory demand for payment.[14] The second servant went prostrate at the feet of the first servant and begged for mercy. He owed the considerable sum of a hundred denarii, but a king's servant in time could have retired that debt. He used the very words of plaintive entreaty the first servant had himself expressed in parallel plight (v. 29b).

Verse 30, the decision of the first servant, is expressive in the Greek. He did *not will* (*ouk āthelen*) to be merciful, but on the contrary (*alla*) threw his fellow servant into jail.[15] He refused to allow his life to be transformed by merciful love.[16] His action expressed the antithesis of mercy. "Unmoved by the august presence from which he has just come, by the memory of a recent benefit, and by the repetition of the words of his own prayer"[17] he carried out a rigid, unmerciful reckoning. He was owed a piddling sum by comparison, and for that matter the granting of an extension represented a realistic arrangement, but he preferred bitter vindictiveness. He had just experienced remission of an unpayable debt yet refused an extension on a manageable debt. So two remarkably parallel scenes have radically different resolutions. The original hearers of the parable, privy to the parallel reckonings, would have been scandalized by the abhorrent action of the unmerciful servant and prepared to say "Serves him right" when the climactic scene concluded. The hearers may not have been quite so ready for verse 35 however.

An Indignant Reckoning (vv. 31-34). Interceding servants distressed about the unmercied servant and furious at the unmerciful servant for his heartlessness reported the whole story to the king (v. 31). These servants serve a dramatic function by setting in motion additional reckoning and anticipating and legitimating the upcoming indignation of the king, underscoring the heinousness of the unmerciful servant's attitude by their spontaneous outcry and gathering in the hearers of the parable for the climactic judgment. The background was set for the synthesis scene.

Upon receipt of the report, the lord immediately demanded the presence of the first servant, and the stage was set for confrontation. With great authority, the master boldly faced his servant in a stunning moment of truth. Only now does the lord make a formal speech, but it is the longest speech[18] by far and is climactic and definitive. He named the servant *evil* and reminded him that he had been forgiven everything he owed *because* (*epei* is causal) he had implored desperately (v. 32bc). The word *parakaleō* often has the sense of "asking for help" and is especially noticeable in the Gospels when used of the sick beseeching Jesus for help (Mark 1:40; Luke 8:41). So the initial mercy came as a response to pleading. The lord had modeled mercying (v. 33b), but the issue is also existential. The unforgiving servant was himself mercied. He knew what it was like to be prostrate and unable to pay—to be altogether dependent upon someone else's mercy. And he knew what it was like to receive mercy when in such dire circumstances. He knew how good it felt to rise from his knees with the weight of the world off his shoulders. Yet he could close his heart to his fellow servant's desperation. The issue is responding to a plea— having a heart ("as I have mercied you," v. 33b).

So the sovereign responded with wrath (v. 34), a classic contrast to his previous compassion (v. 27a). He turned the wicked servant over to the jailors[19] until he repaid everything he owed (cf. v. 30b). *The lord had a soft spot, but he was not a soft touch.* The king's indignant action was none too extreme for a servant without heart who was ungrateful, egoistic, and harsh.[20] In the first scene the lord had evidenced already his preference for mercy. The king was disposed to grace but capable of indignant judgment.

Meaning of the Parabolic Drama

Function of the Parable. The parable itself functions as a *warning* to jolt and awaken. Each of the three dramatic scenes features a reckoning. The sovereignty of the king hovers over the entire narrative. The climactic third scene describes stinging reckoning from an indignant king. This parable, as others, puts an issue into a new perspective—the viewpoint of the kingdom of God. It provides a theological attitude toward an offending person rather than merely a rule of thumb. The story seeks to awaken the hearer to the imperative of forgiving one's offending brother or sister. Failure to do so will bring a thundering denial. Do not imagine casually that hardheartedness toward a fellow is of no concern to heaven. The parable warns negatively. It is a "refusal parable." It exposed a form of ungrateful existence unacceptable in the kingdom. Mistreatment of fellow human beings will not go unrewarded. There is no sloppy *agape* here! The parable moved against cheap grace, against those who imagine immunity from wrath because of covenantal status.

After the parable comes the *application*: "Thus also will my heavenly father do to you unless each of you forgives your brother from your hearts" (Matt. 18:35).[21] Only then with the application was the original hearer brought personally into the parable event. The hearers would have booed the unmerciful servant and sympathized with the unmercied servant and agreed with the king's rectifying judgment. Thus they (and we) would have voted against the heartless servant analogous to the way David did after Nathan's parable of the little ewe lamb (2 Sam. 12:1-7). Suddenly the Parabolist related the parable to the hearers themselves, interlocking the hearers with the story and creating an existential encounter. (Observe the use of "you" and "your" and "each one of you.")

A stress upon forgiving from the heart appears in verse 35, and this is exactly on target in regard to the parable despite the fact that the word *heart* has not appeared. The king explained his forgiveness as *caused* by the desperate imploring of his servant (v. 32). Indeed, his response was so heartfelt that he gave him far more than he dared ask (v. 27). The call for forgiving from the heart "keystones the whole passage, and indeed the New Testament" (as Rom. 6:17; 1 Pet. 1:22).[22] Indeed, the only kind of genuine forgiveness is, and in the nature of the case has to be, from the heart.

Some scholars believe that the parable is primarily a warning about the last judgment.[23] The parable undeniably assumes divine judgment and is a jolting warning. Efforts to make the reference to imprisonment until he repays all he owes (v. 34) refer to purgatory or universal salvation in a far hereafter represent an unduly allegorical exegesis however. The reference belongs to the story and is understood when seen as corresponding to the treatment meted out to the second servant (v. 30*b*). The parable is an eschatological or apocalyptic assessment of heartlessness, but it intended to make an impact upon that historical moment rather than merely give a revelation about the last judgment. At least no explicit reference is so made.

Thrust of the Parable. The story compels *the imperative of forgiveness upon the forgiven.* The forgiven must forgive because forgiven. The indicative of grace emphatically precedes in the parable through the king's mercy, so there is no legalistic distortion. The parable is not open to that misunderstanding because of the antecedent of grace. The disciple does not earn divine acceptance but receives remission first for an unpayable debt. So the indicative precedes the imperative.

The imperative to forgive others does follow grace however. Forgiveness appears explicitly as the clear relational imperative both in the king's speech (vv. 32*b*-33) and in the application (v. 35),[24] and it is predicated upon the indicative of grace. It is a decidedly theological ethic comparable to Jesus' insistence upon the indissoluble linkage between the commands to love God and neighbor (Mark 12:34-40). There is no separating allowable between the disciple's relation to God and to followers. Helmut Thielicke observes that "in the Christian faith nothing remains shut up in the ghetto of our inner life. Everything in it immediately thrusts out and seeks to become an action."[25] Indeed, the fatherhood of God and the brotherhood and sisterhood of humanity are encouraged by the parable, but with the realistic recognition of man's inhumanity to man. The horizontal component of authentic religion reappeared with magnificent monotony in the proclamation of Jesus. "Become merciful just as your father is merciful" (Luke 6:36), he commanded.

So the character of discipleship is defined as an echo of the divine forgiveness. The parable revealed God's will for disciples to forgive offending brothers and sisters times without number because of an amazing grace forgiving *all*.[26]

Assumption of the Parable. The parable assumes the sovereignty of God. It is a kingdom of God parable not merely because it is so named (v. 23), but because the sovereignty of the will of God is presumed throughout. God or Yahweh is pictured in the Old Testament as King by Isaiah (6:5) and Jeremiah (46:18; 48:15) and the psalmist (5:2; 24:7) in terms of his power, greatness and willingness to help.[27] Surely the king of the parable reminded Jewish hearers of God the King. [Note the divine sovereignty in the strength of mercy (v. 27) and the strength of judgment (vv. 32-34).] Jesus believed passionately in the sovereignty of God, desired God's will on earth (Matt. 6:10), and conceived of the Heavenly Father and the Heavenly King as one and the same.[28] The divine mercy seen in the king is a miracle out of God's sovereignty.

Jesus shared in the divine sovereignty by the authority to speak for God both in verse 35 and supremely through the entire parable. There is obvious Christological penetration in verse 35 ("my heavenly father") and in his ministry he created a fellowship of the forgiven (Luke 7:36-50).

Hermeneutical Exploration

The Personal Involvement. The hearer or reader or student of the parable cannot go unscathed or remain blithely uninvolved. Who has not found it difficult to forgive someone who has willfully undermined personhood or position? Eta Linnemann must be heard in her insistence that "our assent to the parable means that we have fallen into contradiction with ourselves. . . . After the word of Jesus has reached us," she continues, "we cannot leave everything as it was and still think everything is in order."[29] The imperative of forgiveness upon us the forgiven breaks into our comfortable working arrangements with life, exposes our cherished grudges, discloses our hidden hostilities, and unmasks our guerrilla warfare. The parable stubbornly insists upon repentance.

The Relevance of Judgment. Such a God as revealed through the parable will not ignore genocide with yawning indifference, nor the crushing of other people by economic clout with divine unconcern, nor the kicking of people when they are down as a matter of no consequence. No one since the beginning of time has lived as if God did not count and gotten away with it. Permissiveness may go on its flippant way, but God's sovereignty must be encountered yet. The reality of judgment does provide meaning to human existence. Human life matters to God; and since Ultimate Reality takes note of human existence, life takes on value. Furthermore, the quality of relations between persons on earth matters infinitely to God. He wills something better because he cares. He wills peace. Also, injustice will not triumph forever or go unnoted.

The Power of Forgiveness. Christian forgiveness lies not merely with the common grace of a sunny disposition, but with the antecedent graces of God. We love one another because God has loved us (1 John 4:11). The parable is at its winsome best with its picture of a king with a heart (v. 27) and a forgiveness that can free.[30] The first servant was given the power of forgiveness, a gift of grace.

In practical terms, the power of forgiveness can come by remembering our awesome debt to God in comparison to an offense done us by a neighbor. "Only the thought of what God has done for us and what he has forgiven us," said Thielicke on the last Sunday of Hitler's Third Reich, "can suddenly lift us above the situation, can deliver us from the lurking reaction of anger and bitterness and give us the royal freedom to forgive."[31] Otherwise we retort with revenge, "the sweetest morsel ever cooked in hell,"[32] or suppress anger to explode later in our interiors or toward another.

The Community of Forgiveness. The evangelist saw the necessity for forgiveness if Christian community were to happen. Jesus was calling a new kind of community into existence, the sort that *cannot be without forgiveness.* It depends upon catching the spirit of the King, else it is hardly his community. The church becomes a new kind of community when the triumph of grace occurs within it. The church is a community of forgiveness that relates redemptively to sinners because it itself is "for sinners only," for those raised to their feet by amazing grace. The Christian naturally relates the mercy of the king in the parable to Christ's gracious act on Calvary and recalls the Lukan word from the cross: "Father, forgive." "God's grace may flow freely toward us," A. M. Hunter reminds, "only when we are channels through which it may flow to others" (Matt. 6:14-15; Mark 11:25; Eph. 4:32; Col. 3:13; Jas. 2:13).[33]

NOTES

1. The Greek *heōs ebdomekōntakis hepta* could also be rendered seventy seven times, a number reminiscent of Genesis 4:24. Luke 17:4 refers to seven times a day.

2. Eta Linnemann, *Jesus of the Parables*, p. 107.

3. It is possible that Matthew 18:21-22, capable of standing independently as a self-contained pericope, has been juxtaposed by the evangelist with the parable. See Linnemann, p. 106; Christian Dietzfelbinger, "Das Gleichnis von der erlassenen Schuld," *Evangelische Theologie*, 32:438 (1959). However, both the incident and the parable are concerned about the inclination to be unforgiving and both highlight the importance of a disciple forgiving a person offending him directly. The parable provides basis for boundless forgiving (18:22) in the example of the compassionate lord (18:27), yet adding as well the note of judgment upon calloused refusal to forgive. Indeed the basis for the forgiveness among fellow servants derives from the generosity of the King. I wonder further if Luke 17:3-4, replete with an offender pleading, is not an accurate historical remembrance fitting hand in glove with the parable pattern in Matthew 18. It may reflect the Lukan emphasis on repentance, however.

4. Eduard Schweizer, *The Good News According to Matthew*, p. 379, says, "Matthew is concerned to help the community really live as the community of Christ."

5. David Hill, *The Gospel of Matthew*, p. 277, wonders if the church were in a position where it may have to judge sternly "those who jeopardize the fellowship by their lack of mercy towards others." See W. G. Thompson, *Matthew's Advice to a Divided Community: Matthew 17:22-18:35*. No. 44 of "Analecta Biblica" (Rome: Biblical Institute Press, 1970).

6. J. D. Crossan, *In Parables*, p. 106.

7. So T. Deidun, "The Parable of the Unmerciful Servant (Matt. 18:23-25), *Biblical Theology Bulletin*, 6:216n (1976), possibly following F. H. Breukelmann.

8. The Greek is stylistically parallel (*splangnistheis, orgistheis*) and would seem definitely intended by the evangelist's diction. Furthermore, this very stylistic contrast appears in another parable belonging to the Lukan tradition (Luke 15:11-32). Hence two special traditions (M and L) report a strikingly similar pattern and provide not only evidence for authenticity but indication of the kind of internal comparison Jesus devised within parables. Note also Matthew 22:7 and Luke 14:21 where the second reaction is wrathful.

9. See Ezra 4:7,9,17,23; 5:3,6; 6:6,13; and 2 Esdras where the term *sundoulos* refers to high officials under the governors. So Jeremias, *Parables*, p. 212.

10. Duncan Derrett, *Law in the New Testament*, pp. 37-41, is insistent that the servants in the parables were major revenue farmers and that the parable portrays consistently a realistic situation in which a tax collector actually owed ten thousand talents in uncollected tax revenues. Earlier scholars have also reckoned with this possibility. The apparent Achilles' heel is the stubborn fact that the account nowhere speaks of tax revenues but does speak of *debt*.

11. Most students are convinced that the assumed setting is non-Jewish because the sale of a wife was prohibited in Jewish law, and no institution of slavery for debt was allowed for fellow Jews (Lev. 25:39-43). An Herodian context is not impossible, but the sum is too large.

12. O. R. Sellers, "Talent," *IDB*, R-Z:510-11 (1962). The drachma was a Grecian silver coin equated with the Roman denarius. So H. Hamburger, "Drachma," *IDB*, A-D:867. Jeremias, *Jerusalem in the Time of Jesus*, p. 91, refers to a Hebrew talent worth as much as ten thousand silver drachmas. It is possible that hearers of the parable may have remembered the tale of Joseph, the son of Tobias, who bought the right to tax Syria, Phoenicia, Judea, and Samaria from the Ptolemy. According to Josephus, *Antiquities*, 12:4, the revenue for that region came to more than eight thousand talents. Derrett, *Law*, p. 33, stresses this connection and insists that the parable's reference to ten thousand talents was quite realistic and not fantastic. However, the critical notes in the Loeb edition are quite skeptical of the sum. Derrett (p. 45) also insists against Jeremias that one of R. Aqiba's parables parallels the Unmerciful Servant. However, in Aqiba's parable the impression gained is that one can ingratiate oneself with God, scarcely a dominical idea.

13. See H. Köster, "*splangnon*," *TDNT*, 7:550-554 (1971). In *Test. of Zeb.* compassion and mercy are used interchangeably (5:1), and the two are beautifully portrayed as "weeping with" (3:5-6).

14. There is a striking parallel in *Baba Bathra* 18:8: "If a man seized a debtor by the throat in the street. . . ." Oesterley, *The Gospel Parables*, p. 97, reported that clutching a debtor by the collar of his toga and dragging him off to prison was Roman custom.

15. Linnemann, p. 110, points out that the first servant could not sell the second servant into slavery because the indebtedness was less than the average price of a slave.

16. Deidun, p. 218.

17. A. B. Bruce, *The Parabolic Teaching of Christ*, p. 406.

18. Thirty words are given to the king's speech as compared to eleven (v. 26), four (v. 28), and nine (v. 29).

19. The Greek *basanistēs* can be rendered jailer or torturer. There were torturers in Herod's household according to Josephus, *Jewish War*, 1:592, 635. Derrett, *Law*, pp. 46-7, related torturers to debtors' prisons whose presence improved the honesty of the debtor regarding personal assets and encouraged his family to make good the debt.

20. So C. Spicq, *Dieu et L'Homme*, Vol. 29 of "Lectio Divina" (Paris: Du Cerf, 1961), p. 61.

21. Many students consider verse 35 Matthaean, and it is quite true that there are several conspicuous elements present characteristic of the evangelist such as "my heavenly father" and the use of "brother" and the second person plurals. Matthew did have a keen sense of Jesus as one who stood closer to God than other men (cf. Mark 3:35 with Matt. 12:50; Mark 10:40 with Matt. 20:23; Mark 14:25 with Matt. 26:29). See G. Schrenk, "*patēr*," *TDNT*, 5:987n (1967). One may also recognize that verse 35 climaxed a lengthy unit in Matthew. However, it is not necessary to conclude that the entire verse is only from the evangelist. E. Linnemann, p. 107, is quite certain that verse 35 does not fit the parable exactly because it makes verse 34 the point of the parable. I believe that the point lies in verse 33 (along with v. 32b) so far as *interpretation* is concerned. Indeed, verse 35 is not an interpretation but an existential application. The parable is an awakening or warning parable like the Rich Man and Lazarus.

22. E. Schweizer, p. 379.

23. They point to the apocalyptic flavor at verse 34 (Rev. 14:10,11; 18:7,10,15; 10:10), the thinly disguised reference to endless punishment in verse 34, and the future tense of

verse 35. Jeremias, *Parables*, p. 213, favors the last judgment as the focus.

24. Forgiveness and debts are often and naturally associated. The Old Testament teaches that sin makes people debtors to God. See Numbers 5:7-8; Jeremiah 51:5; Isaiah 24:6; also Matthew 6:12*a* (debts). And in the New Testament one who prays for forgiveness must be willing to forgive (Mark 11:25; Matt. 6:12*b*). See also Colossians 3:13; Ephesians 4:32. Thus interrelationship of divine and human forgiveness may also be seen in *Test. of Zeb.* 5:3 and 8:1-3 and in Sirach 28:2-5. Matthew 6:15 chimes in with Matthew 18:35.

25. Thielicke, *Our Heavenly Father*, trans. by J. Doberstein (New York: Harper, 1960), p. 112.

26. Observe the prominence of the word *all* in the parable (*panta* in v. 26*c*, *pasan* in v. 32, and *pan* in v. 34). Each usage is in relation to the first servant's enormous indebtedness and is not present in any references to the second servant.

27. G. von Rad, "*Basileus*," *TDNT*, 1:568-571 (1964).

28. See T. W. Manson, *The Teaching of Jesus*, Second Edition (Cambridge: University Press, 1959), p. 163. The heart of Manson's analysis, in contrast to Jeremias' emphasis upon the Father, lay in an extended statement of God as King (pp. 116-284).

29. Linnemann, pp. 112-113.

30. Dietzfelbinger, pp. 441-442, makes a creative, Fuchsian hermeneutical observation that the king offered the gift of time and the gift of freedom, though they are denied.

31. Thielicke, p. 113.

32. Attributed to Sir Walter Scott by A. M. Hunter, *The Parables Then and Now*, p. 68.

33. Hunter, *Luke*, Vol. 18 of "The Layman's Bible Commentary" (Richmond: John Knox Press, 1959), p. 82.

Luke 10:25-37

13 The Parable of the Compassionate Samaritan

The words comprising the parable of the Good Samaritan contain an unaccountable power. The simple narrative has inspired the construction of literally hundreds of hospitals and gained respect even from non-Christians. It has engaged the Western imagination in an almost unparalleled fashion. It has promoted acts of kindness every day of the last two millennia. The story symbolizes applied Christianity and makes unmistakable that compassion is more "than a tingling sensation in the gizzards."

One suspects that difficulty of interpretation lies not with understanding the second most famous parable but with applying it, yet careful attention to the text enriches the traditional interpretation. Sharper focus must begin by grasping the context.

The Life Situation

It is just possible that Jesus was standing on or near the Jericho road when he spoke the parable since Bethany is on the same road and the next pericopé centers there.[1] Certainly the parables usually associated with Galilee are not peopled with priestly sorts whereas this parable may well have been uttered in Judea, a region more related to the Temple. The parable may belong to the later phase of Jesus' ministry after he set his face to go to Jerusalem (Luke 9:51). Very possibly the story anticipated the action of cleansing the Temple and stood in some temporal proximity.

The teachable moment for the parable arose when a scribe[2] engaged Jesus in a dialogue concerning how he could inherit eternal life (cf. Luke 18:18). This leading question may have been typical (see Luke 18:18-30). Students of Rabbi Eliezer are said to have requested him to teach them the ways of life so they might attain to the life of the future world (b. Ber. 28*b*).[3] Jesus, assuming the authority of the Law, pursued the question with another query: what is written in the Law? Georges Crespy, recognizing the transaction, observes, "From being the one who puts Jesus to the test, he becomes the one who is tested by Jesus."[4]

The scribe, learned in Torah, answered with apparent alacrity melding the two love commands (Deut. 6:5; Lev. 19:18) into one: "You shall love the Lord your God with your whole heart and with your entire soul and with all your strength and with your complete mind, and your neighbor as though yourself" (Luke 10:27). This memorable combination, confirmed by Jesus' personal authority in this context and brought together by him elsewhere (Mark 12:29; Matt. 22:39,[5] had evidently been forged already and repeated by the scribe. The famous *Testaments of the XII Patriarchs* contains passages that bring together love for God and neighbor.[6]

Jesus responded most affirmatively with his famous dominical authority that the scribe had "read" the Law incisively and left no doubt that he too so understood authentic life within the covenant. He added, however, that right reading of the Law would not usher in authentic existence but rather enactment of it. Exhortation one (*Do this and you will live*, v. 28) was not merely moralistic, however, because of the nature of covenantal love commands. The second love command (love neighbor) assumes the first (love God),[7] making both *theocentric*. The scribe could not rightly distort the command to love into helping someone in order to win salvation because it would then not have been an act motivated out of genuine love for the person involved. Furthermore, the close connection of the dialogue with the parable serves to link the Samaritan's example to the ministry of Jesus and the proclamation of Jesus to the Old Testament.

The scribe pressed the Teacher further with an essentially exegetical question: Who is my neighbor? The question, which implies that there can be a nonneighbor,[8] reflects an actual debate in the time of Jesus.[9] Leviticus 19 clearly provided for love of fellow countryman (*re'a*, v. 18) and even for the sojourner (*ger*, v. 34). The brouhaha resulted from a lack of consensus as to the precise identity of the *re'a*.

The Pharisees excluded non-Pharisees from their definition of neighbor; the Essenes were to hate all sons of darkness; and a rabbinical saying ruled that heretics, informers, and renegades should be pushed (into the ditch) and not pulled out. Personal enemies were also excluded from the circle (Matt. 5:43).[10]

So the scribe raised a familiar issue out of classic debate. Perhaps he asked a more technical question to show himself no simple man,[11] but it is more likely that he objected to Jesus' neighbors! The seemingly innocuous exegetical question may have been a veiled assault against his controversial ministry to the *Am-ha-ares*, the unclean people of the land. The scribe likely thought that the correct answer must of necessity exclude the "lawless."

Distortion of the parable of the Compassionate Samaritan is more likely when the life situation is ignored or jettisoned unnecessarily. The context of an exegetical discussion clarifies the nature and function of this parable particularly.

Form and Structure

The parable itself is a dramatic story composed of easily separable scenes or moments with a resounding triumph for conclusion. The dramatic situation establishes itself immediately by means of a brutalizing robbery. Powerful narrative features are employed like bandits, coincidence, suspense, contrast in threes, a climactic speech, and unmistakable denouement. It is clearly not an actual event but a stylized story, especially effective because of its realistic detail reminiscent of DeFoe's descriptive power.

Attention to narrative tactic exposes how the parable exemplified the specific situation type. Note the reference to a particular (*tis*) man, priest, and Samaritan (10:30,31,33) as well as usages of past tenses. Observe the specific place names (Jerusalem and Jericho) and the explicitly religious roles. There appears a specific religiosocial structure somewhat determined, a particularity that must be retained. It does not function as the story of any one and subsequent travelers but becomes a comment about authentic religion.

The structure of the narrative tells.[12] It depicts journeys and responses and may be outlined as follows:

> Situation (twenty words; 10:30)
> Response 1 (fourteen words; 10:31)
> Response 2 (eleven words; 10:32)
> Response 3 (sixty words; 10:33-35)

The three travelers are united deftly by the thrice certified point that they saw (*idōn*) the victim. Furthermore, the prepositions that prefix the main verbs themselves convey graphically responses of moving away (*anti*) and toward (*pros*) in verses 31-33, a clue about the nature of compassion. Response 3, fitting the law of end stress, dominates. Significantly, it contains a climactic speech from the Samaritan that functions in a crowning fashion (v. 35). Internal comparison, made explicit later (v. 36), functions among the three responses.

The parable, by all means an answer to the scribe's exegetical question regarding the identity of his neighbor (as I hope to show), interprets and extends the second love command (Lev. 19:18) with that breathtaking approach to the Scriptures characteristic of Jesus. The parable answers the scribe's question at the same time and does far more. Existential excitement exists in the new exegesis that not only has the flavor of discovery but also becomes Scripture itself. One may call the parable in a general way midrashic, though it exceeds its counterparts.[13] While the parable derived much of its direction from the Scriptures (Lev. 19:18; Hos. 6:6-8; 2 Chron. 28:1-15) as a midrash should, it also owed much to the eschatological moment of the ministry of Jesus. Here is a clue to Jesus' stance toward the Old Testament. At any rate it is natural to expect a midrashic parable within a dialogue with a scribe.

The parable and dialogue do transcend the agenda setting of the scribe as Jesus sounded a covenantal call to action rather than merely providing good exegesis. Since the famous parable student Jülicher, many, especially Roman Catholics,[14] have dubbed the parable an example story because Jesus finished by directing to go and do likewise (*homoiōs*, 10:37). Certainly the Samaritan is an inspirational figure and the detailed description of his compassion fairly invites imitation. However, the literary category should be used with reserve because it lacks a certain dynamism and tends to reduce the parable both theologically and literarily.

The Unfolding of the Narrative

Jesus took up the challenge of the scribe's second question (who is my neighbor?) with alacrity and creativity. The scribe had required the fine point that did not yield easily. The Greek word (*hupolambano*, v. 30), often left untranslated, means here Jesus "took him up"

and conveys the flavor of challenge accepted! The parable that resulted, it is well to remember, is a Jesus story.

Situation (10:30). The narrative sets the scene of an unidentified
man descending the treacherous road from Jerusalem to Jericho. He
was probably an Israelite or *Am-ha-ares* but just might have been a
Roman. The actual road descended 3,270 feet or 997 meters. Josephus
reported the distance as 150 stades (*Wars*, 4.475), the equivalent of 19
Roman miles or 17 English miles or 28 kilometers. The entire journey
could have been accomplished in a day. H. B. Tristram described the
desolate terrain memorably as a barren, treeless wilderness with ir-
regular sharp turns in the road providing safe cover for robbers.[15]
Interestingly enough on the old Roman road 5 miles above Jericho
there is a pass called in Arabic *tal 'at el-damm*, the Ascent of Blood.
The original Hebrew name may have referred to red rocks, the red
marl, but tradition has associated it with the blood shed by robbers.[16]
It is an intriguing possibility that Jesus had this pass in mind.

Several robbers ganged up on their victim and brutalized him. He
never had a fighting chance, though he apparently resisted. They
deprived him of his clothing by force, probably plundering his cloak
(*chlamus*), an outer garment made of goat's or camel's hair used by
travelers and soldiers.[17] Possibly they also took the tunic (*chiton*)
worn next to the skin, an indispensable undergarment often used as a
coverlet at night.[18] That clothing itself was valued is demonstrated by
the record of the soldiers casting lots for Jesus' garments (Mark 15:24,
and par.; John 19:23-24) and the fact that garments were taken as
spoils of war (Josephus, *Life*, 334). The victim's purse was surely
snatched if in his possession.

The robbers violated his person further with blows, possibly as
severe as lashing (Josephus, *Life*, 335) or flogging with a stick or whip
(Luke 12:48; Acts 16:23; 2 Cor. 6:5; 11:23). Possibly he was struck
about the head with walking sticks as Jesus was (Matt. 27:30), thus
explaining why he was injured to the extent of unconsciousness. The
severity of the beating can be implied also by the wounds requiring
medication mentioned in verse 33, as well as his prostrate condition of
half deadness.[19] The assailants, by deserting the battered man to his
fate, compounded further their cruelty. One cannot sentimentalize the
crass brutality of these criminals.

The nameless robbers may well have been ordinary Bedouins, but
two other dramatic identifications deserve naming. What if they were

Jews of a Zealotic persuasion? The brigands are called *lēstai* (10:30,36), a word which suggests the "ruthless use of force in seeking the goods of others."[20] Commonly it referred to ordinary robbers, but this same word could refer to a political revolutionary like the violent Zealots.[21] Then the parable would express fundamental opposition to the fashion in which the Zealots think they serve God. Yet another possibility remains that the robbers were undisciplined Roman soldiers. This is allowable because the word originally meant "to gain as booty" and in the Hellenistic world could be used to refer to the mercenary soldier who had a right to plunder.[22] Both of these are exciting suppositions that silence holds at bay.

Response 1 (10:31). A priest responded by refusing to expose himself to human needs. He came riding down the road out of Jerusalem so he may have just come from one of his two annual sabbath-to-sabbath stints in the Temple (cf. Luke 1:5-8).[23] Interestingly, a large number of priests were scribes, a fact that would not be lost on the scribe questioning Jesus.[24] Such a priest enjoyed by hereditary office badges of belonging like direct access to the court of the priests and social station above the Levite. A pecking order can be found in one religious tractate: "A priest reads first, and after him a Levite, and after him an Israelite—in the interests of peace" (Gittin 5:8; cf. Horayoth 3:8).

Upon sight, the priest reacted by complete withdrawal to the opposite side of the road. He put all the possible distance between himself and the stranger. Could it be that he concluded that the unidentified stranger was not a neighbor? Perhaps the victim was a sinner who had forfeited his religious heritage. Could it be that the man appeared dead because unconscious and the priest abhorred uncleanness? Indeed, the Old Testament had served notice that contact with a corpse caused uncleanness (Num. 19:11-16) and directed a priest to avoid contact altogether except for the closest of kin (Lev. 21:1-4).[25] Had he rendered himself unclean for a stranger, it would have been inconvenient and might have cost him income and would have been particularly odious to a priest who valued religious purity so highly.[26] One cannot be sure, but in any event his dissociation put him in enormous tension with the second love command (Lev. 19:18). It may well be that he thought that the stranger was a breathing Jewish brother. Compassion was notable by its absence.[27]

Response 2 (10:32). A Levite exposed himself to human need yet failed to aid. The text describing the response of the second clerical traveler is not precisely the same as for the first and may well favor the picture of the Levite drawing nearer and looking more carefully.[28] He may have expressed heartless curiosity or anemic pity. He too confined his religious practice to the Temple. Compared to the priests, the Levites formed an inferior clergy passing as descendants of Levi. They could take no part in the offering of sacrifice and were forbidden, on pain of death, access to the altar (Num. 18:3). They functioned as musicians and janitors and as Temple police would have had authority to keep out a Samaritan. Some of the Levites were scribes versed in the Law, as Joseph Barnabas, the convert to Christianity.[29]

One interesting possibility turns on a silence in the text. Could it be that the Levite, unlike the priest, was journeying from Jericho to Jerusalem and thus toward Temple service?[30] This would explain why he was exercised to avoid defilement if, indeed, he thought the victim dead, a still undemonstrated theory. At any rate, even apart from Response 3, the parable delivers a pulverizing indictment of a Levite who withheld mercy.

Response 3 (10:33-35). A Samaritan exposed himself to human hurt and was overcome by compassion. The original hearers undoubtedly expected the hero to be a layman, after two dismal clerical failures, but scarcely a Samaritan. Shock, a characteristic weapon of Jesus' parables, likely called forth a bristling from the hearers in this instance. When Jesus celebrated a Samaritan at the expense of Israelites, he touched a raw nerve and put electricity in the air.

The Samaritans enjoyed the lowest rung on the social ladder following after despised trades, Jewish slaves, Israelites with a slight blemish, Israelites with a grave blemish, and Gentile slaves.[31] The Jews often called the Samaritans "Cutheans" to distinguish them sharply from Israelites,[32] and the name *Samaritan* conveyed contempt (John 8:48). Though involvement in commerce with Samaritans was allowed, they remained suspect and were not to be trusted.[33] The Jews separated themselves socially by refusing to associate on friendly terms or use dishes in common (John 4:9).

At the time of Jesus, relations were especially embittered, and the Samaritans were probably forbidden access to the inner courts of the Temple,[34] a striking factor in the light of the parable. Even if the

Temple tax were volunteered, it should be returned: "if a gentile or a Samaritan paid the Shekel it is not accepted of them" (Shekalim 1:5). Indeed, one could argue that the clash between Jews and Samaritans more often than not centered in the Temple![35] The parable is situated in the eye of the storm.

This "certain Samaritan" overcame his own consciousness of kind with a love from the bowels. The Greek word for *compassion* means a heartfelt mercy felt in the inward parts.[36] It is a very special verb in the Synoptics, referring to the attitude of Jesus except in those parables where he uses it himself of others. Contextually compassion is a moving toward (*pros*) human need leading to involvement. Note the specificity of the Samaritan's caring:

> he cleansed and sterilized the wounds with oil and wine;[37]
> perhaps he bandaged the wounds with his head cloth;
> he placed the man on his animal to ride;[38]
> he escorted the man to the nearest inn;
> he nursed the man caring for him;
> he gave the innkeeper two silver coins to cover the
>   robbed man's needs;[39]
> and he promised to return and defray additional costs.

So the Samaritan's action reveals the shape of compassion.

The inn or khan to which the wounded man was taken would have been a simple resting place for travelers (as Jer. 41:17). It would have been a square enclosure with a gateway by the side of which was the keeper's lodge. Only straw for sleeping and water for drinking were provided. Inside the hollow square were rows of chambers open in front for animals. Most of the men would have slept under the open arches beside their beasts.[40] There remains the ruins of an old khan still standing midway between Jerusalem and Jericho.[41]

In the strategic, climactic speech, the Samaritan expresses forcefully his intention that compassion continue through the agency of the innkeeper in his own absence. His compassionate spirit is such that he sets no limits on necessary expenditure and promises to return and pay even more out of his uncalculating generosity (v. 35).

Interpretation

Personal Encounter (10:36-37). Without a break, Jesus pressed the scribe with a kind of forced ranking or multiple choice question:

"Which of the three, do *you* think, turned out to be neighbor to the one who fell into the hands of robbers?" This natural question, on which the scribe must have choked, was put to force him "to involve himself in the implication of the story."[42] Throughout the entire exchange of question and counter question there has been a battle of wills, and the scribe sought desperately to retain the initiative and escape the existential claim of the love command and of Jesus. The scribe's vaunting pride had been taking a beating since the priestly debacle in the story and the winsome warmheartedness of the Samaritan. The scribe would have identified with the priest and Levite[43] and felt emotional distance from the Samaritan. The question of Jesus required him to put together two impossible and contradictory words for the same person: Samaritan (10:33) and neighbor (10:36). The whole thrust of the story demands that he say what cannot be said: Good Samaritan.[44] It was a moment of truth, and the scribe's values and assumptions are in disarray and his being tolled; yet he was scripture student enough to know that his own initial answer (v. 37) required the conclusion that the one doing mercy neighbored (v. 37*b*).

As the scribe's religious horizons broadened when he accepted a Samaritan as a model of the love command, Jesus then asked him to "be a Samaritan."[45] Like "a sovereign command-er"[46] Jesus demanded, "Go and *you do* likewise" (v. 37*d*). To respond willingly to the demand was to begin to accept the lordship of Christ. An academic debate became a meaningful existential encounter.

Answer to the Question. Many sensitive lay persons and scholars have sensed a discrepancy or "deficient logic"[47] between the questions about the identity of one's neighbor (v. 29) and who turned out to be neighbor (v. 36). It is often said that Jesus did not answer the scribe's question but led him to answer another. Such careful reading is consciousness raising because it highlights the fact that the parable goes well beyond the mere information-asking of the scribe (v. 29). However, the tension between the questions can be overdrawn because one is a neighbor to a neighbor. Furthermore, the tension itself communicates the nature of the transaction between Jesus and the scribe. Jesus met the scribe not merely with scriptural interpretation but also with word of God. After all, "A successful parable is an event that decisively alters the situation."[48]

If, as I claim, Jesus did answer the question, what was his answer?

Was it that his neighbor is a Samaritan?[49] Probably not. Was it that his neighbor is anyone in need? Yes, but the answer is more pointed yet. Remember that the Samaritan would have been programmed to distrust/dislike any Jew, yet he had compassion. He loved an enemy. Jesus reveals the kingdom-of-God perspective that *even an enemy is your neighbor.* The scribe surely collided with his pride when he recognized the Samaritan as the hero and as one who could practice the law of Moses, but he was extended far more to see that neighboring could mean loving your enemy (cf. Luke 6:27-36; Matt. 5:43-48).[50] The parable was a revolutionary extension of Leviticus 19:18, not a mere midrash. It also goes beyond Leviticus 19:34,[51] which required a Jew to love the sojourner (*gûr*) as well.[52]

The love command of Leviticus 19:18 *itself* calls for action, and in the parable love is compassion, that is, mercy in action. Go and enflesh the love command. Go and love your neighbor as yourself. Go and show compassion to an enemy. It should be seen that compassion (vv. 33-35) is organically related to exhortation one ("Do this and you will live," v. 28c) and exhortation two ("Go and do likewise," v. 37d). The stress on doing inheres within the parable as well as in the two directives to the scribe. Compassion is something you do. Action is the way to life.[53]

The Samaritan was not so much more liberal-minded as he was more warmhearted. The action of the Samaritan was not merely humanism at its finest for he was exemplar of the second of the two love commands, which were present in his Bible and the heart of the covenant. "The heart makes the final decision. He fulfills his neighbourly duty whose heart detects the distress of the other."[54] The lack of warmhearted action on the part of priest and Levite is painfully apparent, but the kingdom breaks out in the action of the Samaritan: "God reigns where people act like the Samaritan."[55]

Prophetic Protest. The cultic overtones should by no means be allowed to drift away as often happens. The fact that there is specific reference to the road from Jerusalem to Jericho is surely because it is the Temple road and not just any road.[56] The fact that the two travelers were both priestly and not just unidentified travelers is neither accidental nor incidental. The fact that the priest at least was coming from Jerusalem, ostensibly from services, is hardly coincidence. What a damaging comment! Fear of defilement from cultic considerations may possibly have directed noninvolvement, though this may not be in view at all. The role of the Samaritan is intrinsic as well to the cultic comment. He was not just a non-Jew but a *layman* and one disinherited from the inner courts of the Temple. People like the Levite kept him out of the Temple.

The parable was nothing less than a prophetic exposé of the Temple and call to repentance. The villains are decidedly cultic figures, and the Samaritan is an emphatically noncultic figure. The wounded man became a test of authentic religion. The parable exposed the hypocrisy of cultic exclusivism and religious pretension. (Shades of Stephen and Qumran!) The parable is of a piece with the upcoming challenge to Jerusalem and especially the cleansing of the Temple. The Lord of the Temple, like certain prophets preceding, came into open conflict with the Temple itself, that parable in stone. The parable chimes in with Micah strikingly:

> With what shall I come before the Lord,
> and bow myself before God on high?
> Shall I come before him with burnt offerings,
> with calves a year old?
> Will the Lord be pleased with thousands of rams,
> with ten thousands of rivers of oil?
> Shall I give my first-born for my transgression,
> the fruit of my body for the sin of my soul?
> He has showed you, O man, what is good;
> and what does the Lord require of you
> But to do justice, and to love kindness
> and to walk humbly with your God? (6:6-8, RSV).

Christological Penetration. Allegory must not run rampant, especially in such a direct parable, but excessive allegorization has appeared and reappeared.[57] Apparently the temptation to make a simple identification of the Samaritan with Jesus can be overwhelming, and it has even been suggested that the half-dead man is Jesus.[58] That there are Christological implications, however, should not be overlooked.[59]

The place to begin is with the fact that Jesus was the Teller, that furthermore it is his story and meaningful in his moment of history and ministry. His characteristic authority, seen in *the parable as a whole*, is the key. He is a Giver of commands about living, an Interpreter of Scripture with more authority than a scribe, a Maker of the

Scriptures virtually, a Proclaimer of the kingdom (indirectly), and a bold Evaluator of priests and Levites with a high hand. He spoke for God. Furthermore, Jesus saw his ministry directed to Israel. The parable contained a prophetic sting to stir the slumbering conscience of Israel. He saw Israel as in profound need of national repentance and recognized that the cultus was part of the problem. He challenged smug religious complacency from a kingdom of God perspective and revealed reality. The way Jesus sees the world reality is as the Samaritan![60]

Just possibly the scribe was indirectly challenging Jesus' implicit understanding of neighbor and consequent ministry, and the parable defended his own life.[61] Of course, Jesus was the supreme revelation of the neighbor love of God (John 3:16; 2 Cor. 5:19) and *the one* who loved the Father with his whole heart,[62] but such observations are broader theological reflections.

The Absolute Contrast? The clearest opposition abstractly lies between the robbers and the Samaritan.[63] The Samaritan began to undo what the robbers did: they beat the man, the Samaritan poured on oil and wine; the robbers left the man half dead, the Samaritan took him to an inn; they robbed him, the Samaritan contributed financially to his needs. The robbers stood opposite the Samaritan in wounding/healing, also taking/giving. With the brigands there was practice of nonmercy, with the priest and Levite the nonpractice of mercy, and with the Samaritan the practice of mercy. There are those who hurt and those who heal the hurts of others.[64]

Such a reconstruction would likely make the parable anti-Zealotic. The Samaritan loved an enemy, the very thing the Zealots rejected in favor of the opposite. If this view was in mind, it was definitely secondary. It is not the primary intention but an intriguing possibility. In principle, nevertheless, the parable stands in fierce repudiation of the spirit of the Zealots.

The Evangelist's Agenda. Though the dialogue and parable were not constructed by the evangelist,[65] the choice of language is notably Lukan,[66] and the author consciously communicated with a Christian readership. The location and function (*Sitz im Buch*) are significant as the passage appears in the journey to Jerusalem (and Temple) section in the first portion wherein the evangelist is establishing the fact of the fateful journey. The Christian disciples who read learn the radicality of discipleship (9:57-62), hear a call to mission (10:1-16), receive a reassurance of salvation (10:20), overhear a special Christological revelation (10:21-22), discover the special privilege of the Christian era (10:23-24), and note the importance of hearing and responding to his word (10:38-42).[67] Luke preached effectively to his readers.

Several concurrences appear between the parable and Luke's broad concerns. For example, the comments about the motives of the scribe are likely Lukan and reflect good exegesis. The lawyer wishes to challenge the exegetical acumen of Jesus (10:25a) and to justify his own exclusions of some as neighbors (10:29a; cf. 18:9). Another example of a concurrence is clearly the extolling of a Samaritan at the expense of Jewish lepers (Luke 17:11-19) or priests.[68] Probably the evangelist sought to accent the appeal of the gospel to the wider world. His main concern was to call Christians to action, for they too could be like priest or Levite.

Hermeneutical Exploration

Down-to-Earth Compassion. The story of the Compassionate Samaritan illuminates what it really means to accept the lordship of Christ. The Christian life can be lived in a kind of enchanted mist with a determined disdain for relevance, but the parable requires involvement. Compassion is something you do. When the word is used in the Gospels, it is a verb and means action. Jesus significantly chose the word in three of his parables to describe a tangible response to someone in need. He so characterized the acceptance by the compassionate father of the prodigal son (Luke 15:20) and the forgiveness by the compassionate master of an immense debt (Matt. 18:27). In all three parables, there is an internal contrast between compassion and (a) two travelers, (b) an elder brother, and (c) a wicked servant. For Jesus, compassion is a badge of discipleship and not merely a religious amenity. Compassion is, after all, as concrete as a cross. Compassion is Christianity in overalls (P. Scherer). What a theology for medical mission! What a basis for ministry. A. T. Robertson once remarked, "This parable of the Good Samaritan has built the world's hospitals and, if properly understood and practiced would remove race prejudice, national hatred, and war."[69] Churches all over with heart and imagination are discovering forms of ministry, are realizing that they do not exist to be ministered to but to minister, are fashioning weekday ministries, and some are blending it with a genuine evangelism. Compassion then is more than "a tingling sensation in the gizzards," but it is that. One can get out of touch with her or his feelings. This may be especially true of men programmed by stereotypical expectations and who bury feelings until they become like volcanic rock. Compassion does involve a certain warmhearted fellow feeling, a sensitivity to the wounds of others.

Love for an Enemy. The Samaritan overcame his conditioning and prejudices and reached out to an enemy. He refused to be a slave to conventional morality and let his heart lead him to incarnate the love command. There were racial differences. There were national differences. There were religious differences. He was so truly liberated, however, he chose to love an enemy.[70]

We still have a parochial conscience in an age of universal history. We often limit our lives unwittingly because of a narrow "consciousness of kind." Often, however, a whole world of neighbors is discovered by Christian missionaries among others and recommended to any with ears to hear. The parable addresses us, with its revolutionary extension of the love command, to discover neighbors where there is need. It calls us to care about world hunger and to modify regional and even national provincialism. It invites us to reexamine images and caricatures of religious groups other than our own.

The parable offers a kind of value clarification. Throughout the value of the wounded man is at stake. The brigands negated his value. His only value to them was in his possessions they wrested away. When they deserted him on a wilderness road, they betrayed their notion of his worth. The priest and Levite affirmed their own value. The Samaritan affirmed the worth of the stranger to be like that of himself. Values are, indeed, inherent in actions.

Does not the parable speak psychologically of the "geometry of love"? Rollo May calls attention to Adler's interpretation of distances, which he terms a geometry of love. "Friendliness and interest and other aspects of love are indicated by a movement *toward*," he points out, "whereas hate and the negative emotions are shown in movements *away from*."[71] He goes on to point out that in our society these movements may be masked and subtle, but a careful observer sees the shying of one person from or the movement of one person toward another. His own value judgment as a psychologist amounts to an affirmation of Samaritan-like movement.

> The norm and ideal of personality health is . . . a free movement *toward*, the open-armed attitude toward life. . . . The neurotic individual, who is always exhibiting the movement *away from*, is precisely the one who cannot love.[72]

Though Rollo May does not relate the geometry of love to the parable, the correlation once made is electric. The Samaritan kind of movement toward (*pros*) the wounded stranger, both initially and in his promise to return, exemplifies the healthy, open-armed attitude toward life. The priest and Levite and especially the robbers revealed by their movements away an inability to love! Our movements toward and away also telegraph our willingness to love, and attention to our movements may be very illuminating and may eventually stimulate a growth in interpersonal relationships.

Critique of "Religion." The parable exposes any religion with a mania for creeds and an anemia for deeds, an uptightness about orthodoxy not matched by a parallel concern for orthopraxy (cf. 1 John 3:23). The hero was a Samaritan who looked to a shrine deemed worse than worthless. Furthermore, a good merchant—not necessarily a contradiction in terms—expressed real concern, while religious professionals apparently saw religion as ritual. Religious leaders must be shocked into awareness of professional hazards and peril.

"Religion" can be misused as a crutch, as an escape from life. There is that deadening tendency to define religion in terms of private purity and support of structures. Such religion alone can weaken spontaneity, routinize life and sap its vitality, and absorb all religious energy within prescribed parameters. The parable makes clear what real religion is like (as Jas. 1:27) and invites the Christian to examine himself. Incidentally, the meaning for today should not be construed as a negative comment upon Jews and Judaism but upon any inauthentic religiosity.

Identification. There is value in personal identification with the characters: the needs of the wounded, the need for repentance seen in insensitive priests, and the willingness to love on the part of the Samaritan. There is a need to develop empathy, to enlarge sensitivity toward the wounded, even those carrying wounds that drew no blood. The profound helplessness, the hurt of being ruthlessly overcome, the pain of being savagely pummeled, and the fear of dying on a desolate wilderness road belonged to the traumatic experience of this nameless man and to others wounded and hurt and desperately insecure.

To identify with the priestly failures is decidedly unappealing but instructive. Perhaps the original scribe began to identify and then drew back, and possibly some ministers unwillingly feel their lives queried. These failures call up times when weakness prevailed or even expose the pattern of a whole life-style. Albert Camus probed the depths of depravity and man's inhumanity to man and focused on a suave lawyer of Paris fond of himself. One night midnight silence was broken by the sound of a body falling from a bridge into the river. The lawyer stopped but did not turn around. He heard a cry repeated several times. He stood motionless in the crisis. "I told myself that I had to be quick and I felt an irresistible weakness steal over me."[73] No quickness came. Weakness won. He tried to cope by avoiding the next day's paper. Before one races to the hero or identifies with the victim of the biblical parable, it is worthwhile to pause with the priests until there is not so much as a tinge of self-righteousness!

To identify with the Samaritan may be best of all, though fraught with hazards. The Christian must not name the Samaritan unconsciously a Christian and the priests Jews! Neither should one equate himself or herself flippantly with the Samaritan, yet the directive of the Lord is to "go and do likewise"—to be a Samaritan. The positive experience of identifying with such a winsome and warmhearted religious hero has its own capacity to enlarge one's being and to inspire. Indeed, the Samaritan provides clues for vocation in life and a durable ideal that provides lasting meaning to the question, Will it matter that I was?

NOTES

1. So A. Plummer, *The Gospel According to Luke*, "The International Critical Commentary," Fifth Edition (Edinburgh: T. & T. Clark, 1922), p. 286.

2. The actual word used in the text is *nomikos*, in a Jewish context a student of the Law (4 Macc. 5:4). Mark never uses the term and Matthew only once; but Luke chose it frequently (7:30; 11:45,46,52,53; and 14:3) in order to communicate with a Hellenistic audience. W. Gutbrod, "*nomikos*," *TDNT*, IV (1967), 1088, is somewhat misleading. K. Bailey, *Through Peasant Eyes* (Grand Rapids: Eerdmans, 1980), p. 35, calls attention to the deference the lawyer demonstrated both by standing as a social courtesy and by using the title of teacher.

3. Cited by W. Grundmann, *Das Evangelium nach Lukas*, Vol. III of "Theologischer Handkommentar zum Neuen Testament," Second Edition (Berlin: Evangelisch Verlagsanstalt, 1963), p. 222.

4. Crespy, "The Parable of the Good Samaritan: An Essay in Structural Research," *Semeia*, 2:40 (1974). This transaction continued throughout.

5. Some source critics identify Luke 10:25-28 with the Jerusalem incident recorded in the other Gospels and believe that Mark's account is the most primitive. See V. Furnish, *The Love Command in the New Testament* (Nashville: Abingdon Press, 1972), pp. 24 ff. Other scholars, however, opt for a different occasion, such as T. W. Manson, *The Sayings of Jesus* (London: SCM Press, 1949), pp. 259-260; and Jeremias, *The Parables of Jesus*, trans. S. H. Hooke, Revised Edition (New York: Charles Scribner's, 1963), p. 202.

6. The *Test. Issachar* 5.2 conveys the generalized admonition to love the Lord and your neighbor, and one text of 7.6 combines love of the Lord and every person with the whole heart. *Test. Dan.* 5:3 in something of a summary requires loving the Lord through your whole life and each other with a true heart. Since fragments of the *Testaments* were found at Qumran, more students are prepared to see them as pre-Christian, though Christian influence cannot be certainly ruled out. If Jesus were not the first to combine the two love commandments, then it is more plausible that both Synoptic accounts are authentic and separate occasions.

7. In the Greek text, they are written as though they are one. There is not even need to repeat the verb.

8. Duncan M. Derrett, *Law in the New Testament* (London: Darton, Longman & Todd, 1970), p. 225.

9. See H. Greeven, "*plēsion*," *TDNT*, 6:315-17 (1968).

10. R. W. Funk, "The Old Testament in Parable. A Study of Luke 10:25-37," *Encounter*, 26:261n (2, 1965), paraphrasing Jeremias. J. Bowman, "The Parable of the Good Samaritan," *ET*, 59:153n (1947-48), reported the famous event when Hillel summarized the Law for a potential convert (T. B. Shab. 31a): that which is hateful to thee do not do to thy Haber (companion or member of the Pharisaic Haburah).

11. So C. Spicq, "Charity of the Good Samaritan, Luke 10:25-37," *Bible Today*, 6:361 (1963). H. Binder, "Das Gleichnis vom barmherzigen Samariter," *Theologische Zeitschrift*, 15:178 (3, 1959), is convincing in his suggestion that the scribe brought up rabbinic casuistry against which Jesus polemicized.

12. John Crossan, "Parable and Example in the Teaching of Jesus," *Semeia*, 1:74 (1974), pursued a different structure favoring balance and symmetry in the relative length of each portion but leading to a forced and rather artificial division. His article "The Good Samaritan: Towards a Generic Definition of Parable," *Semeia*, 2:96 (1974), is quite provocative from the side of structuralism when he suggests an alternative pattern for

the parable in which the victim was Samaritan and the helper a Jewish layman! Funk, "Structure in the Narrative Parables of Jesus," *Semeia*, 2:61 (1974), patterns the parable in terms of crisis and two responses, similar to the structure commended above but without dependence. D. Patte, "An Analysis of Narrative Structure and the Good Samaritan," *Semeia*, 2:17-18 (1974), described creatively the response of the priest and the Levite as *disjunctional* while the Samaritan entered the wounded man's story and was *conjunctional*.

13. Clearly the second command is hand in glove with the scribal question, and one has only to recognize that the parable completes the triangle. Several scholars nowadays stress further midrash as the definitive form of the parable. E. E. Ellis, "New Directions in Form Criticism," *Jesus Christus in Historie und Theologie Neutestamentliche Festschrift für Hans Conzelmann zum 60. Geburtstag*, ed. Georg Strecker (Tübingen: J. C. B. Mohr, 1975), pp. 311-312, pinpointed the rabbinic commentary as similar to the *yelammedenu* pattern; B. Gerhardsson, *The Good Samaritan—The Good Shepherd?* (Lund: C. W. K. Gleerup, 1958), p. 20, has argued unconvincingly that the parable is a midrash on Exodus 34; also Derrett, p. 227, named it midrash but on Hosea 6.

14. As Spicq, p. 362: "a paradigm, a 'pattern story,' a concrete, particular case illustrating a point of doctrine and presenting a model of religious or moral life to be imitated." The parable as parable then suffers from abstracting reductionistically by committing the "paraphrastic heresy." Also J. Lambrecht, "The Message of the Good Samaritan," *Louvain Studies*, 5:128 (2, 1974): "There is no need of a transposition or application of image to intended meaning and reality." Indeed, it should be recognized that the parable is more direct than some, but transpositions and applications must take place still. Some redaction critics think that the evangelist transformed the parable into a didactic and paraenetical vehicle.

15. H. B. Tristram, *Eastern Customs in Bible Lands* (London: Hodder and Stoughton, 1894), p. 220.

16. I am indebted to Jack Finegan, *The Archaeology of the New Testament* (Princeton: University Press, 1969), pp. 86-87.

17. Bauer, Arndt, and Gingrich, *A Greek-English Lexicon of the New Testament*, Fourth Edition (Chicago: University Press, 1952), p. 890. The very verb used of the robbers stripping the man (*ekduō*) appears in Matthew 27:28.

18. A. C. Bouquet, *Everyday Life in New Testament Times* (New York: Scribner's, 1953), p. 58, names other usual articles of clothing including a belt, sandals, head covering, and waist cloths. He also reports that a person was considered technically naked if only wearing the waist cloth (p. 60).

19. The word translated as "half dead" is a hapax, appearing nowhere else in the New Testament. It appears once in the LXX (4 Macc. 4:11). Moulton and Milligan, *The Vocabulary of the Greek Testament* (Grand Rapids: Eerdmans, 1963), 280, does supply a striking parallel of a woman beaten by her brother and his wife and left half dead. Bailey, page 42, relates the word to a rabbinic category meaning at the point of death.

20. K. H. Rengstorf, "*lēstēs*," *TDNT*, 4:258 (1967).

21. Ibid. Rengstorf considers this quite possible, an idea taken from K. Bornhäuser, and so explains why the victim's life was not taken. I wonder if Luke 22:52 does not provide cannon fodder!

22. Ibid., p. 257. Rengstorf listed these usages but did not apply to the parable.

23. First Chronicles 24:1-19 mentions the division of the priesthood into twenty-four courses. The typical priest would do two weeks a year and three pilgrim festivals. Bailey, page 43, makes a very strong case for the likelihood that the priest, like the Samaritan, rode. The poor walked. No one with status takes such a long hike in the desert. This point is critical actually because it establishes that what the Samaritan did, the priest could have done.

24. According to Jeremias, *Jerusalem in the Time of Jesus*, trans. F. H. and C. H. Cave (Philadelphia: Fortress Press, 1969), p. 207.

25. In a collection of rules about Temple purity attributed to Yosi b. Yoezer (ca. 150 BC), it is decreed that he who touches a corpse becomes unclean (M.Ed. 8:4). Cited by J. Neusner, *From Politics to Piety* (Englewood Cliffs, N.J.: Prentice-Hall, 1973), p. 119, who thinks that this text is probably before AD 70.

26. The argument that the priest avoided contact because it would obviate Temple service is obviously invalidated by the fact that his journey was downward from Jerusalem. That he could bypass a suffering person just after worship leadership is the alarming possibility. Could it be that the original scribe (Luke 10:25) saw in the priest's attitude toward this stranger the spirit of his own question about the identity of his neighbor (Luke 10:29)?

27. Certainly not all priests or Jews were like this one! For instances of caring for lepers and Romans, see Israel Abrahams, *Studies in Pharisaism and the Gospels* (New printing from the 1917 and 1924 originals; New York: KTAV, 1967), Second Series, p. 29. Furthermore, Zechariah, a priest of the tribe of Abijah and father of the Baptizer, was a lovable, devout priest (Luke 1:5 ff.).

28. The pair of particles *idōn* and *ethōn* favor such a reconstruction if *genomenos* is retained. It enjoys textual support from p[45], A C D E G H K M and others, but it is omitted from p[75] B L X and others. For further discussion see Bruce M. Metzger, *A Textual Commentary on the Greek New Testament* (New York: United Bible Societies, 1971), pp. 152-153. Plummer, p. 287, entertains the possibility of the Levite drawing nearer; also I. Howard Marshall, *The Gospel of Luke*, "The New International Greek Testament Commentary" (Exeter: Paternoster, 1978), pp. 448-9, advocates it. The fact that the text changes from way (*hodos*) to place (*topos*) in verses 31-32 also favors the impression that the Levite drew nearer. Bailey, p. 47, raises the possibility that the Levite crossed the defilement line of four cubits perhaps to hear the victim speak so he could find out if he were a neighbor.

29. I am indebted to Jeremias, *Jerusalem*, pp. 207-213.

30. So argued by Binder, p. 189n. For a contrary view see Bailey, p. 46.

31. Jeremias, p. 352.

32. 2 Kings 17:30; Josephus, *Antiquities*, 12.257 indicated that the Cutheans descended from Median and Persian colonists. For another expression of Jewish contempt of Samaritans see T. Levi 7:2.

33. So J. Bowman, "The Parable of the Good Samaritan," *Expository Times*, 59:151 (1947-48), who reports that they milled corn (M. Dem. 3:4; 5:9) for Jews and prepared wine (M. Dem. 7:4). He indicates that they were seen as little better than Gentiles (M. Jer. 3:9; M. Shek. 1:5) and classed with the *Am-ha-ares* (M. Dem. 3:4). See also Ecclesiasticus 50:25-26.

34. So Jeremias, p. 356.

35. Recall the rejection of the Samaritans' offer to help rebuild the Temple (Ezra 4:2), the crusade against the rival Samaritan temple on Mt. Gerizim that aroused hatred (Josephus, *Antiq.*, 13.256), and the defilement of the Jewish Temple (Josephus, *Antiq.*, 18.29-31).

36. H. Köster, "*splangnon*," *TDNT*, 7:548-559 (1971). He calls particular attention to Proverbs 12:10; 17:5; Test. Zeb. 6:4; 7:1,2; 8:3.

37. Oil, considered one of the necessities of life, was used as fuel for lamps (as Matt. 25:3) among other things. Possibly the wine cleansed the wounds while the oil had the effect of softening. The mixture of oil and wine in healing a wound is also attested in the Talmud (Shab. 134a) according to J. F. Ross, "Oil," IDB, K-Q:593 (1962). Bouquet, pp. 84-85, identifies the wine as posca, a diluted drink from a sour, overly fermented wine drunk by the poorer classes; and reports that a writer on veterinary medicine recommended posca and oil for healing wounds.

38. The Greek (*ktēnos*) does not make it entirely clear whether the animal is an ass or a mule or a horse. Josephus, *Antiquities*, 8.241, used the word clearly to refer to an ass, and authorities like Derrett, p. 209, think of two or more asses.

39. Jeremias, *Parables*, p. 205, estimates that a day's board would be about one-twelfth of a denarius. This may be a clue to the length of time required for the man to recuperate and the extent of his injuries!

40. As described by Tristram, pp. 218-9.

41. R. C. Stone, "Inn," *The Zondervan Pictorial Encyclopedia of the Bible*, ed. Merrill C. Tenney (Grand Rapids: Zondervan, 1975), 3:280, adds: "Something more like an inn in the modern sense is in view in this passage. If one may judge from the Khan Hathru, located today midway between Jerusalem and Jericho, the inn of Jesus' day perhaps consisted of a large building, with an arched doorway opening into a spacious courtyard with a well in the center." The Greek word *pandocheion* means literally "all receiving" and is used variously in the New Testament (Mark 14:14; Luke 2:7; 22:11). Early Christians may have avoided inns because they had a bad name (1 Pet. 4:9).

42. L. P. Trudinger, "Once Again, Now, 'Who is my Neighbour?' " *Evangelical Quarterly*, 48:161 (3, 1976).

43. Surely some of the other hearers identified sympathetically with the wounded man in the ditch. Funk, "The Good Samaritan as Metaphor," *Semeia*, 2:79 (1974), continues his long held contention that the audience naturally related to the victim. In favor of this is the fact that no other character was carried all the way through the parable and the probability that the hearers and the victim were Jewish lay persons. However, I have taken seriously the scribe as the immediate audience and believe there was an intentional attack on the hearer's expectation that refocused his "world." Furthermore, from a literary perspective the hearer is invited to see from the viewpoint of the narrator who independently, like a fly on a rock, saw it all. Funk, "The Old Testament in Parable," p. 263, consents as he recognizes that with the call to pass judgment, the hearer is no longer victim, priest, Levite, or Samaritan but judge.

44. Crossan, "Parable and Example in the Teaching of Jesus," p. 76.

45. Crespy, p. 47.

46. Furnish, p. 39.

47. So A. Jülicher, *Die Gleichnisreden Jesu* (Photocopy from 1910 edition; Darmstadt: Wissenschaftliche Buchgesellschaft, 1963), 2: 596. Also R. Bultmann, *History of the*

Synoptic Tradition, trans. J. Marsh (Oxford: Blackwell, 1963), p. 178, saw an artificial blending into the context. He did consider verses 36-37*b* as original. Linnemann, p. 129, seems more inclined to accept as dominical. Funk, p. 267, has it right, recognizing that the disjuncture, far from being inimical to the parable, is necessary to the point! Here is an instance, where one may jettison an attached context and miss in part the parable's significance. Bultmann, p. 178, did this when he saw only a contrast between the loveless Jew and the loving Samaritan.

48. Linnemann, p. 30.

49. So G. Bornkamm, *Jesus of Nazareth*, trans. Irene and Fraser McLuskey with J. M. Robinson (New York: Harper, 1960), p. 112 *f*.

50. So also H. Gollwitzer, *Der Barmherzige Samariter*, Vol. 34 of "Biblische Studien" (Neukirchen-Vluyn: Neukirchener Verlag, 1962), p. 68. He reflects theologically from the two commands that the compassion of the Samaritan is an echo of the divine warmheartedness, that love of enemy arises out of grateful response. God has already put oil and wine on my wounds. Once more care for accuracy and respect for Judaism require that it be pointed out that no Old Testament passage explicitly commands hate of enemies, see though Deuteronomy 7:2; 23:3-6; 25:17-19; Psalm 137:7-9. The Old Testament does refer to national enemies, of course, and also to one's personal enemies (Ex. 23:4; Judg. 16:23; 1 Sam. 18:29; Esther 7:6). J. A. Sanders, "Enemy," *IDB*, E-J: 101 (1962), concludes, "It is only in the New Testament, however, that the categorical imperative is made that a man should love his enemies (Matt. 5:43-44)." He does cite some beautiful passages that approach it (Ex. 23:4-5; 1 Sam. 24:17-19; Job 31:29; Prov. 24:17; 25:21-22). A. Schlatter, *Der Evangelist Matthäus* (Stuttgart: Calwer, 1929), p. 191, pointed out that so long as love is limited only to one's neighbor the possibility for hate of enemies lurks. The problem for Christianity in empirical, historical terms has been in living up to the New Testament (as Gal. 5:14; Rom. 13:8-10; John 2:8).

51. Bowman insists that the theory of a revolutionary expansion of Leviticus 19:18 does scant justice to Leviticus 19:34. He is certainly right that 19:34 reveals a generous tendency beyond mere nationalistic consciousness of kind. One wonders, however, whether the *Ger* included a Samaritan and whether the parable intended so much to require the audience to love the Samaritan.

52. See D. Kellerman, *"gûr,"* TDOT, 2:442 (1975), who points out that the category developed increasingly toward the meaning of proselyte.

53. Jeremias, *Parables*, p. 202. Hence one should be careful about assigning too much to the evangelist.

54. E. Stauffer, *"agapaō,"* TDNT, 1:46 (1964). Spicq, p. 366: "It is a physical emotion experienced at the grief, pain, or misery of others."

55. Lambrecht, p. 128.

56. So Jülicher, p. 598; also Binder, p. 188, who makes a forceful case for the cultic implications generally.

57. According to Gerhardsson, pp. 3-5, the patristic tradition universally interpreted the parable Christologically. The robbed man would be interpreted as Adam or the man fallen in sin, the priest and Levite as the Old Testament priesthood or perhaps the Law, and the Samaritan as the Lord. Gerhardsson himself has not been convincing in his own identification of the Samaritan to the true shepherd and hence to Jesus.

58. Binder, p. 191, spoiling an otherwise good article.

59. Funk, "The Old Testament in Parable," p. 263, recognizes that Jesus is in the penumbral field of the parable, "the off-stage qualifier of the situation" (p. 266).

60. Ibid., p. 264.

61. Cf. Lambrecht, pp. 129-30, who wonders if one day Jesus helped a sinner and the parable was an apology.

62. So Gollwitzer, p. 73.

63. Again the prepositional prefixes are instructive as away (*apo*) is used of the robbers and toward (*pros*) of the Samaritan. Certain structuralists have also noted this absolute contrast. Patte, p. 18, writes, "The Subject Samaritan struggles against the OPPONENT." See also Crespy, pp. 40-42.

64. So Charles Rice in personal conversation. Bailey, page 48, writes beautifully of a clear progression. "The priest only goes *down the road*. The Levite comes *to the place*. The Samaritan comes *to the man*."

65. Binder, p. 176, considers the connection of 10:25-29 to be secondary, that the parable itself is a self standing traditional unit, and that Luke took 10:25-29 from the Markan passion narrative and rewrote it with ethical emphasis. Lambrecht, p. 126, wonders if verse 37*b* is also from the evangelist, forming a kind of inclusion or framing with an emphasis upon doing. He sees a tension to the point of awkwardness between redaction and tradition. These reconstructions are possible, and I have recognized an exhortation one (v. 28*c*) and two (v. 37*b*). However, there are similar tensions between question and answer elsewhere that may well reflect a certain dominical boldness. Furthermore, if the parable may be seen in part as a midrashic comment on Leviticus 19:18 so far as genre is concerned, this strengthens the connection of parable and context. Furthermore, while doing is a stress congenial to Luke it is also so for Matthew as well, and doing is inextricably bound up inside the parable itself.

66. The best demonstration is Binder, op. cit., pp. 178-9n. Hapax appears twice and classic expressions abound.

67. Gollwitzer, pp. 69-70, thinks that the evangelist already identified the Samaritan Christologically and makes right much of the blatant Christological content of 10:17-24. My reading of the literary context, partially dependent upon Gollwitzer, would rather see the parable as an exhortation to action for disciples.

Note the introductory *kai idōn*, a typical Lukan connective formula (2:25, 27; 5:12; 7:12; 8:40; 13:11; 14:3; 24:13) that may relate the passage back to 10:24 (So Binder, 176, citing Zahn).

68. Marshall, p. 449, points out that the emphatic position of *Samaritan* at the beginning of the sentence is intentional and heightens the contrast between the first two travelers and the third. I wonder if the close proximity of Nazareth to the boundary of Samaria afforded Jesus opportunity to see Samaritans as they really were. I also wonder with others if the story of Oded, a kind of prototype of the good Samaritan (2 Chron. 28:1-15), also influenced the parable tangentially. See F. H. Wilkinson, "Oded: Proto-Type of the Good Samaritan," *Expository Times*, 69:94 (3, 1957); and J. M. Furness, "Fresh Light on Luke 10:25-37," *Expository Times*, 80:182 (6, 1969). This would certainly weaken Helevy's celebrated theory that the original parable did not refer to a Samaritan.

69. A. T. Robertson, *Word Pictures in the New Testament* (Nashville: Broadman, 1930), 2:155. On the love of the Samaritan as both spontaneous and enduring, see

Edmund A. Steimle, *God the Stranger* (Philadelphia: Fortress Press, 1979), p. 55.

70. See my article, "The Liberated and Liberating Lord," *Review and Expositor*, 73:284 (3, 1976). The spirit of the Samaritan contradicted Sirach 12:1-7.

71. May, *The Art of Counseling* (Nashville: Abingdon Press, 1939), p. 105.

72. Ibid.

73. Camus, *The Fall*, trans. Justin O'Brien (New York: Random House, 1963), p. 70. See p. 147 also.

14 The Parable of the Persistent Widow

Occasionally Jesus chose a rascal to make a religious point. A refreshing sense of humor, a love for irony, and a winsome willingness to be daring in order to communicate permeate the parables containing a villain. The crooked character added immense human interest and shock value and ensured a hearing. Individuals like an unscrupulous judge contributed dimension to a story and jolted hearers into fresh thoughts, what Crossan labeled "attempts to shatter the complacency of one's world."[1] So Jesus elected burglars and unjust stewards[2] to score his points. In Luke 18:1-8, furthermore, a defenseless widow is pitted against a heartless judge, but in a rather marvelous contest of wills.

Context

The parable itself in its literary context (*Sitz im Buch*) functions as the conclusion of an interesting eschatological unit and provides the transition to the next parable, which also concerns prayer. The two prayer parables were placed side by side by the evangelist for pastoral purposes. In the preceding series of eschatological sayings (17:22-37), the future arrival of the Son of man is portrayed as coming suddenly and unexpectedly, catching some unawares. During the interval before the day of the Son of man, some may grow anxious (v. 22). The parable belongs to these reflections on last things and may even have been connected in the Lukan source.

It is probable then that the parable was given to the disciples as pastoral encouragement. Specificity about the precise setting in the ministry of Jesus (*Sitz im Leben Jesu*) is lacking. It is just possible that the parable came out of the same situation that gave rise to the parable of the Friend at Midnight (Luke 11:1-13), but it is more probable on

242

balance that it belonged to a discourse on the last days directed to anxious disciples.[3] It may be that the exact circumstance is not recoverable, but illuminating background information regarding judges and widows is available.

Background

Legal Setting. The parable depicts a court with a single judge deciding cases, so the widow's suit was most probably a money matter because fiscal dispute was the only kind of case that an individual judge could decide.[4] Since the judge in the parable did not fear God, he was certainly not a scribe and was most probably an Herodian official, a secular metropolitan judge. Regulations in the Mishnah called for three judges in cases regarding property (*Sanhedrin* 1:1; 3:1).

The fact that this judge was characterized as unrighteous invites attention to H. B. Tristram's memorable portrait of a Mesopotamian court scene.

On a slightly raised dais at the further end sat the *kadi*, or judge, half buried in cushions. Round him squatted various secretaries and other notables. The populace crowded into the rest of the hall, a dozen voices clamouring at once, each claiming that his cause should be the first heard. The more prudent litigants joined not in the fray, but held whispered communications with the secretaries, passing bribes, euphemistically called fees, into the hands of one or another. When the greed of the underlings was satisfied, one of them would whisper to the *kadi*, who would promptly call such and such a case. It seemed to be ordinarily taken for granted that judgment would go for the litigant who had bribed highest. But meantime a poor woman on the skirts of the crowd perpetually interrupted the proceedings with loud cries for justice. She was sternly bidden to be silent, and reproachfully told that she came there everyday. "And so I will," she cried out, "till the *kadi* hears me."[5]

This colorful incident from a corrupt Oriental court helps to establish a possible atmosphere.

The *Plight of the Widow.* As it happens the Greek word for widow (*chēra*)[6] means "forsaken" or "left empty" and so she was. The fate most abhorred by women was that of widowhood. In many instances Greek widows were not allowed to remarry and were normally faced with two alternatives.[7] They could return to their family of origin if the original purchase price were refunded, or they could elect to remain in the husband's family in a very subordinated status!

They were mistreated by the socially powerful and even sold as slaves for debt, though the Romans did legislate laws for their protection.[8]

The Book of Lamentations begins with musing about Jerusalem and widows:

> How lonely sits the city
>   that was full of people!
> How like a widow has she become,
>   she that was great among the nations!
> She that was a princess among the cities
>   has become a vassal (1:1; RSV).

Note the connection of widow and vassal in a Jewish context.

It may be that the clothes required of Jewish widows reflected their low social esteem. (Gen. 38:14,19). The clothes of mourning were worn for the whole of life on the ancient principle that marriage is not dissolved by death. No bracelets or earrings or rings or ornaments (garments of gladness) were acceptable.[9] The fact that widows wore a virtual uniform means that the judge in the parable knew quite well that the woman was a widow, and yet he did not care.

The prophets of Israel railed out in courageous protest at the wrongs done to widows (Isa. 10:2; Ezek. 22:7; Job 24:3), and they issued spine-tingling warnings against injustice to widows as something unthinkable (Ex. 22:22; Deut. 24:17; Jer. 22:3; Zech. 7:10). It was dangerous to oppress the widow because God is her champion (Ps. 68:5). Some benevolence was organized for widows from tithes (Deut. 14:29; 26:12) and gleanings from the field as in the case of Ruth (Deut. 24:19-21; Ruth 2:2).

The prophets clearly established God's will for justice and compassion toward widows; and Jesus had special compassion for a weeping widow (Luke 7:11-17), conceivably sensitized by his mother's experience. One of the messianic traits was as Friend of widows. The problem in the parable is that the secular judge has not realized that his role was to serve God by bringing justice to the downtrodden (Ps. 82:2-7). Amos 5 contains a passionate call for justice from the courts. Justice in the courts is indication of the moral health of the nation. The prophet lambasts those who thrust the destitute out of court (v. 12) and promises that the Lord will be gracious if justice is enthroned in the courts (v. 15). A judge who hammers out justice serves God (2 Chron. 19:6).

Literary Analysis

Form. The parable is specific situation, calling attention to a particular kind of judge in a certain city and a particular widow in that city. Past tenses are employed. The parable contains direct discourse in terms of a strong-willed request from the widow and a nervous interior soliloquy from the judge. The parable itself is complete, in contrast to its first cousin (Luke 11:5-8),[10] and is followed by an affirmation and rhetorical question (Luke 18:8).

Characters. Two strongly independent characters clash in the parable, one powerful and one powerless. Many interpreters consider the unjust judge the principal.[11] This metropolitan judge was no Oliver Wendell Holmes. In a word, he was secular and self-sufficient. He is described as neither fearing God nor man, a descriptive device that established the situation immediately. In the soliloquy he so characterized himself (v. 4c) as well, so that his reputation and self-understanding concurred. Not being an elected official this unprincipled judge did not respect persons as persons, was not "person-centered" administratively. Since he did not reverence personhood, it would not matter to him that she was a widow, a category of person needing special sensitivity. Neither did he fear God. God was not a constitutive factor in his existence. Divine mandates regarding justice to "the least of these" were irrelevant. He denied any theonomous existence in favor of a raw autonomy. Not principles but preferences and predilections predominated. A. B. Bruce characterized him as a "lawless tyrant, devoid of the sense of responsibility and of every sentiment of humanity and justice."[12] There seems to be a linkage between disregard for God and the inability to see the divine dimension in the other, and all sin reverts to a lack of reverence. Indeed William Temple used to say that "war breaks out when worship breaks down."

The unconscionable judge's refusal of the widow's request reflects his characteristic failure to treat persons as persons. The fact that the litigant was a widow or that she had a just cause counted for nothing. It has been suggested cogently that the corrupt judge may have refused because of the influence of the widow's opponent.[13] Bribing was not unknown (Mic. 7:3), though clearly repudiated in the Mishnah (Bekh. 4:6). Perhaps her adversary had delivered a bribe, but parallels to other "refusal parables" makes it likely that the main point is willful rejection for a time.

As it happened the socially powerless widow turned out to be equally independent and more forceful. As the determiner in the story, her indomitable spirit overcame a hardened public official. This nameless, but somehow not faceless, widow was not necessarily an old woman because marriage came as early as age thirteen. She was an urbanite who took the initiative in bringing her cause before the court. The Greek of verse 3 indicates that she kept on going back (iterative imperfect). That this grammatical observation is not overdrawn can be seen in other phrases from the *New English Bible* as "for a long time he refused," "this widow is so great a nuisance," and even "who cry out to him day and night" (v. 7).

The widow then was no frail thing too fragile to fight! This woman insisted on her rights persistently, represented her own case, did not give up or become intimidated but stood her ground aggressively. She is the force in the narrative that effects a decision. "It is ironical," Via muses, "that a person of such helplessness in her society should turn out to be a figure of power."[14] Her chances of success to all appearances were nil. She met repeated rebuffs. The unrighteous judge functioned as a blocking character. She could not even count on a sudden attack of integrity from such an insensitive man. Compassion and mercy were out of the question. To the degree that the characters were merely a widow *versus* a profane judge, circumstances compelled despair. J. A. Robertson graphically described the general circumstance: "one of the most helpless and unprotected creatures on God's earth, petitioning a callous beast, who happened to be the city's judge, for justice against some wolf of a man who was taking cruel advantage of her unprotectedness."[15]

Nevertheless this particular widow overwhelmed the judge with uncommon persistence. She broke down his reluctance. She succeeded in bothering him to the point of inconvenience, but it may not be entirely accurate that "she had no weapon but her own perseverance." The parable may have conveyed a joke that would have explained why the judge was apprehensive enough to talk to himself. If so, it surely drew a snicker or so from the crowd. The Greek text very probably should be rendered, "Indeed because this widow causes me trouble I will vindicate her lest coming finally she may give me a black eye" (v. 5). It simply cannot be ruled out that the judge feared a female fist in the face as the crowning blow.[16] The judge was independent but not impervious. After all, she might start using her fist rather than her tongue. The widow is quite a person. She is the more dominating character. Indeed, it is the judge's soliloquy that clarified how decisive was the action of the widow. She is the protagonist who made things happen.

Master Metaphor. Upon close reading, a single image looms into view, the image of *vindication*. In the parable itself, the widow requested that she be vindicated against her adversary (v. 3c) and the judge decided to vindicate her (v. 5a). In the application there is the assurance that God will vindicate his elect (vv. 7a,8a). This master metaphor draws the parable and application together because both concern eventual vindication.

The Greek words for *vindication* (*ekdikeō, ekdikēsis*) often refer to revenge in the Old Testament (LXX). But in judicial process the contextual meaning is to fight for someone's cause or to help someone to justice.[17] So the parable follows ordinary language of the court and is a call for justice and freedom from oppression rather than revenge.[18]

So the key metaphor reiterated throughout unifying parable and application is definitely vindication, a clue to interpretation. The climax of the story comes when the words are reached, "I will give her justice."[19] I am in delightful agreement with a pregnant sentence from J. M. Creed: "The idea of *ekdikēsis* is so clearly interwoven in the texture of this story that if the eschatological element were eliminated from the interpretation, the parable would lose its main force."[20]

Historical Meaning

Challenge. The center of gravity for the interpretation falls for some upon the persistent or importunate widow (as Luke) and for others upon the unjust judge. Any adequate approach will comprehend both and keep the story whole. Neither character is disposable in story nor interpretation. However, the methodology advocated here has shown direct discourse to be a major key and climactic speeches especially revealing. In the judge's soliloquy, it is the widow more than himself who figures decisively. He elects finally to do something against his personal preference or will (v. 4a). She is dominating even in his private reflections.[21]

So then challenge to persistent faith stands at the forefront of the parable. On this reading, the widow becomes the paradigm for the persistent believer. The persistence required is not merely continuing prayer but remaining in prayer and hope for divine vindication. Furthermore, then it was not merely the duty of prayer but encouragement not to give up, not to cave in to the sin of despair. Disciples in tribulation would feel as powerless as the widow as they encountered authorities as powerful and profane as the judge, and they would have been heartened by the widow's monumental determination. When a widow refuses to quit when stymied by the powers that be, why should disciples? A faith that risks against appearances to the contrary is called forth by the parable. The parable calls not merely for regular prayer but for faith in God, a faith that expresses itself in prayer for the coming kingdom. The Lord's Prayer springs immediately to mind: "Thy kingdom come!" (Matt. 6:10; Luke 11:20). So does the fourth Beatitude: "How blest are those who hunger and thirst to see right prevail" (Matt. 5:5, NEB). More specifically, this parable thinks of tribulation and last things and perseverance through the crisis with an unstinting expectation of vindication.[22] The parable is a Last Judgment and/or Parousia parable.[23]

The challenge of the parable is climaxed in the application through the rhetorical question: However when the Son of man comes will he then find faith upon the earth? This application is genuinely open-ended and searching. It is challenge to hearer and reader. Schlatter put it finely, "That he comes is certain; but whether he will find faith is an open question."[24] The parable not only contains assurance but also cause for self-examination. "Election is fulfilled only in obedience."[25] It was disturbing for disciples called directly by Jesus into community to assess the depth of their commitment. Eelection is not a static doctrine but a dynamic process and pilgrimage. The parable by pungent rhetorical question invited faith to the finish.

Promise. The parable assures faith. It asserts pastorally that God will surely vindicate his elect (v. 8a). God hears the cries. God answers prayers. God will aid his people. The parable speaks to a crisis of faith. The believer need never give up on the providence of God. So an unjust judge becomes an indirect revelation of God. The parable is a "how much more" argument (*kal wahomer*) that positively implies that of course God will do more for a genuine supplicant than did the judge. After all, if the judge vindicated the widow who was a stranger to him, God is so much more likely with alacrity to help his own people (as Matt. 2:9-11; Luke 11:11-13).[26]

The promise then is that God will in fact vindicate his anguished elect (v. 8), and he will vindicate them decisively in a sovereign manner. Some understand the promise (*en tachei*) to refer to the *manner* of vindication, and others conclude that it points to the *time*.[27] Does it mean suddenly and unexpectedly or soon and speedily? The idea of suddenness fits the Lukan context superbly. If the parable did, indeed, belong originally with Luke 17:22-37 as appears likely, then suddenness is the natural choice because of 17:24,26,30.[28] In Luke, the suddenness is like lightning (17:24), Noah's flood (17:26-27), the fire that befell Sodom and Gomorrah (17:28-30), and a decisive, unexpected separation (17:34-35). There is not only this insistent announcement of coming judgment in Luke but also a persistent call for readiness and watchfulness associated with prayer (21:34-36). Likewise the parable speaks of vindicating judgment (18:7-8*a*) and calls for watchfulness (18:8*b*).

The parable assured disciples chastened by the prospect of stressful experience that this vindication cannot possibly fail. After all, "It rests in God's hands."[29] God will surely show mercy to his people.[30]

Thoughts on the Character of Election

The parable will not leave the believer at ease in Zion. One who is called responds through an abandoned life with an adventuresome God. Election is not for privilege but risking faith. Indeed, T. W. Manson rightly insisted that the elect "are not the pampered darlings of Providence, but the *corps d'élite* in the army of the living God."[31] Indeed, faith is a struggle. Faithfulness requires persistence, becoming like a widow who did not know the meaning of quitting.

This need to persist is introduced from the outset of the life of discipleship. The call to discipleship has within it implicitly the expectation of a lifelong commitment. The one who accepts Christ pledges to stay around for the finish. Though perseverance has frankly fallen out of much theological talk and lost its dynamic place in understandings of salvation, it is imperative that it be recovered. It is symptomatic and telling that Christians have stopped reading *The Pilgrim's Progress*! It is encouraging that Christians are regaining a sense of the Christian life as one of discipleship and salvation as a process. To this must be added a robust and biblical advocacy of perseverance. Indeed, pastoral care of Christians would take on a greater priority if perseverance received its rightful place. Concern about persons moving to the fringes of the life of the church must be increased. Desire to recover those fading from the church's institutional life can come front and center. Personal decision to stay with Christ from conversion to death and whatever life may hold in between can happen and make appreciable difference (as 2 Tim. 4:7). Calling or election is a call to struggle and hang in to the very last. Faith expresses itself as faithfulness and trust in a sovereign God of justice, mercy, and action. Depend on God and shelve giving up as an option.

Contemporary Meaning: "Hang in There!"

There is a winsome story about plucky Daniel Boone and his wanderings in the forests of Kentucky. He was trying constantly to find new lands for settlers and better roads. One settler asked the great wilderness man, "Were you ever lost in the woods?" He pondered a moment before his reply. "No, not exactly *lost*," he answered, "but I have been *bewildered* for days on end, once for more than a week, but *I kept going on*."[32]

Many others have felt bewildered for days on end but have kept on going. A patient with an emphysemic condition faced bad days and could not look forward to easy answers, yet he spoke with true grit to his minister, "I've just got to hang in there." A budding graduate student faced a stiff penalty for changing majors as he tried to establish himself in a new profession. He faced tough seminars and had stiff proficiency tests to pass. He was beginning to find himself and said, "I've just got to hang in there, and I can do it." A faithful wife cared for her husband through an extended illness. She had gone the second mile. Her minister said he wanted her to know how much he admired her loving care for her husband. Without a pause she responded, "We made vows, didn't we?" Her minister with feeling then added, "You, dear, have kept yours." She quietly answered, "I just try to hang in there." These Christian disciples, like Daniel Boone, have felt bewildered but kept going.

Jesus, who had a tender spot for widows, admired and respected the determined widow in his story who hung in there. He courageously faulted the Pharisee for devouring widows' houses (Mark 12:40); he compassionately healed the only son belonging to a widow

(Luke 7:12); and he lavishly praised the generous widow who threw two mites into the Trumpets or collection receptacle (Luke 21:1-4).

Modern widows must also learn to stand alone and hang in there. Only one wife in twelve will escape widowhood, and there are approximately 10.5 million widows in the United States today. They often confide that "a piece of you dies with him," and that loneliness and memories are companions; but many fight their way valiantly until they can stand alone and find renewed purpose.[33]

The church itself must become far more aware of the plight of the widow and the need to provide a ministry of understanding, opportunities for mutual support among widows and encouragement for them to get involved in ministries through the church and elsewhere. Many widows have found their way and have much to give.

The parable model for hanging in there persistently certainly relates to praying as well as to widows. Prayer really isn't any good unless it is persistent. George Buttrick, saintly in his own fashion, believed, "God cannot be found save by persistent plea."[34] And prayer has been defined in its essence in this manner: "Prayer is . . . the settled craving of a man's heart."[35]

Jesus, model of faith as well as its object, did not dash off his own prayers but sometimes spent the night in supplication. Often our prayers are too light and our petitions of so little moment they are soon forgotten rather than prayed for again and again. David Redding put it memorably that not only is God sales-resistant to random requests but he won't read third class mail.[36] The persistent prayer reflects quality of interest and concern and makes a higher claim. Paul wrote in Ephesians, "Give yourselves wholly to prayer and entreaty; pray on every occasion in the power of the Spirit. To this end keep watch and persevere, always interceding for all God's people." (6:18, NEB).

It is perseverance alone that wins the crown; and the Christian life calls to struggle, to hang in there to the last. The need to persist is integral to discipleship, but God promises vindication for those who persevere. A young mother staying at home for a time with two small ones in diapers demanding so much may feel as powerless as the widow, yet have encouragement to hang in there and not be vanquished. A patient subdued by insidious disease that irreverently crowds and weakens may actually be heartened and helped by the divine encouragement to hang in there. A person may feel that the raft of his marriage is pulling apart and will not stay together any longer and believe that it is impossible to hold on any longer. Sometimes the need is just to hang in there a little longer. There may be a change, a death and a resurrection, a miracle. It may be worth another try.

Upon successful completion of her first flight across the Atlantic, Amelia Earhart made a public address in Boston. She recounted the crucial situation of her lonely journey. She was out about five hundred miles over the Atlantic from Halifax when her engine began to have trouble. It sputtered and backfired and sounded like it was going to give up. She lowered the plane and flew close to the sea, thinking she might make a desperate attempt to float it. She was forced to a quick decision. She decided to go on as long as she could keep the ship in the air, for the hazards of going on were no greater than the hazards of going back.[37] Her commitment to keep going made the difference.

Hanging in there or persevering is a little heralded posture, but for many it makes or breaks. There are times in Christian experience when we need to bow our backs, set our chins, pray our prayers, and keep going with a faith to the finish. God will vindicate his elect.

NOTES

1. Crossan, *In Parables*, p. 119.
2. Dan Via, *The Parables*, p. 159, is especially creative in his association of the unjust steward with the picaresque hero, a kind of harmless rogue.
3. W. Grundmann, *Das Evangelium nach Lukas*, "Theologischer Handkommentar zum Neuen Testament," Second Edition (Berlin: Evangelische Verlagsanstalt, n.d), p. 338, combines Lk. 17:20-18:8 as "The Day of the Son of Man." G. Delling, "Das Gleichnis vom gottlosen Richter," *Zeitschrift für die Neutestamentliche Wissenschaft*, 53:22 (1962), 22, has made the apparently novel suggestion that the parable was addressed to a pious circle within Israel that thought of themselves as elect and who waited for the Son of Man. He draws attention to Enoch 37-71. This theory should be given a period of grace as it were and should not be rejected out of hand.
4. According to Jeremias, *The Parables of Jesus*, p. 153. The word *kritēs* is used as a coordinate to *meristes* or divider at Lk. 12:14.
5. Tristram, *Eastern Customs in Bible Lands*, pp. 228-229.
6. G. Stählin, *"Chēra," TDNT*, 9:440 (1973).

7. Ibid., p. 442.

8. Ibid., pp. 443 & 444. In 2 Kgs. 4:1-7 there is reference to the creditor coming to take the widow's two children for slaves!

9. Ibid., p. 445.

10. The differences in form between the two parables (Lk. 11:5-8; 18:1-8) are quite considerable. The Friend at Midnight story is a *tis ex humōn* parable that calls to mind a general situation in a village. It uses presents, futures, and subjunctives. Both parables have additional application. R. Bultmann, *History of the Synoptic Tradition*, trans. J. Marsh (Oxford: Blackwell, 1963), p. 175, recognized that Luke 18:1-8 is formally different from 11:5-8 yet argued that Luke 18:6-8 is secondary because it has no parallel in Luke 11:5-8. This is to give too little weight to form. The two parables, however, are first cousins (not twins) as both are struggles of will, both are resolved upon less than altruistic grounds after repeated efforts.

11. As J. Jeremias, I. H. Marshall, W. Grundmann, D. Via, M. Tolbert, and E. Linnemann among others.

12. Bruce, *The Parabolic Teaching of Christ*, p. 158. In Lk.'s usages (9x) a judge is not necessarily corrupt, for example, Acts 24:10.

13. So Jeremias. He bases his supposition on analogy to Mk. 6:26 and Lk. 18:13. However, two other refusal parables are more apropos. In the Two Sons there is a temporary refusal (Mt. 21:29), and in the Unmerciful Servant there is a refusal of a plea for mercy (Mt. 18:30). The latter is the closest parallel.

14. Via, "The Parable of the Unjust Judge: A Metaphor of the Unrealized Self," *Semiology and Parables*, ed. D. Potts (Pittsburgh: Pickwick Press, 1976), p. 25. It seems to me that Via chose the wrong character as the primary one and might have had a more interesting psychological analysis along the line of a struggle of wills and an overcoming by the widow.

15. Robertson, "The Parable of the Unjust Judge (Luke xviii. 1-8)," *Expository Times*, 38:389 (1926-27).

16. The same verb means "beat" in 1 Cor. 9:27. The prepositional phrase *eis telos* more naturally translates "finally" than "continually." See K. Weiss, "*hupopiazō*," *TDNT*, 8:590-591 (1972), who insists that the fear of being struck in the face should not be ruled out for certain. Stählin, p. 450, considers it more linguistically probable that the text alludes to the fear of physical violence. A. B. Bruce, p. 616, points out the possibility that the judge is apprehensive of something worse in the future than anything that has yet happened. For the view that the reference is to disgrace and loss of prestige see J. D. M. Derrett, "Law in the New Testament: The Unjust Judge," *New Testament Studies*, 18:190 (1977).

17. Schrenk, "*ekdikeō*" *TDNT*, 2:442-444 (1964).

18. Jülicher, *Die Gleichnisreden Jesu*, 2:286, found the idea of revenge especially present in Lk. 18:6-8, which he jettisoned accordingly. Certainly many texts from the LXX and from Sirach 35:12-36:17 (esp. 35:18; 36:7, 10) favor this position, but the fact that the parable's context is a law court and that usages there have a different nuance provide decisive evidence against revenge as the rendering.

19. So H. G. Meecham, "The Parable of the Unjust Judge," *Expository Times*, 57:306 (1945-46).

20. Creed, *The Gospel according to St. Luke* (London: Macmillan, 1930), p. 222.

21. Not only is there obvious stress on persistence throughout the parable proper, but in the application it is very much implied in the crying to God both night and day (v. 7*a*). In addition the master metaphor of the parable reflects the ultimate concern of the widow, the final speech lionizes her indirectly, and Lk. 18:8*b* can be fitted in. Also Jesus spoke compassionately and admiringly of widows elsewhere indicated.

22. In Mk. 13:19-27 the "elect" appear prominently in the context of tribulation (vv. 20,22) along with a promise of vindication at the Parousia of the Son of Man (v. 27). Both in the parable and in the little apocalypse there is challenge to keep the faith and the promise of divine vindication. Note the cry of the elect also in Rev. 6:9-11 and I Enoch 9:1-3.

23. Some scholars recognize that it is a Parousia parable, as Meecham, p. 307; W. Michaelis, *Die Gleichnisse Jesu*, p. 235. The entire category of Parousia parables has been denigrated unduly by Dodd and even Jeremias despite the three classic predictions of the Parousia of the Son of Man in Mark (9:38; 13:26; and 14:.62(. For a thoughtful recent treatment see G. R. Beasley-Murray, "The Parousia in Mark," *Review and Expositor*, 75:565-582 (1978).

24. Cited by Grundmann, p. 348. C. Colpe, "*ho huios tou anthrōpou*," *TDNT* 8:435 (1972), likens Lk. 18:8*b* to Lk. 17:24, 26, 30 and 21:36.

25. Schrenk, "*eklektos*," *TDNT*, 4:187 (1967).

26. Marshall, p. 674, citing Delling, p. 215.

27. Students such as Delling, Cranfield, and Linnemann take it to mean "speedily." C.E.B. Cranfield, "The Parable of the Unjust Judge and the Eschatology of Luke-Acts," *Scottish Journal of Theology*, 16:300 (.1963), goes on to argue against Conzelmann that indeed the parable as it stands affirms that the Parousia is near. Students favoring "suddenly" include A. B. Bruce, F. Godet, Grundmann, Spicq, Jeremias, and Horst. It is probable that the parable spoke pastorally to Luke's readers regarding what may have seemed to them the delay of the Parousia. Luke has generalized the parable in a helpful and legitimate fashion that extends but remains in the same trajectory as the parable. The evangelist was a good exegete (18:1).

28. So C. Colpe. Cf. Lk. 21:36. Consider also Dt. 11:17; Josh. 8:18; Ps. 2:12; Ezek. 29:5. Note Sir. 27:3. Both the parable and Lk. 17:22-37 focus on the sudden coming of the Son of Man and not merely the Kingdom. Samuel Akande, "The Concept of Eschatological Suddenness in the Synoptic Tradition," (Unpublished Ph.D. dissertation, Southern Baptist Seminary, Louisville, Ky, 1974), p. 80, calls attention to suddenness in the Thanksgiving Hymn of Qumran (IQH 8:18-20; 17:5-7).

29. J. Horst, "*makrothumia*," *TDNT*, 4:381 (1967).

30. The precise translation and punctuation for *kai makrothumei ep' autois* (76) is by no means settled. See Herman Ljungvik, "Zur Erklärung einer Lukas-Stelle (Lk. XVIII, 7)," *New Testament Studies*, 10:289-94 (1964); A. Wifstrand, "Lukas XVIII,7," *New Testament Studies*, 11:72-74 (1964), Horst, 381n, for a clear statement of alternatives. I think the best rendering is one that sees 7*b* as a rhetorical question asking if God will be gracious to his elect.

31. Manson, *The Mission and Message of Jesus* (New York: E. P. Dutton, 1938), p. 599.

32. William Stidger, *There Are Sermons in Stories* (New York: Abingdon, 1942), p. 132. The italics are mine.
33. See Elizabeth Mooney's story in *The Atlanta Constitution*, Sunday, August 9, 1981. See also Betty Bryant, *Leaning into the Wind: The Wilderness of Widowhood* (Philadelphia: Fortress Press, 1975).
34. Buttrick, *The Parables of Jesus*, p. 170.
35. Fosdick, *The Meaning of Prayer*, Revised Edition (New York: Garden City Books, 1949), p. 136. See the larger section on "Prayer as Dominant Desire."
36. Redding, *The Parables He Told*, p. 39. See also David Willis, *Daring Prayer* (Atlanta: John Knox Press, 1977), pp. 130-143.
37. Adapted from Stidger, p. 133.

Index of Names

Prepared by
Michael Fuhrman

Index of Subjects

Prepared by Michael Fuhrman